I0810933

Joseph Holt Mansion

Saving & Restoring the Home of Lincoln's Judge Advocate General

Susan B. Dyer

Acclaim Press
MORLEY, MISSOURI

Acclaim Press
— Your Next Great Book —

P.O. Box 238
Morley, MO 63767
(573) 472-9800
www.acclaimpress.com

Book Design: Rodney Atchley
Cover Design: M. Frene Melton
Cover Image: Jon Rollins

Copyright © 2018, Susan B. Dyer
All Rights Reserved

ISBN: 978-1-948901-06-2 | 1-948901-06-4
Library of Congress Control Number: 2018907736

No part of this book shall be reproduced or transmitted in any form or by any means, electronic or mechanical, including photocopying, recording or by an information or retrieval system, except in the case of brief quotations embodied in articles and reviews, without the prior written consent of the publisher. The scanning, uploading, and distribution of this book via the Internet or via any other means without permission of the publisher is illegal and punishable by law.

First Printing: 2018
Printed in the United States of America
10 9 8 7 6 5 4 3 2 1

This publication was produced using available information.
The publisher regrets it cannot assume responsibility for errors or omissions.

Dedication

To my father, Morton Levi Butler, who was my greatest supporter through one of the most challenging and rewarding works of my life, who always believed in my dream of saving the Holt Home and writing about Joseph Holt and his beloved home.

To my mother, Aggie Harpe Butler, who has given support, traveled with me to book signings and has always encouraged me.

Contents

Foreword . . . 4
Acknowledgments . . . 5
Introduction . . . 22
The Voyager . . . 25
The Dream . . . 28
Being Led by the Muse . . . 31
Delightful Day . . . 34
Holt Home Appraisal . . . 43
Meeting the Publisher . . . 49
Finding Mr. James L. Wimsatt, (Artist) . . . 51
Holt Home Spotlighted on the KY Lincoln Heritage Trail . . . 54
Writing on the Window . . . 57
The 5th George S. Prugh Lecture . . . 60
Byron Crawford's Friendship . . . 81
The Gheens Foundation . . . 83
Valet and Companion to General Joseph Holt . . . 86
Renovation for the Jewel . . . 89
The 7th Annual Holt Home Community Day . . . 96
Indiana National Guard JAGS Onsite Training in Historic Holt Home . . . 99
Speeches Given from the Grassroots Effort . . . 104
Premier Book Signing . . . 107
The Little Black Book . . . 111
The Holt Home Cake . . . 113
The JAGS Gave All . . . 115
The Ida Willis Award . . . 121
Three County Judges . . . 124
Grant Tips . . . 145
The Architect . . . 147
SS *Joseph Holt* . . . 150
Discovering Rose: Judge Holt's Great Niece . . . 155
A Memorable Day for the Fort Knox JAGS . . . 158
Journey to Georgia . . . 161
The Heart of the TJAGS . . . 164
The Lincoln Conspiracy Trial Court Room Revisited . . . 169
The Judge Advocate General's Legal Center and School's Partnership . . . 175
The Kentucky Heritage Council's Lifetime Partnership . . . 177
242nd JAG Birthday Celebration 101st Airborne Division of Fort Campbell, KY . . . 182
Friends of Holt at a Glance . . . 185
Judge Holt's Legacy Lives Again . . . 190
Appendix . . . 193
Index . . . 222

Foreword

It is an honor for me to write this foreword to *Joseph Holt Mansion: Saving and Restoring the Home of Lincoln's Judge Advocate General.* Brigadier General Joe Holt, who served as the Army's Judge Advocate General during the Civil War, had a very close personal and professional relationship with President Abraham Lincoln. It was Lincoln who, impressed with Holt's legal skills, asked Congress to appoint him as the top lawyer in the Army, Lincoln also arranged for Holt to wear the rank of brigadier general—no previous Army lawyer had borne that rank.

Susan Dyer, the author of *Joseph Holt Mansion*, has devoted the last 20 years to saving Joseph Holt's beautiful home, situated on the bank of the Ohio River in Breckinridge County, Kentucky, and restoring it to its antebellum splendor. As she shows in the pages of this interesting book, the Holt home preservation project has meant thousands of hours of fund raising and grant writing, and has involved not just Susan Dyer's tireless efforts, but hard work from many other individuals, including local and state civic leaders, politicians and charitable organizations.

Susan Dyer's work to save and restore Holt's home has been truly remarkable. As noteworthy, she is equally committed to ensuring that history does not forget Joseph Holt, as evidenced by her first book, *Lincoln's Advocate: The Life of Judge Joseph Holt*, first published in 2009. Her devotion to Joe Holt's memory and his home is important to me, because I served as The Judge Advocate General of the Army from 2009 to 2013. While I am many years removed from the Civil War and 'Lincoln's Advocate,' it remains important to me that Americans from all walks of life learn about the legacy of Judge Advocate General Joseph Holt, given his important place in military legal history and our Army.

It is not hyperbole to write that no one in America has done more than Susan Dyer to ensure that Holt is not forgotten. At her kind invitation, I enjoyed the hospitality of the Dyer family in 2013, in a visit to Breckinridge County. There, I gained a greater appreciation of her enthusiasm and persistence in seeking to keep the Holt home restoration project moving forward. I had the opportunity to explore Joseph Holt's magnificent home and to walk the grounds that he enjoyed more than 150 years ago.

I am certain that those who read this book will come away with a greater appreciation of the part played by Joseph Holt in the history of this great Nation—and appreciate equally the tenacity of Susan Dyer's efforts to ensure Holt is not forgotten.

Dana K. Chipman
Lieutenant General, U.S. Army, Retired
38th Judge Advocate General of the Army

Acknowledgments

Thanks to the following for their time and contributions for the success of saving, restoring, and opening the historic Judge Joseph Holt Home for new re-uses both locally, regionally, across the state of Kentucky and our Nation!

First, I thank God, who put it on my heart to save the Holt Home, and for all he continues to do for the continued work of restoration and opening the home to the public. God is the leader of the Holt project!

To my husband Eddie, who has followed me across Kentucky and beyond to the countless invitations to speak for my community about Judge Holt's legacy, military career, and home for the past 20 years with efforts of saving, restoring, and opening the Holt home, and for listening to the numerous bumps along the way ALWAYS WITH POSTIVE ENCOURAGEMENT!

To former Kentucky State Representative Dwight D. Butler, who first believed in saving the historic Holt Home and gave encouragement and advice through very trying and difficult times, who ALWAYS believed the Holt Home could be saved, who prayed many times and was deeply committed to answering phone calls and serving his community. Dwight Butler has spoken at Holt Home Community Days and continues to support this very deserving project!

To Ed Ford, former Public Relations Director for Berea College and author of numerous books, who encouraged me to write a follow-up book on how the Holt Home has been saved and has been instrumental with ideas for the Friends of Holt Home, Inc. for fund raising, and event ideas for the yearly Holt Home Community Day. Mr. Ford developed the idea of a Civil War Baseball game and has been a mentor assisting the author with numerous tasks, who welcomed me to Richmond for several events there with Lincoln's Advocate and has written numerous stories about the author, *Lincoln's Advocate*, and the historic Holt Home, and is editor of the *Joseph Holt Mansion.* Many thanks, Ed, for all you have done!

To David L. Morgan, Former Executive Director and Preservation Officer at the Kentucky Heritage Council/State Preservation Office/Resource for the Holt Home, mentor, and friend, and has assisted with numerous behind the scenes activities to make the Holt project happen and for being a keynote speaker.

To Douglas W. Sikes, publisher & owner of Acclaim Press, who recognized the importance of publishing the first biography on Joseph Holt and working to make this book known nationally, while helping promote the Holt project with the publishing of both books, *Lincoln's Advocate* and *Joseph Holt Mansion.*

To Dr. James C. Klotter, State Historian of Kentucky and a retired professor of history at Georgetown College, author of numerous books, and editor of Lincoln's Advocate, and one of my mentors who was on the Advisory Board of the Kentucky Lincoln Bicentennial Commission. Dr. Kotter has assisted in numerous tasks over the years. I have always been grateful to him for taking me under his wing!

To Mr. and Mrs. John P. Behen (deceased), for encouraging me to attend a Christian Writing Conference in Elizabethtown, who listened to research on Lincoln's Advocate and suggested ideas, who advised me on the 5th George S. Pugh Lecture of Military History on Brigadier General Joseph Holt, and who gave a small collection of Joseph Holt's books to the Friends of the Holt Home, Inc.

To Etta Wilson, publisher and author from Nashville, TN, who made a contact with the voice of Nashville, author John Egerton.

To John Egerton, renowned Nashville author (deceased), who connected me with Dr. James C. Klotter and advised me when Dr. Klotter was in Europe and who came from Nashville to be a part of the First Holt Home Community Day.

To Bruce Kirby, Manuscript Reading Room, The Library of Congress, who spoke with me on many occasions, assisted and helped me locate researchers to assist with the Holt project and the biography.

To Congressman Ron Lewis' Office, including Brittany Fausey, Field Representative, who came for a private tour and attended numerous meetings in our home; Keith Heithpath and Sara Davasher, who assisted with a report and letter to the Department of the Interior; and Sarah Davasher, who helped later when I was doing research on the roads in Breckinridge County and connected to the Transportation Enhancement Grant when she then worked for the Corps of Engineers in Louisville.

To Mary Jean Atchison, former Secretary for the Kentucky Heritage Council/State Preservation Office, who took numerous calls and messages and had David Morgan call me to get things started for the Holt project.

To former Breckinridge County Judge Executive George Monarch III, for hosting the first public meeting in Breckinridge County in efforts of saving the historic Holt Home and to learn of the opportunities of the KY Lincoln Bicentennial Commission, attending meetings in my home with dignitaries with the beginning of the project, writing a letter to the guardian of the private owner to see if they were interested in selling the Holt Home to the county while working closely with the KY Heritage Council/State Preservation Office and David Morgan. Judge Monarch became the "Appraisal Judge "as I named him with the Holt project.

To Lee Stinnett, for getting the contact number of a family member, assisting with several Holt Home Community Day events, attending meetings in my home in the beginning of the Holt project, being Chair of the Friends when we were a committee under the Breckinridge County Historical Society, and helping with fund raisers in 2012 for the Holt Home.

To Becky Shipp (retired) at the Kentucky Heritage Council/State Preservation Office, for assisting during the search for a new Preservation Officer after the retirement of David Morgan as she assisted with information, answering questions, grants, attending meetings, brought the KY Heritage Council/State Preservation Office for their first field trip to the historic Holt Home and attended meetings with former Breckinridge County Judge Executive Ray Powers during the negotiation with the purchase of the Holt Home.

To Dr. Elizabeth Leonard, Professor of History at Coby College and author of numerous books—including *Lincoln's Forgotten Ally*—who came to the Holt Home in January of 2009 for a private tour before restoration began and returned later as keynote speaker at one of the Holt Home Community Days.

To Claude Galloway (deceased), Appraiser for the Holt Home appraisal from Mayfield, KY, who shared and pointed out important details about the historic home that have been used in the preservation and shared with the KY Heritage Council & GRW architects to make sure the restoration is as close as possible to Judge Holt's era.

To Tommy Turner, LaRue Co. Judge Executive, a commissioner on the National Abraham Lincoln Bicentennial Commission, Co-chair of the KY Lincoln Bicentennial Commission, who assisted the author with information about seeking a grant for the appraisal of the Holt Home, invited the author to attend the KY Lincoln Bicentennial Commission meetings, and to speak at numerous Commission meetings on the grassroots effort of saving the Holt Home, some planned with presentations and some on the spot speaking with updates; for his help in making the Holt Home a Legacy Project of the Kentucky Lincoln Bicentennial; and for speaking at the 1st Holt Home Community Day and then returning in 2016 to see the investment the KY Lincoln Bicentennial believed in with the Holt Home (and grant money for its purchase).

To Chris Goodlett, formally with the Kentucky Historical Society, for working with me as I submitted the appraisal grant for the Breckinridge County Fiscal Court. Mr. Goodlett now works at the KY Derby Museum.

To Kenneth Tabb, former Hardin County Court Clerk, who introduced me to the Publisher, Doug Sikes, of Acclaim Press at a Kentucky Lincoln Bicentennial Commission meeting held at Hodgenville, KY. Mr. Tabb had a wonderful dinner and book event/signing for me at the Hardin Co. History Museum in Elizabethtown, KY, sold copies of *Lincoln's Advocate* there, and has attended numerous Holt Home Community Days.

To Mark Dennen, Former Executive Director at the Kentucky Heritage Council/State Preservation Office, for assisting with numerous jobs to assist with the Holt Home project, for sharing at Kentucky Lincoln Bicentennial Commission meetings about the continued progress of the Holt project and the author's work as a volunteer for her community, for attending numerous meetings for the historic Holt Home and the Holt House Steering Committee, for working with the author on research trying to find the original architect of the historic Holt Home, and for making numerous trips to the Holt Home and speaking at the Holt Home Community Day.

To Lindy Casebier, Former Dept. Secretary of Tourisms, Arts & Heritage Council, who was acting Executive Director for the Kentucky Heritage Council/State Preservation Office after the retirement of Mark Dennen. Lindy came to meetings, listened to concerns, accompanied me to a very important meeting, brought KET to the Holt Home to do a segment on the Holt Home, spoke numerous times for the Holt Home Community Day, ALWAYS made me welcome at the Kentucky Lincoln Bicentennial Commission meetings giving positive compliments on the continued work, he worked behind the scenes to assist when we experienced bumps in the road with numerous delays!

To former KY State Senator Dan Kelly, Co-Chair of the Kentucky Lincoln Bicentennial Commission, who worked diligently getting funding for The Kentucky Lincoln Bicentennial Commission where numerous grants were won across Kentucky, including the acquisition grant for the purchase of the Holt Home.

To Paul Smith, KET Producer, who brought a team from KET to do a segment on Joseph Holt and his home and had Dave Shuffett to speak in part of the segment. This can be viewed on the www.jholt-houseky.org home page.

To Carroll Gibson, Former KY State Senator and member of the Kentucky Lincoln Bicentennial Commission, who attended meetings in my home and at the Fiscal Court room, gave kind words for my work at the KY Lincoln Bicentennial Commission meetings, tried to get me on the Commission, made sure I was invited to the KY Lincoln Bicentennial Commission meetings, wrote support letters for numerous grants for the Holt Home, assisted with difficult times along with bumps turning into positive accomplishments, and spoke at the premier book signing for *Lincoln's Advocate.*

To James Wimsatt, (artist) from Owensboro, for giving me a beautiful Holt Home print for my work he drew when he came here in 1972 to capture the beauty of the home, and for using the print for the cover of *Lincoln's Advocate,* and in 2014 also giving a lifetime gift of a license agreement allowing Susan B. Dyer, author, to use in any future books and for the Friends of the Holt Home to use his artwork depicting the Judge Joseph Holt Home.

To former Breckinridge County Judge Executive Ray Powers, for attending numerous meetings during the process of negotiating with the guardian of the private owner and to purchase the Holt Home with grant money while working closely with lifetime partners, the KY Heritage Council. Ray Powers worked diligently in one month's time cleaning out the Holt Home that had been vacant for over 40 years and cleaning up the grounds for the Spotlight of the Holt Home on the KY Lincoln Heritage Trail for the first event for the historic Holt Home in 2009. Judge Powers assisted with tours, attending meetings locally and statewide, made it possible for the

Breckinridge County Fiscal Court to become the entity for the Holt Home, and wrote numerous support letters and encouraged strongly the continued writing for the Save America's Treasures Grant.

To the Breckinridge County Homemakers for serving lemonade and making cookies for the first Holt Home Community Day.

To David Hayes, former editor for the *Breckinridge Co. Herald-News*, who attended meetings and helped with several Holt Home Community Days by being present and taking pictures and writing about the event. For the first Holt Home Community Day, David wrote scripts for tour guides and worked with the Homemakers, wrote ads for the Breckinridge County Guide promoting the event, and articles about progress of the Holt Home and some of the author's events.

To Carol Hinton, Breckinridge County Extension Agent with UK, for assisting with the first premier book signing, carrying in chairs for guests during the entire evening, and for her continued support to spray for insects for the annual Holt Home Community Day that makes everyone more comfortable.

To Tamara Langman, "Costume Designer and Patternmaker" at www.tamaralangman.com, who has made costumes for the Holt Home Community Day for Jaydyn Dyer, granddaughter, and the author, and came from Actor's Theatre in Louisville and spoke about historic costumes at a Holt Home Community Day in 2016.

To Terry Henning, WXBC employee and dress maker, for making several dresses for Jaydyn Dyer, granddaughter and the author to wear at the historic Holt Home, and taking pictures at the annual Holt Home Community Day and doing interviews on site.

To Lee Bramlett of WXBC for getting the word out to the public with continued updates about the Holt Home project, partnering of the U.S. Army JAGS, and continued progress and being present at Holt Home Community Days.

To Sarah L. Robinson, Washington, D.C., for assistance with research from the Library of Congress.

To Charles Allen Wilson, former Breckinridge County Court Clerk, who assisted me with going through deeds in research for the Holt Home and for him bringing Larry Cox, former State Director for Senator Mitch McConnell, to speak with me after I had met Mr. Cox in Louisville.

To Father Greg Trawick, a former Priest in Breckinridge County in 2011, who gave his advice on delivering the 5th George S. Prugh Lecture and prayed!

To Reverend Janet Carden, former pastor at the Harned United Methodist Church in Harned, KY, and dear friend who has prayed for years for the author's work with the Holt Home, speeches and lectures, research, writing, and ALL! Janet prays for the author during important speeches and lectures and listened to the author deliver the 5th George S. Pugh Lecture in its entirety before giving it in Virginia. She has been inspirational to me during all the bumps in the road, the trial and tribulations I have lived through during the most challenging and rewarding journey of my life! Janet is always positive with encouragement, which has truly been a blessing!

To Reverend Rebecca Heid, the author's pastor and friend at Harned United Methodist Church, for her support and prayers for numerous requests from the author. Rebecca has prayed for the speeches and work to be guided by God and for the author to always give her best!

To Retired COL Fred Borch, Historian and Archivist at The Judge Advocate General's Legal Center and School, Charlottesville, VI, who invited the author to deliver the 5th Annual George S. Prugh Lecture in Military History on Joseph Holt, and for giving my husband and me a wonderful tour of the University of Virginia, treating us to a wonderful evening meal with distinguished people from the Army and Charlie Singer, a lawyer from New York, driving us around to our hotel and picking us up for breakfast, then giving a most delightful tour of the JAG School and taking me to meet John W. Miller II, the Commending General at the JAG School in 2011, and for the gifts given to the author after the Prugh Lecture and for the luncheon held in my honor after delivering the lecture. Paying the author to travel was the first of this new career. Also, for giving all when you came to Breckinridge County and paid your own air fare, and car rental and spoke at the 5th Annual Holt Home Community Day in 2013. Thanks for writing numerous articles in the *Sword and Quill* about Judge Holt and his home, and for assisting the author with numerous opportunities for the Holt project, for writing support letters, for talking with me on the phone when you are ALWAYS extremely busy. And for the opportunities that have been presented by the United States Army JAGS because of YOU! It means the world to the author for you to write the introduction to the new book!

To General Dana K. Chipman, Retired, 38th Judge Advocate General of the US Army, for the kindness shown to the author while at the JAG School and for the wonderful dinner, where I had a lifetime opportunity to talk with you personally and shared my heart about Judge Holt, for keeping your promise about coming to Kentucky to view Judge Holt's beloved home and speak where you became the 2nd Judge Advocate General of the US Army to visit Judge Holt's home, which encourages ALL THE TJAGS of the future to give of themselves. What a great example for other TJAGS to follow honoring one of their own as you did when you paid your own air fare and car rental. For the gift you personally bought out of your own pocket and sent for the work of the Holt project "General Orders No. 100 Lincoln and the Lieber Code, April 1863 that hangs in the Great Room of our home, and for the support letters you have personally written for grants for the preservation of Judge Holt's home. For continuing to keep updated with progress and the continued work to make the Holt Home a National meeting place for all the Army Judge Advocates across the nation. To write the preface for *Joseph Holt Mansion* is the kindest gift you can give (your words)!

To General Flora D. Darpino, 39th Judge Advocate General of the US Army, for the privilege and honor to meet with her in the Executive Office in the Pentagon, May 5, 2017. For taking time out of her very demanding schedule to share history of the USARMY TJAGS, and for very kind words spoken about the continued effort and work for Brigadier General Joseph Holt's legacy and the saving and restoring of his Kentucky home that is very important to the United States Army and our American history. For the medal of excellence she gave to the author for 20 years of selfless service for the work of bringing back Judge Holt's legacy and the continued effort to make the Holt Home a national meeting place for the Army JAGS. And for General Darpino's promise, "The TJAGS will work on making it a tradition to send the Judge Advocate General to the Holt Home during their 4-year term because of Holt and his leadership and what his legacy means to today's JAGS!"

To LTC Jeri Hanes, Officer of the Judge Advocate General, Strategic Initiatives Officer, PC, for her willingness to communicate with the author with the continued effort with the keynote speaker invitation for General Charles N. Pede, 40th Judge Advocate General of the United States Army, to speak at Brigadier General Joseph Holt's Home, taking the time for continued communication with her very demanding schedule for the TJAGS, for the kind words spoken about the author's work with Holt's legacy and home, and with continued follow up work with communicating!

To COL Francis King, former XO, OTJAG for General Flora D. Darpino, 39th Judge Advocate General, for his assistance as the PC for communicating with the author with updates to the Judge Advocate General and the TJAG Office about the continued work of restoration for Judge Holt's legacy, Holt's home and the continued accomplishments, and with the request for General Darpino to be a keynote speaker at Brigadier General Joseph Holt's home.

To COL Sean McGarry, JA, former Strategic Initiatives, Office of the Judge Advocate General, who continued as the PC with keeping General Darpino and the TJAG Office updated with continued efforts to make the Holt Home a national meeting place for the Army JAGS and the continued work for Holt's legacy and updates from the Friends of the Holt Home, Inc.

To LTC Jeffery A. Miller former (P) JA, Strategic Initiatives Officer, Officer of the Judge Advocate General, who continued as PC for the TJAG Office and General Darpino, who always answered promptly and kept in the request for General Darpino to be a keynote speaker at Judge Holt's home, who gave the author and her husband a private tour of the Pentagon and invited the author to meet with General Flora D. Darpino after the tour in the Executive Suite of the Judge Advocate General, and for getting permission to take a picture of the author standing next to Brigadier General Joseph Holt, and for giving a tour of the Memorial for 911 outside of the Pentagon.

To COL James Bagwell, Staff Judge Advocate for Fort Knox, who has assisted with numerous wreath-laying ceremonies at Brigadier General Joseph Holt's monument on the Holt grounds, who brought his entire JAG team and the Fort Knox legal community for the first professional development and field trip for Kentucky JAGS, where COL Bagwell praised Holt's works and had the modern day Army compare itself with Holt's service, who worked closely with the Pentagon, TJAGS office to present the Friends of the Holt Home a plaque for their work for the Holt Home and for Susan Dyer, Volunteer President of the Friends of the Holt Home to receive a medal from TJAG Flora Darpino, The Judge Advocate General and a plaque for 20 years of self-less service for preservation of the Holt Home and Holt's legacy from the Judge Advocates Office at Fort Knox, and for being the key-note speaker at the 9th Annual Holt Home Community Day in 2017.

To Todd A. Wayne, CPT, JA, Chief, Client Services, Fort Campbell, KY for sharing with COL Fred Borch (ret.) about the biography, *Lincoln's Advocate,* and recently for inviting the author to be the Special Guest Speaker for the 242nd JAG Corps Birthday Celebration 101st Airborne Division (Air Assault) Fort Campbell, KY, and for him giving a very enjoyable detailed tour of Fort Campbell to the author and her husband after delivering the speech.

To COL Andras Marton, Staff Judge Advocate, 101st Airborne Division and Fort Campbell, for honoring the author after delivering the speech for the 242nd JAG Corps Birthday of the United States Army JAG Corps, by presenting a plaque and medal for her commitment honoring the legacy of General Joseph Holt, and for inviting the author to assist with cutting the cake with the sword. Also, thanks and gratitude to COL Marton for giving a tour of the Sabalauski Air Assault School at Fort Campbell, KY, after the birthday celebration.

To the 113th Army Band from the United States Army Cadet Command and Fort Knox volunteering, providing patriotic music for numerous Holt Home Community Days until the Army band was eliminated.

To COL Edmond Bowen, Staff Judge Advocate at Fort Knox, who spoke at a Holt Home Community Day about Joseph Holt and gave a gift of "General Orders" No. 100 to the Friends of the Holt Home to be placed in the historic home and for serving in a wreath-laying ceremony at Holt' monument.

To Mrs. Edmond Bowen, Jr. for giving the JAG pen off her lapel at a Holt Home Community Day to the author to wear for all the work she continues to do for the Army JAGS.

To COL Daniel Kozlowski, retired, Senior Staff Judge Advocate for the Indiana National Guard JAGS, for seeking information about having an on-site training at Brigadier General Joseph Holt's home and for arranging for the Indiana National Guard JAGS to fly here in three Blackhawk helicopters and having their on-site training with the first new use of the Holt Home while efforts continue to make the historic home a national meeting place for all the Judge Advocates across the nation, and for being the keynote speaker for the 8th Annual Holt Home Community Day in 2016.

To Roger Wilson, former a WO1 US Army, Legal Administrator, Indiana National Guard, Office of the Staff Judge Advocate, now working in Washington, D.C., who came for a tour of the Holt Home, reported back to COL Daniel Kozlowski, (retired) with information about an on-site training at the historic Holt Home and helped plan the professional development for the Indiana National Guard JAGS and was the PC.

To COL Christopher T. Fredrikson, Staff Judge Advocate, and MSG US ARMY Robert Adamove, who did a wreath-laying ceremony at Brigadier General Holt's moment for several years and presented the author with a coin medal from the Office of the Staff Judge Advocate for Excellence.

To Jerome D. Klein MSG, USA Chief Paralegal, US Army Cadet Command and Fort Knox, for assisting with a wreath-laying ceremony at Judge Holt's monument.

To COL Robert J. Cotell, former Staff Judge Advocate, at Fort Knox (deceased), who wrote it in the books for the Office of the Staff Judge Advocate to follow the tradition to come yearly in September for the wreath-laying ceremony at Brigadier General Joseph Holt's grave giving honor to one of their own.

To Breckinridge County Judge Executive Maurice Lucas for always working positively with the author, and the Friends of the Holt Home, Inc. with the cooperative agreement as both work toward grants, archeological training, the continued phases for restoration, for writing support letters for grants, for being actively involved with Student Day and Holt Home Community Day, for speaking at events and onsite for the important JAG events, for making numerous trips to Frankfort for the Holt Home restoration project, for picking up gifts for the Holt Home, for meeting with lifetime partners the KY Heritage Council/State Preservation Office, attending Friends meetings, supporting the President of the Friends, assisting with tours for special guests, giving personal donations for unexpected needs, recognizing the importance of volunteers and working through times of delays with the project to have continued success, and for all the kind words said in behalf of the author's volunteer work.

To Gloria Shepard of Cannelton, IN, for giving permission to include both memoirs of her great-grandfather, Charles Foster Jasper, Valet & Companion to Judge Holt, and her mother, Dorothy Dowell Ramsey, who heard the stories as a child and viewed the Holt mansion while in ownership of the Holt family.

To Donna Sebastian for drawing a picture of the Holt home that hung in the author's classroom while still teaching, and later the picture made appearances across Kentucky while the author spoke about the grass root efforts.

To Warren Greer, former program coordinator for the KY Lincoln Bicentennial Commission, now the Director of the Kentucky Lincoln Heritage Trail Alliance, who assisted the author at the 2006 KY Preservation Conference, and since that introduction Warren has done numerous tasks for the Holt Home project. He ALWAYS made me feel welcome as a volunteer at the KY Lincoln Bicentennial Commission meetings and invited me to attend the KY Lincoln sites meeting prior to the Commission meetings. Warren has attended numerous meetings on behalf of the historic Holt Home and has spoken at the Holt Home Community Day and has helped in many ways to promote the Judge Joseph Holt Home.

To Stuart Sanders, History Advocate at the Kentucky Historical Society, who always welcomed me at the KY Lincoln Bicentennial Commission meetings and was involved with me receiving the Ida Lee Willis Award for Service for Preservation for the Joseph Holt Home in rural Breckinridge Co.

To Iris Larue, a member of the Kentucky Lincoln Bicentennial Commission and Director at the Lincoln Museum in Hodgenville, KY, who befriended the author at the Commission meetings, and KY Lincoln site meetings, has continued to support the work of the Holt Home by continuing to have *Lincoln's Advocate* in the Lincoln Museum since its publication, and has attended numerous Holt Home Community Days; we serve together on the Board of the KLHTA.

To Mr. White, Volunteer from Farmington Plantation, who befriended me at the KY Lincoln Bicentennial Commission meetings when I needed a friend. Work was done to try and find his first name. He will forever be the encourager I needed when I was about to enter out of my comfort zone for the work of Holt and his home.

To Kathy Tabor, former music teacher at Breckinridge County High School, who performed with her beautiful voice and brought the Chamber Singers numerous times to perform selections of the period at the Holt Home Community Day.

To Scott Moore for performing the first violin music at the Holt Home Community Day and for performing at the premier book signing of *Lincoln's Advocate.*

To Steven Boyd, former Director at Breckinridge Co. Chamber, who attended the Friends' meetings, helped with a Holt Home Community Day, and purchased a Sign saying, "Holt Home" on the right-of-away on U.S. 60 guiding guests.

To Jonathan Boyd, former Chair of the Friends of the Holt Home while a committee under the Breckinridge County Historical Society, who assisted with several Holt Home Community Days and spoke and attended three fund raising events for the Holt Home.

To the Kentucky Heritage Council, who wrote a grant that provides the historical marker that interprets Judge Holt's legacy in front of the Holt Home.

To Jackie Miller, who volunteered at numerous Holt Home Community Days and played beautiful flute music.

To Jonathan Bennett, Former Breckinridge County Girls' Basketball coach and presently Assistant Principal at Breckinridge County High School, who organized and developed the Breckinridge County Vintage Baseball team for the annual Holt Home Community Day; who studied the rules, formed the teams, had the uniforms designed, playing the first Civil War Baseball game at an official KY Lincoln site; for all the members of the teams making sure the field was perfect with players volunteering and grooming the field, for Jonathan speaking and explaining the rules, and continuing to give this selfless volunteer service for the Judge Joseph Holt Home.

To Alison O'Donoghue Mattingly, who has performed for numerous years at the Holt Home Community Day with period music as a volunteer.

To former Governor Steve Beshear, a former JAG in his early career, for coming to Breckinridge County for a private tour of the Holt Home, who told the public at a meeting in Breckinridge County the Holt Home was in grave condition and he was going to help. During Governor Beshear's two terms his administration assisted with two $500,000 Transportation Enhancement Grants for the preservation of the historic Holt Home.

To Joe Wright, former Kentucky State Senator of Harned, Kentucky, who has supported the Holt project and worked behind the scenes and continues to give encouragement for the preservation of our national treasure, the historic Holt Home of our most famous citizen.

To Myra Tobin, who has supported the Holt Home project and helped the Friends secure an exhibit for a Holt Home Community Day.

To Shannon Tivitt, former Deputy Chief of Staff for Governor Steven Beshear, for bringing the second $500,000 Transportation Enhancement Grant check to Breckinridge County and speaking at the Holt Home Community Day in 2015.

To Phil Huddleston, former Chief of Staff for Lieutenant Crit Luallen, who worked behind the scenes and made a trip to Breckinridge County to tour the Holt Home.

To Paris Hopkins of Frankfort, KY, who came for a private tour of the historic Holt Home, worked behind the scenes giving encouraging words for the Holt project, and attended the Holt Home Community Day in 2016.

To Sharon Wakefield, former Postmaster at Harned, KY, who assisted the author for years packaging hundreds of Holt cakes mailed across Kentucky and beyond to say thank-you...you are appreciated for your help with the Holt Home.

To the author's sons, Quince and Justin, for their devoted patience with their mother, with the spear heading of the Holt project, for support during grant writing, for support during researching, writing press releases, preparing for the Holt Home Community Day, preparing lectures and speeches, traveling across the state and beyond, writing two books, loading ferns, urns, and supplies for the Holt Home Community Day, helping with final touches for the grounds, and for being positive through some very rough bumps and delays and ALWAYS supporting their mother and the work of the Friends for this most challenging but rewarding project and restoration!

To Jaydyn Dyer, granddaughter of the author, for her willingness to learn about Judge Holt's legacy and the strong American history of Judge Holt and his important legacy to our nation since an infant, For her dressing in period costumes for numerous years at the Holt Home Community Day encouraging today's generation that they will be the torch carriers for the future, to work and protect this American treasure setting in their own backyard.

To Aggie Butler, mother of the author for HER SUPPORT given through many difficult days of the author setting for hundreds of hours at the computer working on the Holt project that has and continues to be non-stop! For traveling with her daughter to numerous book signings, to speaking events, researching events, and making the best black-berry cobbler for General Chipman and COL Borch, and for assisting with the book signing table at Holt Home Community Days for the author when she has numerous other duties.

To my brother Mitchell and sister Yale Lori Butler for their support and for the entire family for understanding the 20 years of work that may have taken moments from you. However, the time spent is for preservation of an American treasure that will remain strong after we are all gone. It will be for the students who walk through the doors and scholars who travel across the nation and internationally to view this remarkable place in Breckinridge County, KY. This work is a gift for the future and I have enjoyed every second that God has given me to do his work and carry the torch for our community!

To Doris Haynes and Jackie Butler for assisting with the Holt Home cakes.

To Jackie Butler, for her creative design of compiling two scrap books for the Holt project and *Lincoln's Advocate* with a collection of newspaper clipping and magazine articles written by Kentucky writers.

To Rick Brown, former Wave 3TV, Production Manager, who gave the author his business card after hearing her speak in Meade County, for inviting the author to appear numerous times on Wave 3TV Listens, discussing *Lincoln's Advocate* and promoting the Annual Holt Home Community Day, for bringing the cameras to rural Breckinridge County to film, and air on the evening news the 5th Annual Holt Home Community Day in 2013, and then to make a segment of this event that can be viewed on the www.jholt-houseky.org website, for coming on March 5, 2016 for the first new use of the Holt Home and stay the entire day to report and air on the Wave 3TV news when the Indiana National Guard JAGS flew here in three Blackhawk helicopters from Indianapolis and held their onsite training in Judge Holt's home.

To Tammy McNeill, Producer at Wave 3TV, who has invited the author to make several appearances on Wave 3TV promoting the Holt Home Community Day and is always so nice to assist with the event helping to get the word across Kentucky about the massive effort of restoration for the nationally significant Holt Home.

To Steve Collins, a Preservation Specialist in Kentucky, chair of the Ida Lee Willis Memorial Foundation, a member of the Kentucky Heritage Council, with numerous roles in preservation across Kentucky who has graciously assisted with good deeds for the Holt Home and has taken time on numerous occasions to speak with the author during bumps in the road, and delays for the Holt Home who will be one of the keynote speakers for the 10th Annual Holt Home Community Day for the "Special Event".

To Renee Wright, a former student and 5th grade teacher in Breckinridge County, who invited the author to speak in her classroom about Joseph Holt and Lincoln's Advocate, and she spoke at Lincoln's Advocate's premier book signing.

To Bob Owsley for support of the Holt Home project, for requesting a private tour of the Holt Home with friends, and for all the kind words said for the work.

To Don Wise, and the Cecilian Bank for their support of the Holt Home project and for purchasing the tax credits from the Friends of the Holt Home, Inc. for the historic Holt Home.

To the First State Bank for their support of the Holt Home Project.

To Elizabeth Parks for her painting of the historic Holt Home and for bringing it to share with the author and then to attend the first Holt Home Community Day, where she presented her artwork to former Breckinridge County Judge Executive Ray Powers.

To Sarah Flood, Director of the Breckinridge County Library, for inviting the author to deliver a speech on Judge Joseph Holt and the efforts to restore his home.

To the Owensboro/Davis County Library, remember—The Civil War 150 Anniversary Lecture and book signing on Judge Joseph Holt.

To Sarah Wardrip, retired teacher of Breckinridge Co. (deceased), who invited the author to Student Day at Hardinsburg Elementary School where the author spoke to fourth graders about Joseph Holt and his home.

To members of the Kentucky Lincoln Bicentennial Commission and Advisory Board, who invested their support with making the Holt Home a "Legacy Project of the Kentucky Lincoln Bicentennial," and placing funding in the Kentucky Heritage Council to be available for grants, thus providing grant opportunity where the acquisition of the Holt Home happened because of the Kentucky Lincoln Bicentennial Commission and the Kentucky Heritage Council who granted funding for the Breckinridge County Fiscal Court to purchase the home and 19.5 acres.

To Joshua Wilks, National Trust for Preservation, who worked his hardest with Breckinridge County Judge Assistant, Kathina Bell and GRW architect Jon Rollins to finalize the SAT grant/ matched mostly with local volunteer time and completed work before the grant deadline expired.

To Congressman Brett Guthrie, who worked diligently on getting the Save America's Treasure Grant through the House of Representatives, spoke at the 1st Holt Home Community Day, and has had his office to assist with numerous bumps in the road for the Holt project.

To Brian Smith, with Congressman Brett Guthrie's Office, who has attended numerous meetings for the Holt House Steering Committee, has assisted on several things for the Holt project, and continues to assist when called upon, and recently gave concerns and requests to Congressman Brett Guthrie from Holt's community and the author for the federal tax credits for preservation to be included in the budget.

To Suzanne Miles, Field Representative for Brett Guthrie, who has attended numerous meetings for the Holt House Steering Committee and the Friends of the Holt Home, Inc., and has been present for numerous Holt Home Community Days. Ms. Miles recently sent requests and concerns to Congressman Guthrie from Holt's community and author about the importance for Kentucky to have the Federal Tax credits for Preservation included in the budget, and updates with the continued success of the project.

To U.S. Senator Mitch McConnell for help getting the Save America's Treasures grant through the Senate and for meeting with the author to discuss the Holt Home project.

To Michael Biagi, Executive Director of the Republican Party of Kentucky, and former Field Representative for Senator McConnell who arranged for a meeting with Senator McConnell to share with him the work of his constituents and the importance of the restoration of Judge Holt's home with its national significance to keep him updated on this important part of American history and the continued efforts for restoration and seeking grants for the home to be opened for Kentucky and the nation.

To Andrew Condia, Field Representative for Senator Mitch McConnell, who has toured the historic Holt home, attended a meeting of the Friends of the Holt Home, Inc. and has shared the numerous accomplishments of the Friends of the Holt Home, and the importance of this nationally significant project with Senator McConnell and recently shared the concerns and requests with Senator McConnell from Holt's community and the author for the Federal tax credits for Preservation to be included in the budget.

To Kentucky State Representative Dean Schamore, who supports the Holt Home project with his presence at numerous Holt Home Community Day events where he has spoken, his presence at the first new re-use for the home with the Indiana National Guard onsite training in 2016, and when he spoke at the 7th Annual Holt Home Community Day on September 26, 2015 when the home received the 2nd $500,000 Transportation Enhancement Grant from Governor Steven Beshear's Administration.

To Kentucky State Senator Steven Meredith for speaking at the 9th Annual Holt Home Community Day lending his support and will be attending meetings for the Friends of the Holt Home, Inc. when his schedule allows.

To Ted Guillaum, Organ Grinder from Nashville, TN, who has attended numerous Holt Home Community Day's, assisted with the Civil War Baseball game, with period music as a volunteer, and by donating beautiful prints of President Lincoln to use for the Holt Home Community Days.

To Rick Stith for doing an excellent job with the sound system for Holt Home Community Days.

To Kent Whitworth, Exec. Director at the Kentucky Historical Society, a state partner with the historic Holt Home, who has assisted with providing the Kentucky History Mobile's presence for Holt Home Community Day's allowing the public to see Kentucky's role in the Civil War linked to President Lincoln.

To Mark Ford from Richmond, KY, who came and played drums as a volunteer at a Holt Home Community Day when the home received the 1st $500,000 Transportation Enhancement Grant.

To Marcheta Sparrow, former Secretary, Tourism, Arts and Heritage Cabinet, who came to the Holt Home sharing great news from Governor Beshear's administration with the first $500,000 Transportation Enhancement grant.

To the Ninth Michigan Infantry reenactors volunteering from West Point, Kentucky for numerous Holt Home Community Days and for having an encampment on the Holt grounds for visitors to enjoy.

To the Frasier Museum of Louisville for loaning a display to assist with a Holt Home Community Day.

To SSG Love from the Fort Knox JAGS for touring the Holt Home and grounds, giving a report back to COL James Bagwell to see about the Professional Development for the Fort Knox JAGS, and for speaking and praising Holt's tireless effort while serving in the Civil War.

To First Class Christian Arbec and Specialist Caroline Bedoy, who studied Holt and gave a presentation on Joseph Holt while the Fort Knox JAGS were present for a Professional Development.

To Kevin and Marla Herford, specialist in historic wallpaper, for coming to the Holt Home and documenting the historic wallpaper.

To MSG, Konrad Nikolao, United States Army Cadet and Command and Fort Knox, Office of the Staff Judge Advocate, who gave a brief talk on April 20, 2017 for the appreciation of the work of saving the Holt Home and assisted with the wreath-laying ceremony at Judge Holt's monument in 2017.

To Jennifer A. Hisgen, COL, JA Command Judge Advocate U.S. Army Human Resource Command Office of the Command Judge Advocate, Fort Knox, for giving the author a plaque/certificate of appreciation for selfless contributions to preserve the historic land mark of such great significance to the heritage of the Judge Advocate General's Corps, February 28, 2014.

To Margaret Rose Badger, g-g-g niece of Joseph Holt who came here, toured the Holt Home with her sister, Cathy Rose (daughters of Joseph Holt Rose), and Dr. Elizabeth Leonard in January 2009, who gave family photos of the historic Holt Home that have been used with the restoration, and included in this book.

To Kim Nyberg, Madison IN, Consultant for the site use plan of the Holt Home, who has worked with the community and the Friends of the Holt Home for the new re-uses of the Holt Home.

To the people in Breckinridge County who came to the two days of meetings and discussions with Kim Nyberg, consultant for the site base plan, of what the Holt Home will become (funded by the National Trust Grant, 2015) written by the author.

To John Nyberg for letting the Friends borrow a form as a guide for creating a document for gifts to the Friends for the Holt Home.

To both Kim and John Nyberg for doing an analysis of the historic wallpaper, some rooms from President James Buchanan's era with five rooms with original paper still on the walls.

To General Pete Chiarelli, retired, Vice Chief of Staff who wrote thanking the author for a copy of *Lincoln's Advocate* and the importance of Brigadier General Joseph Holt.

To Chris Rehmert, Greenville, OH, retired from the Army whom I met at the KY Book Fair in 2009 who has kept in touch over the years, has given encouragement about numerous accomplishments, shared about Grant Hall in Washington D.C. and other important items involving the Army.

To Jim Askins, serving former U.S. Senator Jim Bunning, who attended meetings in the beginning to assist with the saving of the Holt Home.

To Rusty Cheuvront and Marty Tichenor(retired) from Brown-Forman, sending thanks for The Friends of the Holt Home receiving a grant to restore the original Holt fence.

To Suzi Bartholomy, writer for the *Owensboro Messenger-Inquirer*, who came here and did a story that the Associated Press picked up and has continued to partner over the years. Ms. Bartholomy has traveled numerous times to the historic Holt Home to do featured stories about the progress, events at the home, the lectures given by the author, about the author traveling to the JAG School and the effort that continues to make the Holt Home a National meeting place for all the Army JAGS. The Owensboro Messenger has been a wonderful partner with the Holt Home!

To Barry Bernson (retired) Channel 41 Louisville, who came to Holt, KY, and did a story about Joseph Holt, the author, and the beginning efforts to find funding for the Holt project. Mr. Bernson also assisted the author in a press release.

To Fred Bennett formally of Holt, KY, who talked with the author about the Holt Home, shared pictures of his mother's Marguerite Bennett and called to donate the half-acre corner lot where the Holt School once stood that the Breckinridge County Fiscal Court now owns.

To Michael Bostic MSGUSA, Office of the Staff Judge Advocate, who assisted with a wreath-laying ceremony at Judge Holt's monument.

To the Breckinridge Co. Historical Society for their support and for letting the Friends be an umbrella under them until we became a 501(c)3 non-profit organization, and for their support of the continued work of saving a national treasure. Many thanks to the members whom have given the author support and for the organization naming Susan Dyer Historian of the Year 2017.

To the Brown-Pusey House of Elizabethtown, KY, for assisting with a letter written to A.M. Brown, friend, from Joseph Holt.

To Bruce T. Butler, 46th Judicial Circuit Judge, who wrote several support letters for grants for the historic Holt Home, and who gave advice several times when needed.

To Ann Bowne (deceased) of Owensboro who supported the Holt project and invited the author to speak to the Owensboro DAR and opened her Cloverport home for the event.

To President John Roush and Susie Roush of Centre College for touring the historic Holt Home and for their continued interest in Joseph Holt's importance to our nation as Holt attended Centre College and loved debating there.

To Clifford Dowel, Louisville, who gave the author a gift (picture of the Holt church), and who has written articles about the Holt home.

To Jordan Eakin for his assistance on helping design a flyer for one of the Holt Home Community Days and his photos gifts of the historic Holt Home to the author.

To Larry Elliott, who has portrayed Judge Joseph Holt for the Holt Home Community Days and for coming to the Breckinridge County Schools portraying President Abraham Lincoln and tying together Joseph Holt's connection, and for working with the Friends on Student Day at the Holt home.

To Barbara Bradley, Division Administration Assistant, Owensboro Community and Technical College for connecting me with Suzie Bartholomy.

To the *News-Enterprise*, Elizabethtown, KY, for their partnering, Ben Sheron for writing numerous articles about Judge Joseph Holt, and the restoration of his home. To former staff writer John Friendlier and others for writing numerous stories about *Lincoln's Advocate*, the author, the Prugh Lecture, the Conspirator where actor Danny Huston portrayed Holt in 2011, and for getting the news out to readers. The News Enterprise continues to be a wonderful partner.

To the *Meade Co. Messenger* and staff writers, Brandenburg, KY for covering the Holt Home Community Days, for former writer Larry See, Jr. writing a story about the author and the invitation to deliver the 5th George S. Prugh Lecture, and for the continuing partnering for the Holt project.

To the *Daily News*, Bowling Green, KY, for writing an editorial about the author and efforts of saving the Holt Home.

To Byron Crawford for writing a featured story about the author in the *Courier-Journal* and *Kentucky Living* magazine about the author as a Cooperative Hero and coming to rural Breckinridge County to speak at the finale of the fund-raising campaign for the Friends of the Holt Home.

To Celia Lynn Reid, of Owensboro, KY, who was the first teacher to bring a class to tour the historic mansion of Judge Holt's, and for writing stories about the Holt Home and author.

To *Kentucky Monthly* magazine and Editor Stephen M. Vest, for helping to promote the Holt Home Community Days, and for writing a featured story about the author and the efforts of the Friends of the Holt Home.

To *Kentucky Living* magazine for partnering throughout the years of continued restoration and efforts helping to get the word out across Kentucky, for coming to a Holt Home Community Day and doing a featured story about the Friends and the author and continued efforts of restoration for the Holt Home.

To Tiffany Cashman, editor of the *Breckinridge County Herald-News*, for her gallant work with keeping the region updated on continued progress of the Holt Home restoration, the annual Holt Home Community Day, the partnering success of the Army JAGS, for being on site when events occur and the author's continued work with the TJAGS, grants, and new book, along with The Friends of the Holt Home and the Breckinridge County Fiscal Court.

To Fortcampbellcourier.com for "Covering the JAG: Army's JAG Corps" celebrating its 242nd anniversary and guest speaker, the author.

To Craig Potts, Executive Director, Kentucky Heritage Council/State Preservation Office, for speaking at numerous Holt Home Community Days and assisting Breckinridge Co. Fiscal Court and the Friends of the Holt Home, Inc. with a lifetime partnership with the historic Holt Home and making the author an honorary member of the KY Heritage Council/ State Historic Preservation Office at a Holt Home Community Day, and his continued efforts with trips to the historic home and guidance for success.

To the Kentucky Heritage Council and staff for their assistance since the beginning of the lifetime partnership in December 2008 and Facebook page, with their continuous updates with the Holt Home Project, and special thanks to Diane Comer, Public Information Officer, for all the work she does with the partnership that helps the rural community of Breckinridge County; for all the times she assists with questions, concerns, grants, trips to the historic Holt Home, attending numerous Holt Home Community Days, and assisting with the first Holt Home Community Day.

To Charlie Corbett, who diligently helped the Friends become a 501(c)3 non-profit organization and assisted with a county wide fundraising campaign in 2012 and continues to assist with necessary fund raising and helps to keep things moving for the Holt project! For assisting the Friends with cleaning the Holt grounds and making them presidential looking. Salutes to you, Charlie!

To Ken Distler for bringing the Kentucky Home Guard Band to help with the Holt Home Community Days.

To WXBC and Lee Bramlett for your support with the Holt Home project and Holt Home Community Days, for reporting the updates and accomplishments of the project, the continued efforts with the U.S. Army JAGS and with the interviews keeping the public updated on continued efforts, progress, lectures and speeches on Holt and the new uses for the Holt Home, and for your continued effort to be present for very important events.

To the Brook Dyer Family originally from Holt, KY, for donating one of the original Holt Chapel chandeliers from Tiffany's in New York, ordered and payed for by Joseph Holt when the Holt Chapel was built that will be placed in the restored Judge Joseph Holt Home and other gifts, and assisting the author with a collection of newspapers of the early roads in Breckinridge County that helped on research of a Transportation Enhancement grant.

To Mr. Bill Thompson, Breckinridge County teacher of McDaniel's (deceased), who worked diligently to get the Holt Home on the National Register in 1976.

To Verbal Thompson his wife (deceased), who gave the author their collection of information on Joseph Holt and his home.

To Bob Bell and the 12 Regimental Colored Heavy Artillery, Camp Nelson for speaking, setting up camp, and bringing their Civil War Cannon to a Holt Home Community Day.

To Don Wimmer, editor of the *Hancock Co. Clarion*, for supporting the Holt Home Community Day's yearly event by writing an article in the newspaper and for being a wonderful partner; also, for photographing the pictures for the Holt Home for the National Register in 1976.

To Mark Buckles former student from Grayson Co., KY/CEO/Heritage Media of Kentucky Inc., who invited the author to speak on K105 to help promote the Holt Home Community Day, Holt's legacy and *Lincoln's Advocate* and has assisted numerous years with the community calendar promoting the yearly event and for being the MC at the premier book signing of *Lincoln's Advocate*.

To Becky Wethington, chef from Cloverport, KY, who assisted the author by catering the *Lincoln's Advocate* event.

To Alisia Whitfield, for catering the Indiana National Guard JAGS onsite training.

To Veronica Ent, member of the Friends group, who has assisted with Tourism to pay for the Indiana National Guard JAGS luncheon, and banners for JAG events, assists with Student Day and numerous other tasks.

To Down Home Florist, who has supported the Holt Home project and *Lincoln's Advocate*, and makes the yearly wreath for the wreath-laying ceremony.

To Towne and Country Pharmacy, and Laura Willoughby who has supported the Holt Home Project and *Lincoln's Advocate* by having copies available in the pharmacy.

To Karen Diehl for supporting the Holt project, *Lincoln's Advocate*, and for suggesting the author to make project boards out of media clippings telling the story of the project, *Lincoln's Advocate*, and the quest for restoration written by others from newspapers and magazines from across the state and beyond.

To Miller's Flowers, who supports the Holt Home Community Day and assisted with flowers for the Indiana National Guard JAGS luncheon.

To Patty Owen, Rough River Dam State Park Gift Shop, for inviting the author to place *Lincoln's Advocate* in the gift shop.

To Rough River Dam State Park for assisting the Friends of the Holt Home, Inc. with complementary lodging for a special guest and partnering for a Holt Home Community Day.

To Thomas and Joyce Wheatley (deceased) of Cloverport, KY, who assisted with a fundraising campaign for the historic Holt Home and collected the second highest donations from the Cloverport magisterial district to help make the first TE grant match.

To the Thomas and Joyce Wheatley family for donating a Lincoln bedroom suite of museum quality furniture to the Friends of the Holt Home for the historic Holt Home.

To Jon Rollins, GRW architect from Lexington, KY, who has guided the Breckinridge County Fiscal Court and the Friends of the Holt Home, Inc with guidance from the Kentucky

Heritage Council for restoration of the Judge Joseph Holt Home.

To Jimmy Piper, GRW architect, who has made numerous trips to the Holt Home and has assisted with restoration of the Holt home.

To Sheila Wayne, a dear friend, formally of Evansville, IN who now lives in Tennessee, who shared with her son Captain Todd Wayne about Joseph Holt, the first biography, *Lincoln's Advocate*, and the efforts to save his home. She also did some research for the author to help locate a gentleman who has spent decades researching Liberty Ships.

To Bill Hultgren of Erie, PA, who was with the 42nd Infantry in the Army in WWII and spent a lifetime of collecting pictures of Liberty Ships who located for the author a picture of the SS *Joseph Holt Liberty Ship*, a namesake of Joseph Holt written about in this book.

Kathryn Arinage, Librarian, Hawaii and Pacific Section, Hawaii State Library, assisted the author in finding better pictures of the SS *Joseph Holt Liberty Ship* crew and skipper.

To Alex/with E/Reference Librarian Hawaii State Public Library, Honolulu, HI, who connected the author to Kathryn Arinage.

To Joanna Hinton, Former Executive Director of Preservation Kentucky, who assisted the author and applied from Preservation Kentucky for the historic Holt Home for 11 of America's Most Endangered Places, and for Preservation Kentucky listing Judge Holt's home as one of the Most Endangered Historic Places in Kentucky in 2006.

To Leah Rubalcaba, Community Relations Officer for Joint Base Myer-Fort McNair, Washington, D.C., who assisted the author with information about the open house at Grant Hall and permitted the author's request to sit in Judge Holt's chair.

To Dr. Paul Severance, COL (Ret.) U.S. Army Professor of Military Science who portrays General Hancock, a teacher at the National Defense University who shared stories about the scaffold where the assassins were hanged at Grant Hall.

To Jessica Burdette and Michael Gish, who assisted with the Holt Family Trust. To the Holt Family Trust who restored the Holt Family Cemetery and transferred the ownership to the Friends of the Holt Home, Inc.

To Reverend Ken Jesse who prayed numerous times as requests were given and thanks for the many prayers and the great encouragement with the Prugh Lecture the night before it was given.

To Greg Hicks, Henderson, KY, webmaster for www.jholt-houseky.org who keeps the public updated with continued progress of the Holt Home project and events and has assisted the author with pictures and took time out of his busy schedule to meet deadlines.

To Angie Fugue BCATC for assisting with her students the beginning of the Holt website and for volunteering numerous times at the Holt Home Community Day with students.

To the 114th Light Artillery, who bring their wonderful canon to the Holt Home Community Day for visitors to enjoy.

To Neil Tindle, (Ret.) Guidance counselor Cloverport Independent Schools for locating Joseph Holt's signed Bible in French.

To the Guilderoy Byrne Band for playing at a fund-raising event for the Holt Home and playing traditional music at the annual Holt Home Community Day.

To Dr. Judy Piece (ret.), Professor at Western Kentucky University and former member of the KY Lincoln Bicentennial Commission who volunteered as a Civil War Story teller at a Holt Home Community Day.

To the Breckinridge County Cattleman's Association for their continued support with cooking at Holt Home Community Days!

To Breckinridge County Sheriff Todd Pate and Deputies for assisting with numerous Holt Home Community Days and for driving by the historic home to check on it numerous times.

To the Hardinsburg Fire Department for assisting with a ladder truck for inspection of the original roof to be replaced.

To the Breckinridge County EMS for being present at Holt Home Community Days.

To Breckinridge County Public Schools, Cloverport Independent Schools, and the St. Romuald Interparochial School, who are partnering with the Friends of the Holt Home, Inc. for Student Day at the historic Holt Home yearly event.

To Stephens Hopkins, who completed the 501(c)3 for the Friends of the Holt Home, Inc. And has supported the Holt Home project.

To Grant Lucas, UK college student, who has helped the author with numerous computer tasks. Many thanks, Grant!

To Pam Whinnery, Paducah KY, for donations from signing and selling her cookbooks: Recipes of Kentucky Celebrities with proceeds going for restoration of the Judge Joseph Holt Home.

To Pat Henderson, Irvington, KY, who has assisted with support, behind the scenes, for the restoration of the Judge Joseph Holt Home, with ideas for fund raising for the Friends of the Holt Home, Inc. and for attending numerous Holt Home Community Days.

To Sherry Stith, former Executive Director at the Breckinridge County Chamber of Commerce, for placing *Lincoln's Advocate* in the Chamber for visitors. And helping with the Boy Scouts for the Holt Home Community Day, and many other tasks.

To Judge Kelly Easton member of the Friends group for portraying Judge Joseph Holt yearly as a volunteer and being the Master of Ceremonies at the Holt Home Community Day, and for assisting the Friends with numerous other tasks.

To Paul Joseph O'Donoghue member of the Friends group for taking care of the trees on the Holt grounds, for performing as a volunteer and assisting with getting the Breckinridge County Band and Chamber Singers to perform at the Holt Home.

To Cleo Lee, member of the Friends group, for assisting with getting the Holt home ready for the yearly event and giving donations when sudden needs arise for the Friends.

To Kathina Bell, Breckinridge County Judge Assistant, who keeps record of volunteer time, prepares the final program for the yearly event, and does paper work for grants received.

To all those who assisted with the Friends' county wide fundraising efforts in 2012, for all the diligent work you did, for assisting with helping the Friends make a match for the TE grant, for all who came to the events and supported the causes, and for all of those who gave donations!

To the people who have given donations, beautiful, period furniture, encouraging words, and attended the yearly Holt Home Community Day event.

To the Foundations who have invited the Friends to submit grants for the restoration of the Holt home. All grants received are very much appreciated!!!!

To the Friends of the Holt Home and the Breckinridge County Fiscal Court, state partners, foundations, and persons who have assisted and for all of those who will help in the future with their volunteer time, and their gifts, we appreciate you!

To Monica Frank, former manager of the gift shop at Rough River Dam State Park, who first included *Lincoln's Advocate* in the gift shop there.

To Alice Glover for volunteering at several Holt Home Community Days.

To Andrew S. Effron, former Judge for the U.S. Court of Appeals for the Armed Forces, in Washington, D.C. and the 4th Annual George S. Pugh Lecturer, who befriended the author at the JAG School and continues to communicate.

To Elizabeth Roach, former scheduler for Governor Steve Beshear, who continued to keep the author updated with possible visits from the Governor, and always answered in a timely manner.

To Dr. Philip B. Mink, University of Kentucky, who did the radar testing for the Friends of the Holt Home, for the Holt Family Cemetery.

To Don Wojcik, Denver Service Center Planning Division, National Parks Service, for coming to the historic Holt Home on a bitter cold morning and touring the Holt home and Holt family cemetery.

To Virginia Carter, former Director of the KY Humanities Council, for inviting me to be a featured speaker in the KY Humanities Council Bureau of Speakers and including an article about Joseph Holt written by the author in the *Kentucky Humanities* magazine and for the kindness shown to me during the KY Lincoln Bicentennial years in Frankfort.

To Ben Chandler, former Director of the KY Humanities Council, for touring the Judge Joseph Holt Home with Warren Greer.

To WULF radio for inviting the author to speak on the Breckinridge County news for the Holt Home Community Days.

To Hardinsburg Post 5831 for assisting with Holt Home Community Days.

To Tommy Newton, Assistant Director Media Relations, Western Kentucky University, for assisting with getting the word out about Holt Home Community Days and sharing the news with the region.

To John Campbell, Public Relations Fort Knox, for assisting the author for numerous years with the partnering of the Office of the Staff Judge Advocate and the 113th Army Band for the Holt Home Community Days.

To Patrick Kennedy, Kentucky Heritage Council/State Preservation Office(retired), for assisting the author with numerous transitions between Preservation Officers.

To Charlotte Schmidt, (retired) Public Affairs Officer, Fort Knox, who assisted the author with numerous requests for the Staff of the Judge Advocates, the 113th Army Band and for personally attending a Holt Home Community Day.

To Howard Gleason, Public Affairs Office, Fort Knox, for assisting the author numerous times with Holt Home Community Day requests.

To Cindy Henning, Meade Co. Archaeological Historical Society, for inviting the author numerous times to speak and attending Holt Home Community Days.

To Richard Waitman, retired Army lawyer from Hancock Co., who invited the author to be the Special Guest speaker at the Annual Hancock Co. History Dinner who has attended numerous Holt Home Community Days and supports the project.

To Kyle Heavrin, former student of the author, formally with MCRECC, now with Kenergy who assisted the author getting an article in the *Kentucky Living* magazine to help promote the Holt Home Community Days.

To the MCRECC for their continued support with partnering for the Friends of the Holt Home, Inc.

To Kelly Mattingly, Internet Manager Brandenburg Telephone Company, for assisting the author numerous times through the years.

To all the students whom I have taught, from my heart I have given my best, and have given 20 years of my life for the saving and restoration of Judge Joseph Holt's home. I will continue to give 110% as efforts continue to make the Holt Home a National meeting place for all the Judge Advocates across the nation.

To all the organizations, foundations, businesses, the people, guests, scholars, and others who have supported the Holt Home project with their presence at Holt Home Community Days, with their kind words, support, and gifts, thank you!

To all the organizations, individuals and others whom have invited the author to speak and help promote *Lincoln's Advocate* and the work of the Holt Home Project, thank you!

Introduction

Brigadier General Joseph Holt, who served as the top lawyer in the Union Army during the Civil War, is an important figure in the history of American military law, and this is one reason that the efforts to preserve his Kentucky home are worth reading about. A second - and equally important - reason to read Susan B. Dyer's *Joseph Holt Mansion: Saving and Restoring the Home of Lincoln's Judge Advocate General* is that it tells a great story of perseverance and dedication. Over the last 20 years, Susan Dyer has spearheaded efforts to save Joe Holt's beautiful antebellum home in Breckinridge County, Kentucky. While much of the book is about Ms. Dyer's role in fund raising and grant writing, and making speeches and giving talks, the book does not overlook the many contributions made by others in Kentucky and elsewhere, including local civic leaders, politicians in Frankfort (the state capital), and Army lawyers in the Indiana National Guard, at the 101st Airborne Division, and working in the Pentagon in Washington, D.C.

Susan Dyer's earlier book about Brigadier General Holt, titled *Lincoln's Advocate: The Life of Judge Joseph Holt* and first published in 2009, has sold thousands of copies and been read by many Americans. But because *Joseph Holt Mansion* is a complement to *Lincoln's Advocate*, it is appropriate to briefly summarize Holt's remarkable life so that the reader will understand why Susan Dyer has devoted so many years to restoring his home to its former splendor.

Born in rural Kentucky in January 1807, Holt attended St. Joseph College and later moved to Louisville where he studied law. After being admitted to the bar, he established his law practice in Elizabethtown, Kentucky.

In 1835, 28-year old Holt moved to Mississippi to seek fame and fortune. In those days, Mississippi was very much the American frontier and, in this age of King Cotton in the southern United States, a young man looking for success quite naturally thought he might 'make it' down south. Holt handled cases involving land, slavery, and the rights of flatboat owners. He also handled some criminal cases, although civil law was his chief interest.

Holt quickly established a reputation as an eloquent speaker. His coal black hair, tall and graceful figure (he was 6' 2" in height) and magnetic voice were such that when Mississippians learned he was about to speak in court, they would race down the street to hear one of his legal arguments. His ability to marshal facts in support of his arguments and his superb command of the English language (one historian describes Holt as "stunningly articulate") made him one of the best orators in the nation. Remember that in Holt's day and age, where newspapers were relatively scarce and there was no television, radio, Facebook or Twitter, a man's speaking ability was very much a measure of his success and status in society.

Having achieved financial success, Holt left Vicksburg (where he had ultimately established his law practice after arriving in Mississippi) and moved back to Kentucky in 1842. While he continued to practice law, Holt also got involved in politics. During the administration of President Buchanan, Holt lived in Washington City (as the District of Columbia was then known) and served as Commissioner of Patents, the Postmaster General, and finally as Buchanan's Secretary of War.

Holt quickly developed both a warm personal and solid professional relationship with Abraham Lincoln after the 1860 election. Both men were from Kentucky, and both were lawyers. Most importantly, the new Republican president and Holt were committed to preserving the Union.

With the outbreak of the Civil War, Lincoln looked for ways to use his powers as president to deal with American citizens who opposed the Union war effort. Lincoln wanted to arrest citizens suspected of disloyal activities and imprison them, and he turned to Holt for a solution. The answer turned out to be using military tribunals – so-called military commissions – to prosecute outspoken Confederate sympathizers, "Peace Democrats," and American citizens who were actively aiding the Confederate war effort. Ultimately, the Army arrested, tried, and imprisoned civilians for offenses that previously could only have been tried in civilian courts. At the time, no one could be sure that the trial of civilians at military commissions would be upheld as legal. In the 1864 *Vallandingham* case, however, the U.S. Supreme Court, "taking its opinion bodily from the argument of Judge Advocate General Holt," refused to review the decisions of military commissions – thereby approving of Holt's solution to dealing with disloyal citizenry. Not until 1866, with the end of the Civil War and the termination of any need for trying civilians by military courts, did the Supreme Court reverse itself and rule that civilians could not be tried by military courts.

In the meantime, Lincoln was so impressed with Holt's legal skills that he arranged for Congress to appoint him as the Judge Advocate General of the Army in September 1862. Lincoln also arranged for Holt to have the rank of brigadier general – the first time in history that the Army's top lawyer was authorized to wear stars on his shoulders.

During the Civil War era, Judge Advocate General Holt did much more than supervise the administration of military justice in the Army and provide legal advice to President Lincoln. He also personally conducted the prosecution of high profile trials. These included the trial by court-martial of General Fitz-John Porter for disobedience of orders and the post-war trial of Andersonville prisoner of war camp commandant Henry Wirz. Holt also played a prominent role in the military commission that tried the Lincoln assassins. Working with Secretary of War Edwin Stanton, he organized and supervised the prosecution of the seven men and one woman who had been part of a conspiracy to murder, or at least do harm to Lincoln. *Lincoln's Advocate* devotes more than a few pages to Holt's involvement with this important criminal prosecution.

While Holt was a fearless supporter of Lincoln and the Federal government, he paid a price for his Unionist sympathies. His brother, Robert, who also had moved from Kentucky to Mississippi, was a die-hard slaveholder who believed fervently that his adopted state and the Confederacy must be free to secede from the Union. Joseph Holt's unswerving loyalty to Lincoln and to the Union caused a permanent rupture between the brothers. In this the Holt family was not unique; other families in 1860s America also found themselves divided by the war.

Before his death, Lincoln had offered Holt the office of U.S. Attorney General, but Holt declined to leave his position as the Army's top attorney. He continued to serve through the administrations of Presidents Andrew Johnson and Ulysses S. Grant. Grant was so impressed with Holt that he offered to make him the Secretary of War; Holt also declined this cabinet position.

Before he left government service, Holt was brevetted a major general for his faithful, meritorious and distinguished services during the Civil War. In 1875, at his own request, he was retired from active duty. To this day, Joseph Holt has the record as the longest serving Judge Advocate General in history. He also is the only Judge Advocate General to serve three U.S. presidents—Lincoln, Johnson and Grant. And if one remembers that he also served in the Buchanan administration as Commissioner of Patents, Postmaster General and Secretary of War, Holt was a remarkable public servant. After retiring from government service, Joseph Holt remained in Washington, D.C. He died there in August 1894.

As for the 'Holt House,' its foundation was laid by Joseph Holt in the 1850s, on property that had been in the Holt family since the early 1800s. Situated on the banks of the Ohio River, the home is a beautiful brick and stone mansion and Holt spent many happy hours there when he and his family were not in Washington, D.C. As Susan Dyer explains in the first pages of this book, she decided in 1997 that it was her mission in life to restore the dilapidated structure – which had been vacant for more than 50 years – to its antebellum beauty. Over the last 20 years, she has worked tirelessly to do just that – and those who read the pages of this fine book will come to understand the efforts of the many men and women who have been a part of this preservation journey.

The story of Holt the man and his mansion on the Ohio River are intertwined, and Susan Dyer is to be commended for writing books about both. *Joseph Holt Mansion* is a remarkable story of dedication and deserves to reach a wide audience.

Fred L. Borch
Regimental Historian & Archivist
The Judge Advocate General's Corps, U.S. Army

The Voyager

Having stopped by the Judge Joseph Holt Home in the summer of 1997 my life started changing. Still a teacher at the Breckinridge County Middle School my life was overwhelmed. God had placed on my heart to save Judge Holt's home. With this tremendous enhancement, I could not rest. At school, my thoughts lingered to the artist's drawing of the historic home that hung on my classroom wall. Day after day I faced that picture as my heart called out to do something.

On a Sunday afternoon drive in 1997 while I stood in the middle of Highway 144 and stared at the historic Holt Home it touched my heart. It was as if the home was speaking out to me, seeking my help. Its latest visitor thought if she wrote a book, then maybe, just maybe, it would bring attention to the home and it would be possible to save this irreplaceable home for the children who did not know about their Lincoln connection.

First view of the home while driving in 1997

So, the journey began in 1997 to carry the torch for the restoration of the Holt Home and to bring back Judge Holt's legacy. The work of research and writing of Lincoln's Advocate took 12 years along with numerous duties as a volunteer for my community where thousands of hours have been spent on writing grants, giving speeches, and lectures on Holt's career and the Holt project, attending meetings and meeting with local, state and national officials on the most wonderful journey of my life empowering me to do tasks that numerous people said could not be done. However, if you have courage and believe in a dream and God is your leader anything is possible. With the 20-year journey becoming a full circle with a unique team, Edward Ford of Richmond Kentucky inspired me to write how the Holt Home has been saved. This second book includes stories of real people as they happened. Some are almost unbelievable. Mr. Ford encouraged me to write this amazing story from a 20-year collection of notes, over 60 large binders and a mountain of recorded conversations along with several computers and numerous flash drives so others can read and be encouraged to save their history. If you are positive and believe in the dream of saving your history, it can happen. However, be prepared to work the hardest you have ever worked and don't let anyone discourage you! Smile a lot, keep the faith and pray often. And you must form a great team. It takes teamwork to be successful. However, it takes a leader who believes the dream of restoring your history can happen. And it takes much teaching of what preservation is and how grants work.

Please enjoy the most wonderful journey that has not only changed my life but the life of Holt's own community!

Being a teacher who taught writing and worked with portfolios I labored with my students in groups and daily writing was shared. I thought if I could share my love of writing maybe it would empower my students to write about topics they loved. After sharing with my classes what I had written they begged for more. "Tell us more, Mrs. Dyer." Day by day I could feel a continuous force behind me, driving me, even when I became exhausted. Night after night I could not sleep and would find myself up on the computer surfing the Internet to find out anything I could about Judge Holt. All of this became part of *Lincoln's Advocate*. Not being satisfied that he was usually referred to in the footnotes of biographies, and in short passages written by an unkind pen, pens of writers from the South after the Civil War had ended. The writers forgot to say at the beginning of the Civil War most Kentuckians wanted the Union and slaves. But when the crisis ended, Kentucky went more pro southern and writers and historians purposely forgot Joseph Holt.

Time passed as I worked on the computer thinking the only way to find out about Joseph Holt's untold story was to research myself and find out what kind of life he lived and what he truly was about. After searching in my local library, I found a vertical file which had some newspaper clippings about Holt that someone else had written, however, in the next few months when I traveled back to examine and copy the papers most had been taken and the file was almost empty. A grand search continued in libraries and archives across the state. One night being restless once again I went to the computer and typed in the words… Papers of Joseph Holt. Suddenly, before my eyes a program called "Voyager" appeared. It had listed the papers of Joseph Holt. Everything was organized telling what was in each container located at the Library of Congress.

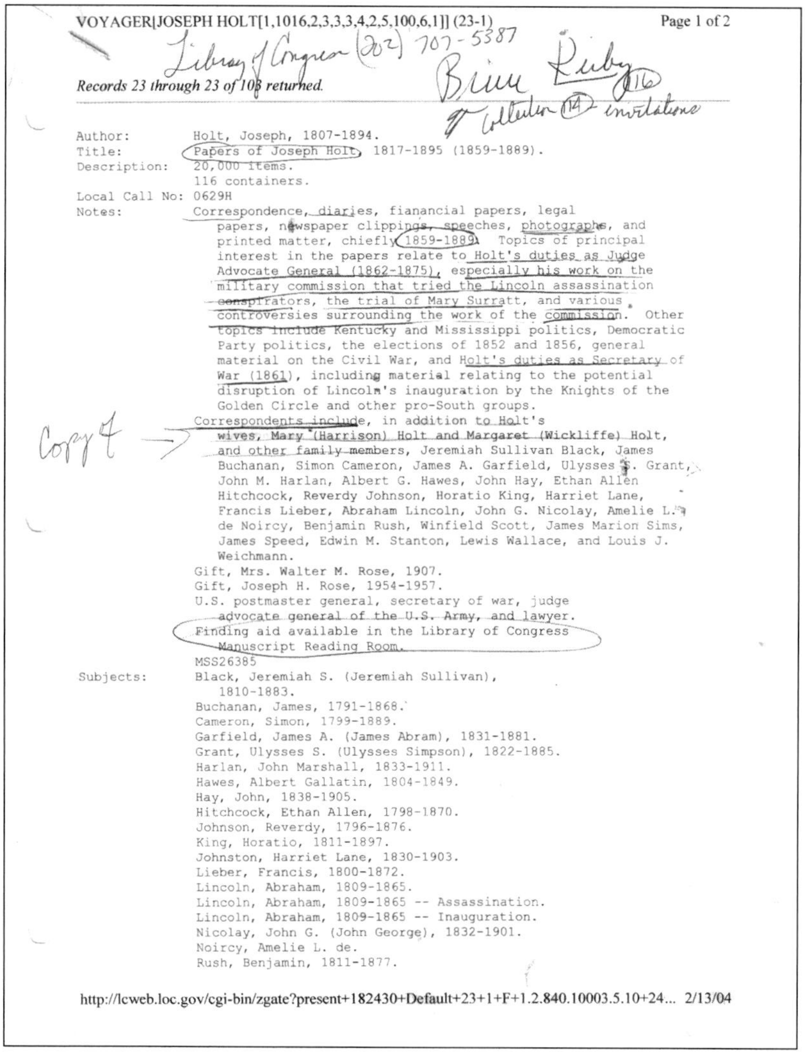

VOYAGER|JOSEPH HOLT[1,1016,2,3,3,3,4,2,5,100,6,1]] (23-1) Page 1 of 2

Records 23 through 23 of 103 returned.

Author: Holt, Joseph, 1807-1894.
Title: Papers of Joseph Holt, 1817-1895 (1859-1889).
Description: 20,000 items.
116 containers.
Local Call No: 0629H
Notes: Correspondence, diaries, fianancial papers, legal papers, newspaper clippings, speeches, photographs, and printed matter, chiefly 1859-1889. Topics of principal interest in the papers relate to Holt's duties as Judge Advocate General (1862-1875), especially his work on the military commission that tried the Lincoln assassination conspirators, the trial of Mary Surratt, and various controversies surrounding the work of the commission. Other topics include Kentucky and Mississippi politics, Democratic Party politics, the elections of 1852 and 1856, general material on the Civil War, and Holt's duties as Secretary of War (1861), including material relating to the potential disruption of Lincoln's inauguration by the Knights of the Golden Circle and other pro-South groups.
Correspondents include, in addition to Holt's wives, Mary (Harrison) Holt and Margaret (Wickliffe) Holt, and other family members, Jeremiah Sullivan Black, James Buchanan, Simon Cameron, James A. Garfield, Ulysses S. Grant, John M. Harlan, Albert G. Hawes, John Hay, Ethan Allen Hitchcock, Reverdy Johnson, Horatio King, Harriet Lane, Francis Lieber, Abraham Lincoln, John G. Nicolay, Amelie L. de Noircy, Benjamin Rush, Winfield Scott, James Marion Sims, James Speed, Edwin M. Stanton, Lewis Wallace, and Louis J. Weichmann.
Gift, Mrs. Walter M. Rose, 1907.
Gift, Joseph H. Rose, 1954-1957.
U.S. postmaster general, secretary of war, judge advocate general of the U.S. Army, and lawyer.
Finding aid available in the Library of Congress Manuscript Reading Room.
MSS26385
Subjects: Black, Jeremiah S. (Jeremiah Sullivan), 1810-1883.
Buchanan, James, 1791-1868.
Cameron, Simon, 1799-1889.
Garfield, James A. (James Abram), 1831-1881.
Grant, Ulysses S. (Ulysses Simpson), 1822-1885.
Harlan, John Marshall, 1833-1911.
Hawes, Albert Gallatin, 1804-1849.
Hay, John, 1838-1905.
Hitchcock, Ethan Allen, 1798-1870.
Johnson, Reverdy, 1796-1876.
King, Horatio, 1811-1897.
Johnston, Harriet Lane, 1830-1903.
Lieber, Francis, 1800-1872.
Lincoln, Abraham, 1809-1865.
Lincoln, Abraham, 1809-1865 -- Assassination.
Lincoln, Abraham, 1809-1865 -- Inauguration.
Nicolay, John G. (John George), 1832-1901.
Noircy, Amelie L. de.
Rush, Benjamin, 1811-1877.

http://lcweb.loc.gov/cgi-bin/zgate?present+182430+Default+23+1+F+1.2.840.10003.5.10+24... 2/13/04

Voyager

A few weeks passed and I called the Library of Congress. A young man named Bruce Kirby answered the phone saying, "Manuscript Reading Room, Bruce Kirby." I began with my name and explained I was researching for a book I was writing about Joseph Holt of Kentucky. Mr. Kirby was nice to me as I explained I had been working for over seven years trying to find a young picture of Joseph Holt and his wives. I told him I knew what container the pictures were in, if he could see if they were there. Mr. Kirby explained he worked there but it was not his job to search for items and he told me he would be glad to send me a list of people who did help with research. I asked him if he would just this one time look for a Kentucky teacher it would be so kind. Bruce Kirby said, "Mrs. Dyer how do you know what box the pictures are in?" There are over 20,000 items here on Joseph Holt and scholars come daily to study the works of Joseph Holt." I told him how it had happened and how I had typed the words …Papers of Joseph Holt on a search and a program came up called "The Voyager" showing me listed items in the Manuscript Reading Room at the Library of Congress. His words were, "I do not understand how that happened but just this one time I will go and search for only two or three minutes and you will have to hire a researcher to assist you."

It felt like eternity as I waited. Thinking how close I was to finally being able to see what Joseph Holt looked like in his prime, not the picture taken of him only a few years before his death. Everyone wants to be remembered at his or her prime, the golden years. The voice on the phone said, "Mrs. Dyer you're not going to believe this but I have found what you are looking for and I will make you a copy on plain paper and mail to you. You can examine the photos and then place a formal order for the photos with a much better quality. This is unreal," the voice said. After that day, there were numerous phone calls to Bruce Kirby with updates about the Holt Home Project, the first biography written on Joseph Holt, and numerous accomplishments that continued. Bruce Kirby personally knows the challenges and the tremendous work behind saving Judge Holt's legacy and home.

Not long after this the photos arrived. Time was spent looking at the photos putting the words that had been written and spoken over a century and half with a face full of promise and youth. The sparkle in the eyes of both wives showed they were both southern belles.

In a phone conversation with renowned author John Egerton, of Nashville, TN I told how the pictures were in the Library of Congress. Mr. Egerton said, "Tell me once again Susan how you found the pictures," I responded, "I typed in the words.... Papers of Joseph Holt and a program called The Voyager appeared. With it was listed the works of Joseph Holt and the numbered containers." Mr. Egerton said, "Susan, I believe you, I have worked with the program "Voyager"; it is an Army Program. It has been obsolete for over twenty years." So now with the restoration of the Holt mansion near completion, here's the rest of the story...Another unexplained occurrence happened.

The Dream

The dream placed on my heart by God empowered my life. From that moment, everything changed, and the massive work began. The thoughts filled my mind with what was possible. There was no peace for when I was teaching at the middle school I could think about nothing else. When everyone was sleeping, I was wide-awake learning everything possible about Joseph Holt. After experiencing the Sunday afternoon drive in 1997 my heart felt the loneliness and the pain Judge Holt's home had felt for over half a century.

Days passed as the passion grew, the love of the home becoming stronger daily. Discussion after discussion arose with my husband about saving Judge Holt's home. In all honesty he told me, "There is no way to save this home. It is privately owned. And it would take a fortune to restore it. We don't have the money to purchase it." However, being a strong lady the idea of writing a book to bring attention to the home was the beginning, hoping to get the local community interested.

Everything started at the same time. Doing research, and writing the book. I thought if I could write a book it would hopefully bring our small, rural community together. After spending an exhausting day without results in our local archives something caught my attention. It was titled, "A Talk on Joseph Holt by John P. Behen in 1962 for the Hardin County Historical Society. What a find! Finally, a clue. Quickly arising with dust-covered hands I had the talk copied and hurried home. Discovering this gentleman had given a good time line of Joseph Holt's life up to mid-life. But it was a beginning. After reading the talk numerous times an idea appeared. Find this man, and talk to him. The search began with not much luck. Phone calls after phone calls I began to think maybe Mr. Behen was no longer living. One day I called the Elizabethtown Community College and asked if anyone knew John P. Behen. Finally, a nice lady told me Mr. Behen used to come and speak to the college. I was told that he was almost blind, and she thought he had died.

Refusing to believe that I called 411 and could not believe what I heard, "John P. Behen the voice said." I explained I was writing a book about Joseph Holt and said I had found where he had given a talk to the Hardin County Historical Society in 1962. The conversation continued, and an appointment was made with Mr. Behen to discuss Joseph Holt. Sparks ignited as the excitement rose. Finally, I was going to meet someone who had studied Joseph Holt. The manuscript was gathered along with copies of the talk delivered in 1962.

Upon meeting Mr. John P. Behen and Mrs. Behen I was amazed. They were both so nice and their library of books impressive. We talked, had coffee and the stories emerged of the adventures Mr. Behen and his wife had forty years earlier. He was excited to see the copy of his talk. He shared his adventures to Washington D. C. to examine the papers of Joseph Holt. And explained he had been asked to give a talk to the local historical society in Elizabethtown about Holt.

At last a historian had been located. I also learned Mr. Behen had once lived in Cloverport, Kentucky and had been a neighbor of my mother, Mary (Aggie) Harpe Butler when she was a small child growing up there. I asked Mr. Behen if he would help me, and he agreed. While there Mr. Behen told me about a Christian Writing Conference scheduled in the United Methodist Church where he attended in a few months. He encouraged me to attend. Going to the Christian Writing Conference in Elizabethtown, Kentucky was a wonderful way to connect with other writers. Courage was gained as I walked through the doors. When signing the register, I questioned myself, "What am I doing here?" Feeling nervous and afraid I signed up for one of the sessions, and the day lingered on slowly. Noticing one of the publishers was meeting with writers at the end of the day I thought it would be interesting and exciting to speak to someone who knew the world of writing and publishing.

Exhausted and tired I went to my car and sat there. Thoughts came to me, "you might as well go home." "But then a voice told me, you're never going to get anywhere by sitting in this car. Get up and go speak to Etta Wilson." Upon entering the church once again I noticed there was a schedule and times to speak to Mrs. Wilson. I stood in line and there were not any spaces left to sign up to talk. Mrs. Wilson said, "Next." Courage came from deep within my heart. I told Mrs. Wilson I did not have an appointment but really had to speak to someone. She was the kindest lady and motioned for me to sit down.

The sketch drawn by Donna Sebastian that made debuts across Kentucky speaking about the dream of saving the Holt Home.

The manuscript was opened, and I began to explain how the story of Joseph Holt had never been told. How he had served three presidents and I wanted to bring back his history and his home. Showing Mrs. Wilson the picture of the Holt Home caught her attention. She said, "Where is this home? It is beautiful." As we continued to talk she told me this story needed to be told and she knew the person who could help me write it. His name was John Egerton, a prominent southern writer from Nashville. She promised to make a contact for me and to call back in a few weeks.

My heart raced as the line of people grew. The appointments were only twenty minutes each and I had occupied over one hour of time without an appointment. Walking to the car too excited to wait until I reached home I phoned my husband. The next few days the thought came to me that I would never hear from Etta Wilson again. She proved me wrong and left a message on my answering machine. It was unbelievable that she had done what she said she would and did not even know me. I remember her saying, "This story must be told, and John Egerton could co-author the book with you."

Taking a deep breath my fingers nervously dialed Etta Wilson's number in Nashville. She answered the phone and we talked. She told me she had contacted John Egerton and he would be glad to speak with me. This took more courage than I thought but when Mr. Egerton answered the phone his voice was reassuring. However, he told me he was too old to start a project like this and burst the bubble. His words of encouragement were to contact Dr. James C. Klotter. John Egerton told me he had worked with James Klotter and he would not steal my work. I was advised to find James Klotter.

Upon securing a phone number, phone call after phone call was made. And finally, James Klotter came into my life. After leaving numerous messages I discovered James Klotter was the KY State Historian, a former professor at the University of Kentucky, former director at the KY Historical Society and now was a professor of history at Georgetown College. However, as each day passed thoughts arose that Dr. Klotter was not going to answer the messages left.

On an August morning in 2005 Dr. Klotter returned my call. I explained how John Egerton had given me his name, and told me I needed advice and what had been put on my heart to save. Dr. Klotter agreed to meet with me at the Joseph-Beth Book store in Lexington at the Kentucky section. The memories of that day pressed in my heart like flowers in a book. It was a day that will live forever. I told him about the dream and how everyone had said it was impossible to save the Holt Home. After meeting, and sharing lunch with Dr. Klotter, his wife and my husband, Dr. Klotter and I talked for over one hour as he sat silent for a long period looking straight into my eyes and said, "Do you really think you can do both things at the same time? Save the Holt Home and write a book?" My answer was, "I don't have a choice. I cannot have peace until I do something." Silence set in as I wondered what he thought. The quietness lingered. Finally, Dr. Klotter said, "Susan, I am going to help you. Start by sending me a few chapters at a time. I will edit and advise your writing. While you are doing this start sending a few chapters to different publishing companies and check out bookstores. Search for books that are like yours. Look for publishing companies that might be interested in your subject."

And so, the writing continued with a mentor who edited and guided the writing, who understood the significance of saving Judge Holt's Kentucky home.

Being Led by the Muse

For my birthday and anniversary for five years in a row my husband asked where I wanted to go, and of course the answer was always Bardstown as research continued on both of Holt's wives. It was late in the evening about twenty minutes before dark when my husband and I were traveling in Bardstown. As we were approaching a beautiful cemetery with thousands of tombstones it caught my attention. My feelings told me I should go there this evening. "Let's stop at the cemetery", I said. My husband wasn't very fond of the idea and told me, "It's almost dark and you are not going to find anything here." However, I could not be convinced to pass it by. "We have to stop. We have passed this cemetery so many times and there is a strong force drawing me here. It won't take long." My husband finally pulled the car over and sat at the entrance of the St. Joseph Cemetery. He was very skeptical saying, "What are people going to think of us going to a cemetery at this time of the evening? We can come back in the morning when it is daylight." But I continued, "The sunlight has scattered, and the beginning of darkness is approaching. Twilight is here, and the dark is beginning. Please just give me a few moments." Convincing as I was the car made its entrance into the cemetery as passersby continued up the busy highway.

Not a breeze was blowing through the open car windows. What a sight before us! Streaks of light floated in the atmosphere. The quietness gave serenity to the stillness surrounding the tombstones of past lives, lives of people long gone and most forgotten. The historic tombstones gave insight to the people of the past. What were the chances of finding a grave with only ten minutes left of light? Quite overwhelmed, I gazed reverently upon the tombstones. But which one was Margaret's? Was she even buried here? Only I believed someone was calling out to me. The car was steered slowly to the first divide. Eddie said, "Which way? I remarked, "Turn right". The car continued as my husband said, "We are going on a wild goose chase. We are just wasting our time." I stayed focused searching the layout of the cemetery and remembered the letters I had read. Examining every detail of graves for as far as my eyes could see. Time was running out! Fragments of dusk decended as I nervously saw the next divide approach. Decision time once again. I knew the words before they were spoken, "Which way?" My husband said. "Turn right, and the car made its path as the automatic headlights came on our Mark VII, and shone over the darkening graveyard. At this point, only seconds remained, and this emotional adventure would end.

With courage in my heart, I would not quit; it was not the first time someone had told me I could not do something. I was determined to find the grave of Joseph Holt's beloved second wife, Margaret. Opening the car door, I told my husband I was going to find Margaret. Eddie's response was, "Get back in this car." I didn't listen, and continued walking, not being afraid as I hurried down the narrow road of the St. Joseph Cemetery. Walking, the feelings grew stronger. Something was guiding me. I could feel the persistence of wanting to touch Margaret's tombstone, to find her name engraved. I continued along until I saw a rusty fence with several tombstones. Could this be the one? Could this be where Margaret lay? Is this the place Joseph Holt wept privately after the rest of Margaret's family returned to Wickland on that sad August day in 1860? Was it possible this was the day to finally view the burial place I had read about? I had almost relived the journey of Margaret's life, the adventures, the sadness, the sickness, and the great love for Joseph Holt she

Finding Margaret Holt's grave

had, including one remembrance of when Margaret wrote to Joseph of how she was getting better and road on horseback to see Mrs. Speed. "She has been so kind to me this summer in sending nice fruit and I take great pleasure in visiting there."

In view of a family gravesite with the headlights glaring with an almost blinding effect, I raised my hand to shield the brightness and walked closer. A majestic pine sheltered a family's gravesite with a Victorian fence protecting it from intruders. Another family site was across the narrow drive way. I continued in the darkness with camera in hand. Walking beneath the Cedar tree my attention caught a glimpse of the name engraved, the first stone I read in the entire cemetery - Margaret Wickliffe Holt, wife of Joseph Holt. Hurrying, I examined the name with only moments of twilight remaining. And then it happened. The moment only a writer and researcher could experience - locating the person you hoped to find and bring back - giving readers a chance to know and appreciate a fine, well-bred Kentucky lady - giving them insight into what life was like then and through the painstaking work of reading the letters that had surfaced, bring a living history once again into the twenty first century to new lovers of history and the historians of the future.

What happened next was the warmest feeling - the connection of two women born centuries apart, both with dreams in their heart, with the drama of their lives becoming one. One living their life and the other writing about it and finding the importance of sharing it with others. With that exhilarating climax of the night I rushed back to the car with blinding lights flashing in my eyes as I told my husband, "I found Margaret's grave!" He could not believe it and ventured out of the vehicle to see for himself."

Elated and so grateful, I returned to Margaret's grave. I moved my hand over the name: Margaret Wickliffe Holt. Making as many pictures as possible with the flash I spoke quietly, "Margaret, I am Susan Dyer and I have found you." As I read on the tombstone the birth date of February 15, 1821 and the death date August 14, 1860, I had a flashback of how the very first meeting for the Holt Home Project was held in Breckinridge County on February 15, 2006 the anniversary of Margaret's birthday. Another clue found linking the story together.

Visiting Margaret's grave after being restored

Margaret, wife of Joseph Holt

Smith Harrison home, home of Mary Harrison, Holt's first wife

Mary Harrison Holt's grave site in Bardstown, KY

Wickliffe Family Cemetery in Bardstown, KY

Visiting Mary's grave

Delightful Day

Taken from a journal: On December 13th, 2005 Brittany Fausey from Congressman Ron Lewis' office, State Representative Dwight D. Butler and I journeyed to view the Holt Mansion. Brittany said, "I had no idea this home was this huge! I can only imagine what it used to look like and all the people who came here. It is grand! It is one of the grandest homes I have seen. Usually someone calls to try and get a school, or a small home restored. (Nothing to this extent.) Driving out in the country I was totally surprised to see this home. It is beautiful and will be more beautiful." Brittany couldn't understand why anyone would not want to see it restored.

The three of us walked slowly to the gravesite of Joseph Holt on a brisk day. I unfastened the gate. Brittany, the first to visit his tombstone called out in a frightening voice, "Oh my!" Representative Dwight D. Butler and I hurried to see what had startled Brittany. As she stood gazing on the majestic stone with an eagle soaring over Joseph Holt's monument she couldn't believe her eyes! Her face was so intrigued. "My birthday is January 6th, the same as Judge Holt's." I told Brittany I would never be able to forget that.

"It is meant to be; you were sent to us," I said. "How strange it is that your birthday just happens to be the same as Holt's."

Brittany shared with Kentucky State Representative Dwight D. Butler and me that Keith Heithpath from Congressman Lewis' office had already written an inquiry to the National Parks. Brittany said she would do a report and submit it to agencies in the government and would communicate with Sara Davasher who helps find monies to restore historical property.

Brittany expressed how wonderful all the work was that had been done to save the home. The discussion continued about checking on the status of a home being listed on the National Register to find out if owners had to follow certain guidelines. Brittany and Representative Butler were amazed with all the research. It was suggested by Representative Dwight D. Butler to make him a copy of the research, so he could be informed about Holt. I told Representative Butler I would make a copy of all the research up to date within a week's time. Work began for a copy of the research including photos for Representative Butler. As his constituent, I told him I would speak to anyone, write letters, do everything professional and ladylike, and even travel to Washington D.C. if necessary to save Judge Holt's home.

Representative Butler voiced he would have loved to have had the research yesterday when he met with Governor Ernie Fletcher. The tour of the grounds continued for thirty minutes. As we stood in the middle of the road the story of the Ginkgo tree Henry Clay likely gave to Holt was mentioned. Both Brittany and Representative Butler enjoyed skimming through the pages of the massive notebook of research.

For the first-time Brittany and Representative Butler saw a picture of a young Joseph Holt. Representative Butler said, "We shouldn't let this history slip away from us." With his copy of the research he could discuss it with people. He wanted to talk to the Governor about the home. He told me to keep digging and find more clues. The grave condition of the Holt Home was noted by the group. A discussion led to see if Representative Butler could find out who owned the graveyard. I mentioned it was once part of the estate and could never be sold. It needed attention, as it was in grave condition also. A picture was given to Brittany Fausey of the inside of the home, and how it looked in 1972 and a copy of Keith Heighpath's letter explaining everything. The group discussed how Representative William Natcher of Kentucky tried to help restore the Holt Home thirty years earlier and how the owners declined. The conversation lingered at the graveyard.

Riding back with Brittany I expressed, "I can't forget this home or Joseph Holt," and shared an image in the window at the Holt Home. The picture had been taken earlier on a disposable 35 mm camera. Upon viewing the printed pictures, I thought wow! What is that in the window? The printed photograph showed an image in the window resembling Joseph Holt with a judge's robe."

In the future, the same photo was shared with Kentucky State Historian, and Professor of History at Georgetown College, Dr. James C. Klotter. I was hesitant at first when I visited with Dr. Klotter in Lexington. On one of the many drives to the Holt Home I stopped by the edge of the road and took a picture. This picture caught my attention, as it was taken with a disposable camera bought at Wal-Mart. Upon receiving the finished photos, I was amazed at an image in the window, unaware of the presence of someone there when I took the picture. I showed it to Dr. Klotter and his comment was, "It looks like Judge Holt to me." We both thought it certainly was very strange.

Continuing the drive back to Highway 60 Brittany shared she felt it was for me to save this home. She said sometimes certain people are brought in to do positive jobs. She asked how I became interested. I told her one day as my husband and I were driving by on Kentucky Highway 144 and stopped in the middle of the road my heart became attached. I felt the pain and could feel the home drawing me to save it. It was as if the home longed to have its life back when it stood as the "showplace of Breckinridge County." Brittany was told how on HGTV sometimes where old homes are showcased on Restore America, they "choose" their owners.

I explained, before meeting Brittany and Dwight, that on that morning I prayed Christians would help restore and save this home. Brittany told me on the drive back she was a Christian. She looked straight into my eyes and said, "I am a Christian. I feel I have been sent here to help save this home." Brittany asked for my contact information, said this was not the end of the prayer but only the beginning. New at this job, Brittany had been working in the position as a Field Representative for only eight months and said Representative Dwight Butler was very helpful to her.

Recorded in my journal: "I told Representative Butler and Brittany the roof was of heavy medal. We all noticed the broken windows and the home's needed attention. I told them about the former village on this plantation; church, school, slave quarters, depot, carriage houses (how Judge Holt had the best horses and the most elaborate carriages), and about the summerhouses. In Judge Holt's personal letters housed in the Manuscript Reading Room, it mentioned his pride of owning only the best animals and how people sought the honor of riding in his carriages. Letters tell how city visitors longed for the country, to travel down the Ohio River from Louisville, to stay in a most welcoming place, the center of the community, to visit, taste the best wines, be entertained by classical music, enjoy delicious foods, and relax in the gazebo, touring the exotic gardens where visitors would stroll for hours and rest under the most beautiful trees collected around the world on Judge Holt's travels and as gifts given to him by the elite.

Being humble, Joseph Holt longed for time to trim his hedges and care for the sanctuary of the grounds that people traveled from Owensboro and Louisville to view. Visitors lingered for days upon days, not wanting to leave this place nestled by the river. This grand lady stood majestic and will once again!

Now the work began. How could a small, rural community save something as beautiful, and grand as the Judge Joseph Holt Home without experience in preservation?

Many doors were knocked upon and I talked to anyone who would listen and when they would not listen I was just a nice lady and went to someone else. After this visit I was asked to write a letter to the Department of the Interior telling them and describing the importance of Joseph Holt's career and legacy and to express the neglected condition of his beloved Kentucky home. Not long after sending the letter I was excited upon receiving an answer from the United States Department of the Interior.

The letter read:

United States Department of the Interior
National Park Service
1849 C Street, NW
Washington D.C. 20240

Honorable Ron Lewis
House of Representatives
Washington, D. C. 20515

Dear Mr. Lewis:

Thank you for your letter of December 7, 2005, and the accompanying correspondence from your constituent, Ms. Susan B. Dyer, concerning the Joseph Holt House and Chapel in Breckinridge County, Kentucky. We appreciate your interest in this property and Mrs. Dyer's commitment to its preservation.

The Holt House and Chapel was listed in the National Register of Historic Places on July 12, 1976. Properties listed in the National Register may be eligible to receive grants, tax credits for rehabilitation, and other forms of financial assistance. To obtain information about these programs, we recommend that Mrs. Dyer contact the Kentucky State Historic Preservation Officer, who serves as a partner of the National Parks Service in administering the National Register and related Federal historic preservation programs. The Kentucky State Historic Preservation Officer is:

Mr. David Morgan
Kentucky Heritage Council
300 Washington Street
Frankfort, Kentucky 40601

Sincerely,
Joe Wallis
for Janet Snyder Matthews, Ph. D
Associate Director for Culture Resources
And Keeper of the National Register of Historic Places

After receiving this letter, I bundled the courage and rehearsed what I would say to David Morgan. And was tested with patience as I called weekly explaining the necessity of speaking to him. There was such a kind, sweet voice on the other end of the line each time I called. The weeks passed as I was told the message would be given to Mr. Morgan. Finally, after weeks of persistence in phoning the Kentucky Heritage Council/ State Preservation Office I knew the voice on the line and this time when Mary Jean Atchison answered she said, "Susan, we have your name and your number." My reply was very direct. "I know you do but I am going to call every week until David Morgan talks to me."

Not long after that on a Friday in late January I finally received a call from Mary Jean saying David Morgan was going to call me that day. I had planned an outing but stayed home and waited as the day passed. My thoughts were, "Has another day been lost?" Late in the afternoon the phone rang and as I checked the number calling I knew it was from the Kentucky Heritage Council State/ Preservation Office. This was my chance at last to speak from my heart to somehow convince David Morgan that Joseph Holt was important and his home was a Kentucky treasure that needed help.

Taking deep breaths and speaking to the person whom could help I gave the performance of my life. Mr. Morgan asked many questions, and I answered every one. David Morgan told me he would help, and I had his attention. He said he would come to Breckinridge County and speak to a group explaining the possibilities available because of the Kentucky Lincoln Bicentennial. He told me he would come but I would have to organize the meeting, find the meeting place, take him to the Holt Home before the meeting, prepare a fifteen-minute talk about Judge Joseph Holt and his home, and I was to have refreshments for the crowd along with driving directions with only two weeks of planning.

This was one of the happiest days! The day had been long sitting close to the phone, and while waiting for the call I enjoyed reading letters from Joseph Holt to his wife, Margaret Wickliffe, a

Kentucky's governor's daughter. Each letter was signed, by Joseph Holt, "from my heart of hearts!"

Later that day traveling on for an outing after speaking with David Morgan I ventured into my favorite store. Normally, I did not view this section of the store but today was different. As I strolled past the home section the item on the top shelf stopped me in my tracks. Frozen, for the moment, I thought, "Is this a sign?" Is Judge Holt's spirit with me? Does he know what I am trying to do?" Focusing back, I carefully examined the beautiful item. It was a reproduction of a Victorian lamp, burgundy in color with the stand part marble and the base in bronze with three figures under the lamp balancing the composition. The shade of the lamp was made with two hearts, on each side out of puffed material. The lamp still shines on the continued work as a memory of the day David Morgan first called to help. The heart of heart's lamp is a constant reminder of days spent reading numerous letters signed by Holt to Margaret Holt his second wife, as "my heart of hearts"!

Quite frightened with the agenda assigned to me for the first public meeting for the Holt Home, I phoned Dr. James C. Klotter. After an encouraging conversation with my mentor, Dr. Klotter told me, "You must have a heart like a lion and a stomach like a goat to do this kind of work." The massive work began as Dr. Klotter and David Morgan advised me. All research on Holt was reread and studied diligently as I prepared the speech to inform the citizens of Breckinridge County the possibilities available with the connection of Judge Joseph Holt and his home.

Dr. Kotter shared with me he was on the advisory board for the Kentucky Lincoln Bicentennial Commission. He told me the last meeting he attended, the group had spoken about a woman trying to save Judge Holt's home. He said, "I believe that woman is you, Susan". This truly inspired and stirred my feelings as the tasks continued.

David Morgan advised me to contact people from the local historical society and citizens who might be interested. Numerous hours continued with phone calls explaining the upcoming meeting and inviting citizens. I bravely phoned Breckinridge County Judge Executive, George Monarch III and asked if the meeting to inform the public about the possibility of saving the Holt Home could be held at the Breckinridge County Fiscal Court Annex? The judge responded positively and said, "Yes". I also invited the daughter of the family who owned the Holt Home to the meeting. The contact number of the daughter was given to me by Lee Stinnett from the Addison community.

On the afternoon of February 15, 2006, I became very nervous when I called the judge's office to speak to him and was told he was at the doctor's office probably with the flue. Shortly, Judge Monarch returned my call sounding very ill, saying, "Susan, I may not be there tonight." I replied, "I need you there, tonight, Judge Monarch. Please try and come!" After the conversation, I put my thoughts to the speech and remained positive about everything. My mother helped with the refreshments, and the judge's office was to provide the coffee.

Waiting patiently at the Hardinsburg United Methodist Church parking lot, I envisioned how the evening would transpire. It seemed like only minutes and a state car pulled beside me. Shifting into the Mark VII Becky Shipp, David Morgan and I had a delightful time as our trio enjoyed the drive and stories of Holt and how hard it had been trying to locate information and getting people to listen. Mr. Morgan enjoyed the stories. He told how inspiring it is to have the love and courage to save history, for the future, explaining that before you can learn about the present you had to understand the past.

Our group arrived barely before dusk. To be respectful to the private owners we parked the car by the Holt graveyard and walked in the middle of the highway viewing the historic Holt home from the road and right of way, David Morgan's words were, "It's amazing, and we have to save it." Darkness came quickly, and time pressed us to get back for the first public meeting.

Driving back to Hardinsburg went quickly. Upon arrival, the parking lot was completely full. David Morgan stated, "This is unreal". Normally when we travel to a community there will be five or six people to show and have an interest. This is wonderful." Finally, a parking place became available as we walked into a hallway filled with people wearing smiles.

After the visitors and local citizens were welcomed I began a journey continuing today as an advocate for preserving the community's history of Judge Joseph Holt and his legacy. As I began to gather my notes, David Morgan asked quietly, as he leaned across the table, "Do you plan to tell us all of that?"

"I answered, "Yes, you said there would be fifteen minutes for a talk about Judge Holt and his national significance and legacy."

The talk....

Guide for Meeting

Thanks for everyone attending tonight. I would like to welcome our guests: David Morgan, The Kentucky State Historic Preservation Officer, and Director who serves as a partner with The National Park Service, along with Becky Shipp from the Kentucky Heritage Council.

Background for Joseph Holt and his Birthplace:

Joseph Holt, a famous son of Breckinridge County was born on January 6, 1807 and lived life like we dream about living. His father, John Holt, was an attorney in Hardin County in 1802, assisted in supervising the construction of the first courthouse, and was Mayor and a member of the Fiscal Court before moving to Breckinridge County.

In 1804, the Holt family moved to Breckinridge County where John became the Commonwealth's Attorney. John Holt was the Justice of the Peace and served as Surveyor and Overseer of Roads. From 1831 through 1835 John Holt inspected tobacco at the public warehouses around Stevensport. He also enjoyed farming the lovely river bottoms at Holt.

Eleanor, Joseph's mother, was widely read and a strong leader in the church. She was a very spirited lady who prepared her children for college. With the help of her father, Richard Stephens, Joseph's reality of attending college at St. Joseph became possible in 1822. Debating was Joseph's favorite subject in college and being on the college debating team helped him prepare for his future.

It is not clear if Joseph Holt graduated from Centre College at Danville. From the time, he left home, he made his way to social and financial betterment that his parents wished him to have, and by 1825 Holt was studying law in Lexington with one of Kentucky's most famous attorneys, Robert Wickliffe.

By 1828 Joseph Holt opened his first law office in Elizabethtown, and became an active, committed supporter of Andrew Jackson's Democratic Party. He soon won a name for his speaking ability in competition with many notable rivals.

In 1832, Mr. Holt gained professional success in Elizabethtown. He then moved his practice to Louisville where he also took a job as assistant editor of the Louisville Advertiser. He was then appointed by the Governor as Commonwealth's Attorney for that judicial district for two years. Three years later Holt, now twenty-eight and Prosecuting Attorney for the Louisville Circuit moved his practice to Vicksburg.

Competition at the Southern Bar was great! Over the next several years Holt's Vicksburg law practice continued to thrive. His reputation magnetized his observer's recognition of his masterly courtroom style. One biographer stated. "There was nothing sparkling in Holt's courtroom's presence. It was the driving force of his sincerity he gave to deliver such power over his audience." Holt's cases were not won by humor, cleverness, or glamour, instead "Holt spellbound the jury by the crushing weight of evidence he would bring to bear on the case."

While pursuing his law career in Mississippi, he continued to expand his commitments to the Democratic Party. Mr. Holt spoke at the National Democratic Convention held in 1835, one year before the election and defended a controversial vice-presidential candidate, Richard M. Johnson, against the attack of his opponents in a speech that further enhanced Holt's fame as an effective speaker.

Joseph Holt was described by J.O. Harrison as tall, lean, dark complexion with dark hair, blue eyes and very prominent features. Money, prestige, and law were not the only things that he thought about then. In April of 1839, Mr. Holt returned to Kentucky for a visit and fell in love and married Mary L. Harrison, daughter of Dr. Burr Harrison and Elizabeth Harrison, for whom Elizabethtown is named.

Holt seemed to have lived a work-centered life in Vicksburg, even undermining his own health with the demanding pace he kept. During the time in Mississippi, both Holt and his wife, Mary, were diagnosed with tuberculosis. Their health seriously eroded by 1842. Holt deemed it fortunate, and was able to economically retire from the law and return with Mary to recuperate. They lived a relatively quiet life at 233 East Walnut Street in Louisville, where they both struggled to regain their health and strength.

Only Joseph was successful. Mary died four years later plunging Holt into a period of deep, private despair. In his sadness and loneliness Joseph toured for the next seventeen months in Europe and the British Isles.

Two years later he began to resume a more active life. He became involved again in the Democratic Party policies to some degree and began to give political speeches on the affairs of the day.

Touring and work restored his lust for living and on April 2, 1850, Holt married his second wife, the beautiful daughter of Governor Charles Anderson Wickliffe of Bardstown. The couple left New York on The American Eagle and set sail for London to tour Europe and the Middle East for their wedding trip. By the messages in their corresponding letters from New York, Washington, and Wickland the strong bond of love shown through very much. Judge Holt had a very loving heart for his beloved Maggie as he called her. And Margaret referred to Joseph as her beloved husband.

Joseph Holt continued his interest in politics. The Wickliffe family was honored to have Mr. Holt as their son-in-law, proud of his brilliant mind.

Holt was dedicated to the Democratic Party in 1852 and 1856. Then in April 1857, he and Margaret moved to Washington City where Holt accepted his first appointment from Democrat James Buchanan.

According to Stanford University Press, Holt served U. S. Commissioner of Patents, U. S. Postmaster General and U. S. Secretary of War in President Buchanan's Administration. Holt joined the United States Army as a colonel and President Lincoln named him Judge Advocated General of the Union Army. He became Chief of the Bureau of Military Justice for the United States Army. Mr. Holt was the sitting Judge Advocate General for the trial of the Lincoln assassination conspirators from May 8 to July 15, 1865. He retired from the Army on December 1, 1875. Mr. Holt helped save his native state, Kentucky, from seceding from the Union during the Civil War by giving numerous speeches throughout Kentucky: namely Louisville, Hardinsburg, and Elizabethtown. He also devised the plan to incorporate blacks as soldiers for the Union Army during the Civil War.

The Library of Congress Manuscript Division has 20,000 items, 116 containers of the Papers of Joseph Holt. There contained are general correspondents and related materials, and numerous others. Bruce Kirby, a young man who works in The Manuscript Reading Room told me every day scholars come to study the works of Joseph Holt.

During WW II, Liberty Ships built by the United States Maritime Commission were named after prominent (deceased) Americans.

Any group who raised $2 million dollars in War Bonds could suggest a name for a Liberty Ship. Our nation named a Liberty Ship after Joseph Holt. It was called the SS *Joseph Holt.*

Lincoln 's *Avengers, Justice Revenge and Reunion After the Civil War* by Elizabeth D. Leonard, a recent book, has 154 references to Joseph Holt. The Professor of History at Colby College states Joseph Holt has been grievously overlooked by biographers and historians, and if one studies Lincoln they must also study Holt.

It is now our turn to try and plan things to recognize and honor this man who dedicated his life for the betterment of our country.

How is the situation now?

Time is running out! The Holt Mansion could add charm, and delight to Kentucky's list of fine and preserved southern homes. As well as bring numerous tourists to Breckinridge County. This home has not only regional, and state interest but national interest as well.

The home is begging for the life it once knew where queens and kings entered through its doors. Throughout the years important people came to social events there. Servants greeted the visitors as they approached. The foyer sparkled in the wing, with the sight of beautiful gas chandeliers. Red velvet drapery with gold tiebacks adorned the walls.

What guests saw dazzled their eyes! Stairwells free standing with encasements making a complete circle to the third floor with handrails made of walnut gracing the spindles of oak trim.

All the walls of plaster are twelve feet high having massive decorative woodwork. The baseboards are thirteen inches high.

In the center of the ceilings are decorative plaster medallions from which the ornate light fixtures hung each holding three kerosene lamps.

There were six fireplaces with heavy metal mantels fitted with a coal grate, which were used for heating the house.

The doors and windows are ten feet tall. The windows were decorated with cornices of wood, trimmed with gold leaf. Lace curtains hung at the windows with swags at the top. The home had a red, green and blue room.

Within the rooms could be found the finest of furnishings of cherry and walnut. Elegant mirrors decorated the home throughout, as it was the showplace of Breckinridge County.

Upon Joseph Holt's death in 1894, the estate went to his nephew Washington D. Holt. Washington Holt's wife Vanda sold the estate at the death of her husband in 1910 consisting of 500 acres then, and the house for $25, 000 dollars.

Fred Dutschke bought the home in sad condition due to years of neglect. After buying the house he tore down the slave shacks and added three new rooms. The house then contained fourteen rooms, three porches, and cellar. Nine of the rooms measure twenty feet by twenty-two feet.

In August of 1943, Fred's son Herman Dutschke inherited the home. He sold the property to Shirley Terry in 1960. Around 1965, after the death of Mr. Terry, the house was sold again. It was bought by the four children of Ida Dutschke Hendry. Today, the property consists of 156 acres and house belongs to Mrs. Louise Doda from Doe Valley, Brandenburg, Kentucky.

The Joseph Holt Home and Chapel were both entered in the National Register of Historic Places on May 12, 1976. The church Joseph Holt built in honor of his mother has been torn down. The National Historical Preservation Act of 1966 provides for an expanded National Register to record the tangible evidence of our national, state, and local heritage that merit preservation.

U. S. Representative William Natcher of Kentucky had funds available thirty years ago to restore the Holt House. At that time, Mrs. Doda and her sisters, owners of the home were not interested in the offer from the state.

Since then the Breckinridge County Historical Society has tried numerous times to help, but the owner declines. She finally did permit the county to place a marker of Joseph Holt in front of the home and then later had someone remove it. The Breckinridge County Historical Society then placed the marker by Judge Holt's gravesite. This site was willed as a small 1.2 acres where Holt and family members are buried and cannot be sold. It is in a Trust Fund with the National City Bank of Owensboro and today the trust has been moved out of state.

With the planning of the Lincoln Bicentennial Celebration of 2009, Mr. David Morgan from the Kentucky Heritage Council is here tonight to present a possible plan for Breckinridge County to participate in the Lincoln celebration with links to Lincoln/ Holt, and slavery issues as well as Joseph Holt's birthplace, possibly receiving good sums of money for preservation. I have contacted Mrs. Pam Hawkins, daughter of Mrs. Doda in charge of her affairs, with the information about tonight's meeting and the possibility of her family getting money to preserve the historical home of Joseph Holt's birthplace if they are interested.

Joseph Holt will be 200 years old on January 6, 2007. His gravesite needs attention now!

Joseph's headstone is very large and topped with a bronze eagle, the symbol of America. The eagle stands on top of two crossed cannons. The cemetery is surrounded by a thick brick wall that is now beginning to crumble. There is a large iron gate at the entrance.

Around 1878, Joseph Holt added a wing to the right side of the house and a front porch to the original house built in the 1850's. The porch has a very decorative iron cornice and an iron railing top center.

The Holt Mansion has been waiting since 1894, begging to be restored to its glorious day's when it entertained the most distinguished people in America as well as Europe. Historians must make it what it once was. Once again, the voices could be heard of people living and being merry in the most pleasant environment near the river, amid the long, rolling fields of green and the sweet smells of goldenrods in the south.

Please help restore this legacy!

Thank you.

Now, I would like to continue thoughts and concerns with Mr. David Morgan guiding us.

David Morgan spoke to the crowd and provided the reassurance that the opportunity existed for the Judge Joseph Holt House to be a part of the Kentucky Lincoln Bicentennial Celebration. He explained the Judge Joseph Holt House had a strong connection to Lincoln and grant opportunities would be available for the next few years.

Adjourn / Refreshments

The story about the red napkins!

The excited crowd enjoyed refreshments. Conversations lingered. Happiness was in the air. The people gradually went home, a few at a time. Lee Stinnett waited until the crowd disappeared and shared that he might be able to help us contact a family member of the Doda family.

All items of paper plates, napkins and materials used for the evening were being bundled to carry home when I noticed something unusual on the serving table. I called my mother to the table, "Look at this!" My mother said, "How did that get there?" My answer was, "Someone spilled coffee on one of the unused red table napkins left in the stack, and it's another heart." My mother told me to keep the napkin and put it in a plastic bag with the coffee spill shaped like a heart. The napkin remains today from the February 15, 2006 meeting as a reminder of the continued journey for our community whom have given their hearts to save their history for their children, for the future, for Kentucky, and for the nation!!!!

Eleven years later, on April 4, 2016, I found Brittany Fausey who now is an attorney with Anspach Meeks Ellenberger LLP in Toledo, OH. I sent a one-page update of all that has happened since she came in 2005 to assist.

I have learned with preservation you always want to keep people as the circle continues. Brittany said "I absolutely remember you. The Holt Home project still crosses my mind on occasion. I loved working as a Field Representative. I met so many amazing people, including you!" You are a 'mover and shaker.' Anyone should want you on his/ her side. You get things done! It fills my heart with so much happiness to know that you've made so much progress. Congratulations!!!! I remember touring the house that day. The www.jholt-houseky.org website looks great too! I hope you are well, and I hope Dwight Butler is well also. Admittedly, I've lost most of my connections in Kentucky. It will always feel like home."

Good communication with people you meet with time invested is one of the keys to successful work in preservation projects. You learn something beneficial from all the people you meet. And the more people you meet the more opportunities you have for continued delightful days!

Susan Dyer knocking on doors after the first public meeting working to gain partners.

Holt Home Appraisal

Calculating the square footage of the home

A meeting was held in my home on June 29, 2006. Attendees were local Breckinridge Countians along with Breckinridge County Judge Executive George Monarch III, David L. Morgan, Executive Director at the KY Heritage Council/ State Preservation Office, KY State Representative Dwight D. Butler, and Congressman Ron Lewis's Field Representative, Brittany Fausey. The meeting's purpose was to discuss the proper way to contact the owner of the Holt Home in regards to purchasing and restoring Judge Joseph Holt's Home.

Since the Holt Home was privately owned the family had to be contacted. The director at the Kentucky Heritage Council / State Preservation Office at the time David L. Morgan suggested the county judge George Monarch III to write the guardian of the private owner to see if there was interest in selling the home. A proposal letter was sent on August 21, 2006 from the Breckinridge County Fiscal Court and citizens of Breckinridge County to the guardian of private owner, Louise Doda to investigate purchasing and restoring Judge Holt's home.

The Breckinridge County Fiscal Court and citizens worked closely with the Kentucky Heritage Council/ State Historic Preservation Office and the Kentucky Lincoln Bicentennial Commission to make this project one of the highlights of Kentucky's participation in the national celebration, which continued through 2010.

On September 26, 2006 Judge Monarch received a response from the proposal letter saying Mrs. Doda's guardian/lawyer Kevin Ford would be happy to consider the August 21, 2006 proposal if Breckinridge County's Fiscal Court and citizens would submit a proposal for property with house that was to be purchased and a specific price.

To continue the process an appraisal had to be conducted. Volunteers worked carefully selecting a qualified appraiser who was certified to appraise historical homes. Mr. Claude Galloway from Mayfield was selected. He worked with people through the Commonwealth working to receive grants, stating he would not pressure for the money. Mr. Galloway said he would wait several months to be paid.

After this a letter was written to Judge Tommy Turner. The letter discussed how the Holt Home Steering Commission was working on an apprais-

Lee Stinnett, member of the Holt House Steering Committee and Claude Galloway, historic appraiser

The only remaining grate in the home

Upper view of the staircase

Bedroom on the second floor

View of the iron works on the front porch with ornate trim

The Holt House Steering Comittee

Grave condition of the stair tower before restoration

Coming down the west staircase

Third floor (virgin timber)

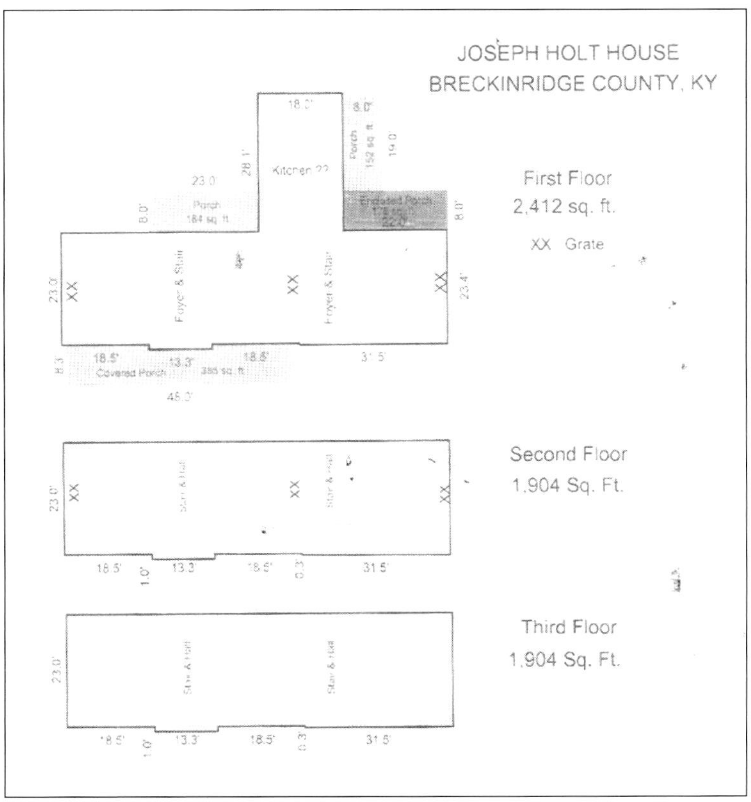

Square footage of the Holt Home from the appraisal

Spear header, Susan Dyer

al on the Holt Home and desired acreage to make a good offer to the guardian/ lawyer of Mrs. Doda. The Commission found an appraiser, Mr. Claude Galloway who would appraise the home and land for $2,500.00 and he agreed to wait patiently for several months for his services. Mr. Galloway said he would be able to appraise the Holt Home and property by the 23rd 24th, or 25th of October.

The Steering Committee worked with David Morgan and were asked to see if Judge Monarch and the county would pay the fee. Judge Monarch's answer was, "wait until after the election." He said he would bring this before the Fiscal Court when they met. He suggested to wait on the appraisal until November 20-24, 2006. After speaking with Mr. Morgan, the committee felt they needed to complete the appraisal as soon as possible and send to the lawyer/guardian, Kevin Ford, before Mr. Morgan retired and left his office.

Then the Holt Home Steering Committee spoke once again to Judge Tommy Turner to see if there were any possible grants connected with the Kentucky Lincoln Bicentennial Celebration that could be used for the appraisal. With advice from the Executive Director at the KY Heritage Council State Preservation Office the committee scheduled the appraisal as soon as possible to know the money was available to pay Mr. Galloway for his services. As time was essential for the project to be successful, numerous calls and emails were sent seeking help to direct the committee to money through grants that could be used to pay for the appraisal.

An email was sent to Judge Tommy Turner on Thursday, October 12, 2006 about mini- grants. His reply came quickly stating there were some mini-grants, but he was not sure if this would qualify or if the time frame of the mini-grant would be any more favorable. Judge Turner suggested chatting with Warren Greer of the Kentucky Abraham Lincoln Bicentennial Commission to see what the possibilities were, and, to ask David Morgan to speak with Warren.

Judge Turner shared since the appraisal would not be completed until the last of October, the appraiser could do the work and then submit a bill for it. Since there is usually a thirty-day grace on the payment for such services, it would be the last of November before payment was due. And this would fit into the county's time frame.

I completed the grant application and mailed to Chris Goodlett at the Kentucky Historical Society, hoping to win the grant to pay the bill. Mr. Goodlett E-mailed saying he received the application on November 9, 2006. A phone call came shortly after the grant was submitted and received as all grants were in review. To completely qualify for the grant, expenses for $2,500.00 had to be proven to match the budget of the grant submitted to make the 50-50 match for the appraisal and had to be scanned and E-mailed within hours. My husband asked who was going to pay for the appraisal if we did not win the grant. My answer was, "I guess I am."

I collected the receipts spent for $2,500.00 and more for expenses along with receipts for research on the Holt Home, Joseph Holt and the beginning research for *Lincoln's* Advocate, the first ever biography on Judge Joseph Holt and submitted to the Kentucky Historical Society hoping the receipts would make the match. With the November election Judge Monarch was defeated and the matter of the court matching the grant was not brought up at Fiscal Court. Now the Holt Steering Committee had a $2,500 bill to be paid.

The appraisal began on October 23, 2006 being completed on November 17. Members of the Holt Home Steering Committee were present for the appraisal with permission from the guardian.

The following are notes from the appraisal taken on November 23, 2006. Pictures from the day can be viewed.

Mr. Galloway inspected the Holt Home and surrounding property. He said the inside was in good shape, sound, and all the trim was in tact. All the iron fireplaces had been pulled loose from the bases. Only three ceiling medallions original to the home were left.

It was difficult to see the downstairs even with flashlights. In one of the downstairs rooms an iron grate was left but someone had tried to pull it out of the wall and left it. This one was probably not in as good condition as the others.

The stairs were still sound, no squeaking, in fact, there was no squeaking in the entire home.

Mr. Galloway said he thought the kitchen was original to the home (architect Jon Rollins later confirmed it was built at a later period,) and the cellar door on the north side of the kitchen and the small porch was an add-on in later years. The back porch or terrace was original to the home and not in good condition.

There were two sections of stairwells. Three or four spindles were missing but they were tied together with strings. The sides of the stairs are chalky white. While in the foyer, a flashlight was shinned upon the wallpaper. It had several layers, but the underneath layer was the same as a reproduction of off white (Victorian wall paper.)

Also under the stairs there were five or six layers of wallpaper, and the underneath colors were of deep black and red velvet. Research says in Joseph Holt's home there were red velvet drapes with lace.

The second floor was in good condition. The stairs are gorgeous. A lot of the plaster has been pulled off where you can see the tiny strips of wood under the plaster. Also, a closet had been built in the home on the second level since 1997 when I was given permission for a private tour by Mrs. Doda from the caretaker.

Some of the glass from a window was lying on the floor. Mr. Galloway told the group the rooms had been used in the past, and was not considered an attic.

He spoke about the certain type of guttering made into the roof to help the rain run off the home. And pointed it out to the group. He said the roof was a very thick metal type. Now, there didn't seem to be any leaks except for windows missing glass.

One of the down stairs rooms was still painted blue. During Holt's life, the research showed there was a blue, green and red room. Mr. Galloway found some of the original sidewalks after the research on the home was shared about brick sidewalks.

He also thought he found the indention of where the circular driveway used-to-be and said it probably circled around the huge tree in the front. He commented how the front steps were made of a low-grade marble.

Claude Galloway was impressed by the Gingko tree. One large limb had broken off since the last trip to the see the Holt Home. However, the tree is still okay. For preservation sake Mr. Galloway said he would preserve the outside of the home first. Shared the bricks were at least 15 inches thick and the house in front was not square. Probably when they started laying the brick they got up to a certain point and realized it was not square. Mr. Galloway voiced that he and his son would be returning to the site again and work on the outside to complete the appraisal. He received permission from David Minor, caretaker on this day to do so. Said he would be finished in about three weeks and would send information to me.

Mr. Minor was very nice and shared the lawyer's address. The day was bitter cold as to bite the bones of anyone who dared a tour on this extremely blustery day in October. The appraisal on site lasted for the extended time of 2 ½ hours. Those who observed this historical beginning were Kentucky State Representative Dwight D. Butler, Becky Ruskowski, David Minor, Breckinridge Co. Judge Exec. George Monarch (was attending a luncheon and could not attend,) Historic Appraiser Claude Galloway, Lee Stinnett, and myself.

The last deed of the home along with pictures of the inside and out were given to Mr. Galloway. I offered to buy Mr. Galloway lunch, but he declined. David Minor shared before he became involved a family member took light fixtures and fireplaces and sold them. One member of the committee found part of the Victorian fence in the closet.

The home was filthy, with lots of junk downstairs but the upstairs was tidier being harder to carry items up the spiral steps. The home was so predominantly dark no one could view what the kitchen was like, even with flashlights. In part of the kitchen someone had painted a complete brick wall a very bright pink. Mr. Galloway said work needed to be done soon on the exterior. In contrast to the condition of the house, the spirits of the Holt Home Commission were warm and bright with promise of the sun shining once again through the clouds on this bitter cold October day where a true jewel had been neglected for decades, but now was on the radar to be saved for the ages!

Good news and progress came. With the proof of paid expenses for my research the Breckinridge County Fiscal Court, a government institution, I won the grant submitted for them as a volunteer for a matching 50-50 grant of $2,500.00 for the appraisal of the Joseph Holt Home through the Lincoln Bicentennial Commission placed in the Kentucky Historical Society! I received notification on Thursday, January 18, 2007 with congratulations as a grant recipient including an invitation to appear and to invite the Breckinridge County Judge Executive Ray Powers and KY State Representative, Dwight D. Butler and Kentucky State Senator Carroll Gibson on February 12, 2007 in Frankfort at the State Capitol Building to celebrate the birthday of Lincoln - to be in the ceremony recognizing grant recipients - witness the unveiling of the Kentucky Lincoln Commission's new website and a history day for Kentucky Lincoln sites. The event was planned by the Kentucky Lincoln Bicentennial Commission and held in the Rotunda from 1:00-3:00 p.m.

Footnotes:

E-mail from Chris Goodlett, KY Historical Society/ Congratulations on your successful Lincoln Bicentennial grant application

Addendum to Appraisal Report of the Holt Home Property

Date of Initial Report November 18, 2006

Date of Addendum December 11, 2006

Pictures taken at the Rotunda and on the Holt Home Appraisal Day

David Minor (deceased), former caretaker, Lee Stinnett, and Clause Galloway, historic appraiser

Meeting the Publisher

There was always excitement on the days the Kentucky Lincoln Bicentennial Commission met. It had become routine to awaken before sunrise for the long trip to Frankfort. However, today would be different, the first meeting as always was with the Kentucky Lincoln sites which would meet today at Lincoln's birthplace in the morning and dismiss for a luncheon at the Kentucky Lincoln Museum in Hogensville.

Upon arrival, I was greeted by the other Lincoln site supporters in the state as I went to learn for my community how to become an official Kentucky Lincoln Site, serving as a volunteer, representing the Judge Joseph Holt Home. I was invited to attend regularly by Warren Greer, Program Coordinator for Kentucky's Abraham Lincoln Bicentennial Commission at the Kentucky Historical Society. There were always refreshments available to make everyone feel comfortable, and the group was very warm and friendly. At the quarterly meetings, all site representatives would give updates on what was happening at their individual site. There was much to learn, and it took courage to attend when the Judge Joseph Holt home was not an official Kentucky Lincoln site until February 12, 2007.

Kenneth Tabb, then, the Hardin County Court Clerk was seated by me and in conversation Mr. Tabb learned I was writing a biography on Joseph Holt. Mr. Tabb shared this with some of those present during the meeting. After the two-hour discussion, the group was dismissed and headed back to downtown Hodgenville for the prepared luncheon. As always, the food was delicious, and the time too soon expired.

The Kentucky Lincoln Bicentennial Commission always started promptly at 1:00 p.m. On this day before the group settled in for the Kentucky Lincoln Bicentennial Commission meeting, Kenneth Tabb brought over a tall, attractive gentleman dressed as if from New York, quite stylish, to introduce. As I extended my hand for an introduction Mr. Tabb said, "Susan, this is Doug Sikes, publisher from Acclaim Press. Doug, Susan is writing a book about Joseph Holt. And we're having a book signing this evening at the Hardin County History Museum for Robert Prather on Jonathan Swift, and Doug is the publisher. Why don't you come to the event?" What excitement!

Soon the meeting was called to order. At the very beginning Kentucky State Senator Carroll Gibson gave kind words and shared the work with the Commission I was doing for the community with the Holt project. During the middle of the meeting Judge Tommy Turner said, "We will now hear from Mrs. Holt." During the time of the Kentucky Lincoln Bicentennial it became common practice for Judge Tommy Turner, Co-Chair to ask me to give updates without notice. An update was given to the Kentucky Lincoln Bicentennial Commission on the progress of the Holt project. The publisher and others sat in the audience and listened about community effort and the urgency of saving this Lincoln connection.

After the meeting, Lindy Casebier, Deputy Secretary of Tourisms, Arts and Heritage Cabinet would most often speak with me as we had met at David L. Morgan's retirement party where I had shared the need for guidance about saving the Holt home. After speaking to numerous members and friends whom I met during the Kentucky Lincoln Bicentennial years, the crowd left the building. Walking down the street to my Jeep the publisher approached and said, "You did a great job in there!" Tell me more about your book. So briefly, I shared the main elements and the intriguing story of Holt. Mr. Sikes invited me once again to come to the book signing that very night at the Hardin County History Museum. I was asked to go home, get the manuscript and return that evening. Doug Sikes explained he wanted to see my research, pictures, and manuscript.

How unbelievable is this for a writer to have a publisher approach her, invite her and want to examine her writing and research! Most writers are lucky for a publisher to even talk with them. The journey home was rushed as the outline of the biography needed to be polished, and I needed to be refreshed.

Traveling back to Elizabethtown that evening my thoughts were, "Is this really happening? A publisher wants to see, and view my writing? He wants to sit down and look through my manuscript!" Mr. Kenny Tabb helped to host the book event at the Hardin County History Museum that evening. Memories of that event are fondly remembered with a nice crowd, good food, walking upstairs and listening to the author speak.

During this time, Mr. Sikes told me that when Mr. Prather started signing books downstairs we would go into the side room and he would have a table for viewing my work. The publisher was amazed with the pictures especially of the home. He turned through viewing the massive manuscript loaded with portraits and continued smiling. When finished, he said, "I want to publish this book. When will you be finished?" The response was, "I am writing a grant now and I have two more grants to write for the Breckinridge County Fiscal Court." I told Mr. Sikes the grants must be completed now as we need money for the purchase of the home." Mr. Sikes stated, "I will wait for you! Finish your grants, keep me updated and let me know how the writing is coming along."

Every three or four months I gave the publisher updates on the status of the grants. And late at night after working on grants for the county as a volunteer, work continued completing the biography. However, work for the county government for the Holt Home was done first. It was long and tiring, but worthwhile! And the biography finally was completed after twelve years of research, writing, editing, rewriting and compiling the work.

With the biography finished the publisher came to our home once again. The day was happy as Mr. Sikes sat at the kitchen table and read through much of the manuscript. He said, "I can't put it down!" I like your writing style. He also examined very carefully the edited manuscript by Dr. James. C. Klotter, Professor of History at Georgetown College and the Kentucky State Historian. He said, "Susan there is one thing I want you to do." And I asked, "What?" Mr. Sikes told me he wanted me to write one more chapter after the biography was completed. He wanted me to include a chapter about the execution of the Lincoln Conspirators where Judge Joseph Holt was the prosecuting judge. Doug Sikes told me I had two weeks to research and submit the chapter to him for examination.

Many sleepless nights followed. I remember reading numerous works about the Lincoln Conspirators all night long, about the execution and making notes and finally writing the final chapter becoming the first chapter of the biography. How relieved to hear the publisher's words, "I like it!"

Everything following the published work has been a wonderful, continued journey! At the first Holt Home Community Day on August 15, 2009, my friend Mary Jean from Frankfort was manning the table where we were selling the newly published *Lincoln's Advocate*. While I was away from the author's table to give a talk Mary Jean asked Mr. Sikes what I was like to have as an author. Doug Sikes responded, "I have never had one like her!"

Finding Mr. James L. Wimsatt, (Artist)

After admiring the print of the Judge Joseph Holt Home in numerous locations in the community, a quest began to locate one. The search started by visiting antique shops across Kentucky, and asking everyone how to find a print.

Years passed without a trace. One day at home after questioning many people and without results an idea came. Call 411. Call the last city James L. Wimsatt lived. Dialing 411 took courage especially asking for the name for the second time of someone I had been told was deceased and no one knew what had happened to the artist.

The operator asked, "What city and state?" My reply was, "Owensboro, Kentucky." "What listing? The operator asked." "James L. Wimsatt," I stated with hope and courage. Just then a voice said, "Hello". And I said, "Mr. Wimsatt, this is Susan Dyer from Breckinridge County. I have been trying to locate you for years. I am writing a biography on Joseph Holt and am trying to save his home. I have admired the print you did of the Holt Home and would love to buy one."

At first Mr. Wimsatt thought I was a telemarketer and did not want to talk with me. He asked again, "Who did you say you were?" That time I caught his attention when I mentioned the Holt Home and said I was from Breckinridge County. I explained I wanted to buy one

Gift from Mr. Wimsatt

of his prints. He said, "I am sorry but I do not have any more."

The conversation continued with, "I am so proud of you for what you are doing and am so sorry there are not any prints left." I told Mr. Wimsatt that it was okay and at least I had found him. He shared he and his wife had been in Florida for twenty years and had just returned to Owensboro. A few days passed and I received a phone call from Mr. Wimsatt saying he had discovered a print, only one left. And he would bring it to me the next time he came to Hardinsburg.

Two days later the Fed Ex truck delivered a most cherished surprise. A print of the Joseph Holt Home, no. 134, the last one! The print had been waiting for the one who longed for it. Autographed by Mr. Wimsatt it read, "Good Luck & Best Wishes to Susan Dyer. -Jim Wimsatt."

Treasured so much, my husband had the print framed in a Victorian reproduction for Valentine's Day and it proudly hangs today in our Great Room. On completion of *Lincoln's Advocate*, my personal request was made to Mr. Doug Sikes, Publisher from Acclaim Press for the print of the home to be a part of the book cover. On one of his numerous visits to my home the publisher also liked the idea of using the print.

After a planning committee meeting for the First Annual Holt Home Community Day in July of 2009 Doug Sikes took a picture of the print in the Victorian frame outside Judge Powers' office in Hardinsburg. He stood directly over the print where it was placed on the ground. With his massive camera, the flash went puff, and that became the photograph that proudly shows Judge Holt's Kentucky home on the cover of *Lincoln's Advocate*: The *Life of Judge Joseph Holt*.

Since that moment in time numerous accomplishments have occurred for the Holt project. And a wonderful friendship developed with Mr. & Mrs. James Wimsatt including visiting his home, telephone conversations, cards sent back and forth to each other as the relationship and the successful work of the Holt project continued.

Mr. James Wimsatt and wife Trudy continue to pray and are kept updated with all the wonderful accomplishments of the efforts to save the Holt Home. Mr. Wimsatt has attended events where I continue speaking about the legacy of Judge Joseph Holt. And finally, at ninety-three years old, returning to the 3rd Annual Holt Home Community Day on September 24, 2011, he witnessed Judge Holt's Home receive $500,000 for a Transportation Enhancement Grant. That day he shared it had been thirty-nine years since he drew the print of the Holt Home and was on the grounds! Mr. Wimsatt continues to appear when he is able, yearly at the Holt Home Community Day. He had the privilege to meet COL (Retired) Fred Borch, now Historian and Archivist of the JAG School and LT. General (Retired) Judge Advocate General Dana K. Chipman, the 38th Judge Advocate General of the United States Army at the 5th Annual Holt Home Community Day in 2013 where he gave them a gift of pictures he took of the U.S. Army Generals gathered together in Europe while serving in the Air Force in WWII. Mr. Winsatt has become a very close friend and to the Holt Home as well.

In an earlier interview, Mr. Winsatt was asked about the time he came to Breckinridge County to capture some of the historical remaining treasures such as the Holt Home and covered bridges before they were lost and torn down. He explained how it took three or four different trips to the Judge Joseph Holt Home, invited there by Bill Thompson, a former teacher who diligently worked to get the Holt Home on the National Register in 1976.

James L. Wimsatt's talent was first honored for the Holt project on the cover of *Lincoln's Advocate* and he stated that at the age of 97 when interviewed for the third time on February 25, 2015 that it is such an honor to be remembered for your artwork.

Some of the experiences of drawing the Holt print were shared for the very first time with me during the February 25, 2015 interview. The question was asked, "What was it like when you were here on the grounds of the Holt Home, drawing the sketch?" Mr. Wimsatt's narrative began, "I have never shared this before... being an artist I had never experienced anything like this... not until

Left to right: Mr. Kenny Tabb, retired county court clerk, Hardin County, Susan Dyer, and Mr. James L. Wimsatt, artist

now have I shared what happened.... I was having a very difficult time in capturing the turnings and beautiful moldings on the home." Many attempts were made and some of the drawings are included with this chapter and the sketches were kept. "I did not want people to think I was kooky or something. However, even though it was 1972 and being 97 when telling this story in 2015 it is very clear in my mind today. The feeling of someone beside me was present and I knew I was not alone. The presence became so strong, an image of a woman appeared to me not in the flesh but so strong I began drawing what came to me. Who was this person? What did she want? Why was she there?" Mr. Winsatt was asked, "How did you feel about her presence?" He replied, "A good feeling came from her. It was warm and then the drawings of the turnings came to me easy, without difficulty. After her image came and was drawn, the sketches were completed on scratch paper and then the print was completed without delay or difficulty. I never thought much about the Lady's image that appeared to me in 1972 until I was asked about the sketches I did and the drawings leading up to the final product of the Holt print."

Sometimes, I refer to the home as "The Lady." The Lady will soon be what she once was. And now Judge Holt's home can share the vision of the Lady who assisted artist, James L. Wimsatt capture the elegance the historical architectural print - with blessings from the past!

Mr. Wimsatt said he always felt Judge Holt's presence was there from the first glance of the historical home, "The Holt Home is something you would expect to see in Washington, D.C., not in Kentucky."

In 2014 a great gift was given, a license agreement for Mr. Wimsatt's generous offer allowing Susan B. Dyer and the Friends of the Holt Home, Inc. to use his beautiful art work depicting the Joseph Holt Home. Time really is golden as the print continues to portray the majestic qualities of the only home Judge Holt ever loved listed on the National Register as nationally significant in history, politics, and architecture and the only place Joseph Holt ever called home.

Holt Home Spotlighted on the KY Lincoln Heritage Trail

What a time to be spotlighted! With the Kentucky Lincoln Heritage Trail revamped it was perfect timing in 2009 to give the Joseph Holt Home just what it needed: attention, love, respect, and visiting and viewing by Kentuckians who had watched the home slowly fall from grace over the past forty years. Without a paint brush's touch, or maintenance keeping the beautiful, historical mansion maintained for decades this opportunity presented itself as an introduction of the Holt Home to the public to bring awareness of the grave condition the home had fallen into.

The Judge Joseph Holt Home was included on the Kentucky Lincoln Heritage Trail with recognition at the Rotunda in Frankfort as an official Kentucky Lincoln site, February 12, 2007.

During the Kentucky Lincoln Bicentennial celebration in 2009 all official Kentucky Lincoln sites were to choose a date to be spotlighted on the Kentucky Lincoln Heritage Trail. Holt's home had only been purchased in December 2008 for Breckinridge County Fiscal Court through grants from the KY Heritage Council/ State Preservation Office placed there by the Kentucky Lincoln Bicentennial Commission. The first grant was for $108,000. Not many citizens realized that grant was almost lost, but an extension was done, and the grant saved. Then, I wrote a second grant for another $50,000. Both grants combined made acquisition possible for county government.

The spotlighting of the Joseph Holt Home would assist with the awareness of the needs of restoration of this historical jewel. However, the home had to be groomed for guests, cleaned and needed dramatic restoration.

With only a few dates remaining to choose from and a massive clean up of the home needed, August 15, 2009 was the date chosen by Breckinridge County Judge Executive Ray Powers and me.

Extensive work was done to clean out the home consisting of garbage, old appliances, and debris, and to clean for safety for the public to view. Judge Powers arranged for inmates to assist with the cleaning of the home and the grounds. The workers took pride diligently working with the home making it look remarkable. Briers and tangled weeds were removed so visitors would be able to walk around the home. There was also an urgency in the planning because there was only

Holt home spotlighted on the Kentucky Lincoln Heritage Trail

The lines were heavy all day

Pictured left to right: Master Sgt. from the Office of the Staff Judge Advocate, Susan Dyer, Col. Robert Cotell (deceased), Deputy Secretary of Tourism, Arts & Heritage Cabinet, Lindy Casebier, Secretary of Tourism, Arts & Heritage Cabinet, Marcheta Sparrow

Office of the Staff Judge Advocate, Fort Knox

one month to pull off this event. The small committee worked with a handful of volunteers and was told by Judge Tommy Turner, Co-Chair of the Kentucky Lincoln Bicentennial, one of the numerous speakers that day, that the Holt Home was one of the most successful events in the Lincoln Bicentennial Celebration. The estimated crowd was over 1,500 people, causing a traffic jam in the middle of a county road on Kentucky Highway 144 in Holt, Kentucky.

That morning was beautiful as the sun filled the sky with gracious color. Driving to Holt was a dream as Tuscany: A Romantic Journey on CD was played from home to the event. I felt a nervous, emotional lump in my throat. Numerous prepared writing pieces promoting the event were crammed into one month, along with learning how to draft press releases, and writing articles for Kentucky magazines hoping and praying people would come. Driving down through Holt's bottoms with Mary Jean, a guest and friend from Frankfort, the excitement was strong! Cars were lined everywhere. I rolled down the car window and asked, "Where can I park?" My Jeep was loaded down with a wreath for the wreath laying ceremony, books and numerous items for the event. Michael Davis from the Breckinridge County Historical Society answered, "Anywhere you want." The event was to begin at 9:00 a.m. but people were coming on the grounds before the final touches had been added.

The night had been short as the evening before the first premier book signing of *Lincoln's Advocate* had taken place where over 200 people attended. Doug Sikes, Publisher from Acclaim Press told me he had not had anything like this in the twenty years he had been in publishing. There was not a seat left. Chairs had to be carried in during the entire book event for a reception of violin music with hors d'oeuvres, and brief messages from political and civic leaders as well as the author and publisher.

The first Holt Home Community Day will long be remembered by all who were present as the people stood in line for most of the day to tour the unrestored home and purchase the first biography ever written on Holt. The open house welcomed local talent along with homemakers serving lemonade and cookies. Judge Powers and the committee expected around 250 people to attend the event. However, "People want to see interesting places!" And they came, and stayed, and the community took ownership of Holt's beloved home on that day as they had been waiting for decades to open its doors and share the rich history of how this home, "Is the only home in America today that tells the complete story of the Lincoln Conspiracy Trial", where Judge Holt had the tremendous responsibility of prosecuting the conspirators who had slain the very president who had appointed him to that office, President Abraham Lincoln". This was the beginning for numerous locals to find out the many mysteries, legends and historic events surrounding the home.

The immense project of research on the home and Holt began in 1997 along with labored grant writing, volunteering, and championing restoration of the Holt mansion. Today, the Holt Home has wonderful support with numerous state agencies, along with a non-profit organization, The Friends of the Holt Home, Inc. who work in a cooperative agreement with the Breckinridge County Fiscal Court who owns the home.

Today, Joseph Holt's home has become the people's home! It belongs to Americans as it tells the story of the most famous citizen of Breckinridge County who gave his undivided best to three presidents; President James Buchanan, President Abraham Lincoln, and President Ulysses S. Grant, the United States Army and our nation. And only recently has Holt's memory been restored and honored as it should be. The annual tradition has been established now to celebrate and honor, the man, Joseph Holt and his legacy for our state and nation on the fourth Saturday of September.

Speakers at the first Holt Home Community Day

Visitors of the day

Judge Kelly Easton portraying Judge Joseph Holt

Union Soldiers

Writing on the Window

Writing on the window

On a cold winter day, the Fed Ex truck backed up to the Great Room of the Dyer house. The deliveryman was taking his time as he seemed to have several packages. It took two trips to get all the packages inside the house.

It was a delivery that marked the beginning of a journey. It would be a trip of enlightenment and inspiration and an excursion into an experience that could not be rationally explained. It would be something beyond reality.

Waiting until the truck pulled away, I hurried to search out the name of the sender. The label read Sarah L. Robinson. It was from one of the researchers working with me for information on Joseph Holt. As I opened the first package, my face lit up as I touched copies of letters written by Mary, Joseph Holt's first wife. Reading pages as fast as I could, the faded old English manuscript soon caused my eyes to ache. I learned, however, of the passion Mary had for Joseph. First, reading of Mary as a schoolgirl who was longing for Joseph Holt to appear. The letters told of an aching heart of a young girl who longed for the company of a gentleman who long since had visited Kentucky. The letters explained how Mary Harrison spent each day and what she had been reading.

The letters gave personal insight into Mary's heart and soul. If she felt sadness, then the reader felt sadness. When she spoke about a party with the elite, you could feel you were in the presence of the guests.

Stories continued as the pages of Mary's life unfolded to the reader, another woman longing to know what Joseph Holt's wives were like. First, to learn about the first wife before she became Mrs. Holt, to learn about her dreams and visions she had as she explored the possibilities of what her life would become as she spoke of herself in a letter dated December fifth, 1837:

> "One faint say of hope that I may again see is at last given me. Oh, hope, 'sweet southern of our sorrows' why ever forsake me? I will cut short this sentimental strain and tell you why I did not answer your first letter although you do not ask it of me.
>
> "It has ever been the repeated advice of my Father, never to correspond to a gentleman under any circumstance, never to place myself in his power as I may believe his heart as pure as heaven.
>
> "For often is myself deceived in the one they think most perfect and often an ever flowing of the little fountain of their affection they find out their error and are left to regret that they had ever been so liberal in

their vows of friendship. Poor weak creatures they are and only think that I am one of them. You have made me a disobedient child; the sin may rest upon you. You still talk of the gulf the fates have thrown between us. I beg of you that you will not believe the fates, have so much to do with your happiness, deprived more upon yourself and I am sure yours will be a bright destiny, but think not that I am vain enough to flatter myself that the writing of my fate with yours would add one ray to its brilliancy. You say, I do not know myself tis true. I do not but how much more are you deceived in me. Would you always be blinded to my fates, I should not attempt perhaps to enlighten you, for it is my greatest wish to be all you would desire! I am neither beautiful nor gifted and when it is too late you may find out that all your struggles for a palace is for one who does not possess the accomplishment necessary to advise such a station, and can only lament the many days she has possessed."

After taking two summers to read the entire letter collection of not one wife, but both Mary Harrison and Margaret Wickliffe Holt, I realized the two inspirational women in Joseph Holt's life must have come to me through the spirit of a muse to speak, to guide, to show me the treacherous path in a world of creativity. Even though it felt strange, it really happened, and these strong women were like a candle bringing the light seeming to live in my life as truly guardian angels. No matter what is written, this experience shows how important these two women were and how they should be honored in the memory of a man who loved them both dearly.

Both wives brought their lives back by sharing their most private thoughts, their desires, and experiences. It was an experience of living life with them, reading about their tribulations, their joys and sorrows, the grandeur of life with its peak moments, giving the reader insight as if they truly experienced tasting the marvelous foods, traveling the exciting, adventurous journeys, and the gratifying privilege of being married to Joseph Holt and living a life people can only dream about two centuries later. These gracious women opened the doors to let readers experience living in the nineteenth century and understand the commitment and patience that future women can learn from and hold close to their hearts as these moments of their lives will forever be remembered. Their lives are pressed into pages written for the future, an experience of their journey of life forever pressed into the art of letter writing.

To obtain the privilege of a close connection with these women, much work was committed by the diligence of not quitting when eyes became tired, when they hurt from trying to interpret the faded handwritten letters, by studying old English handwriting and using magnifying glasses, reading glasses, trying to determine some ink smears and words that have become obsolete or changed in meaning since the writing.

The task included such things as keeping letters in order, reading and interpreting them, writing many of the letters over, which took countless hours, so the stories could be remembered and included in the biography of *Lincoln's Advocate: The Life of Judge Joseph Holt*. It also was the experience of feeling the pain and happiness of these women that gave encouragement to continue until every letter was read. Each new day gave hope as the day must dawn with new adventures and more stories that would be told that were special to Joseph Holt, who kept track of everything important in his life. After the project of reading the love letters of both wives, it was a gratifying feeling to accomplish this goal.

Two days after putting the letters back in spiral notebooks, I felt relieved. But, never could have imagined what I would experience next, how I would feel to see, to witness with my own eyes a thank-you from the past.

At first, I stood transfixed as I stared at the window. A lowercase letter "h" had mysteriously appeared on the glass. I wondered how it got there, but, then, I realized there was something familiar about it. It was somewhat like an Old English letter in a style I had seen in hundreds of handwritten letters. Mary Harrison and Margaret Wickliffe Holt had fashioned the letter in the same manner.

How was this possible? How could a stylish letter appear on the window? It wasn't there yesterday. The excitement built as I moved closer to the massive fixture directly over the new master bath, built after two tornadoes had hit our home in 2004. The letter looked as if it was on the outside of the glass. But, how could it be on the outside of a two-story window?

Examining the marking, it dawned on me that perhaps someone else or another presence was aware of what I was doing. I reasoned it could be a statement of appreciation, a realization of the time, arduous labor and dogged determination that transposing hundreds of personal letters required, an affirmation that preserving this phase of history was worthwhile and I was being encouraged to continue.

I could hardly wait until my husband and sons came in for lunch to show them the letter on the window. Of course, our sons were skeptical and told me, "a bird just passed over and that explains it." But after examining it, my husband said, "The window is two stories in height, so no one could have written from the outside without being raised on a high lift or a piece of machinery to get there." Also, another point was the writing appeared to be done from the outside and if a person had done it as a prank the writing would have been written backwards, looking out the window from the inside.

That weekend the entire family came for a birthday party and were shown the writing on the window. Comments such as, "let's wipe off the writing from the inside," but that could not be done even though it could have been written from the inside. Upon close examination, the writing appeared as though it was between the glasses. My mother told me to take a picture, to show, to have a record of what had happened.

I returned daily to the writing on the window, an inspiration that good things were to come. The window received hard hits with penetrating rain, high winds, blowing snow and the gravest effects of weather. However, from March 4, 2005 through December 5, 2008, the "h" stood firm and remained as if it had been painted with a magical touch. On the afternoon of December 5th, I received a phone call from Breckinridge County Judge Executive Ray Powers informing me the historic Holt Home and surrounding 19.5 acres now was in possession of the citizens of Breckinridge County and a dream had finally become reality.

On returning home the following day, I went again to view the writing on the window, but to my surprise, the letter was gone. But, not really. It had disappeared into the pages of my heart. The memory would remain there forever, giving strength for all the future challenges for the restoration of the new jewel in Kentucky's Civil War Crown.

The image revealed to me that many things are possible that we cannot explain, but when we have help to light our paths they become reality, when we believe and allow angels to guide us.

The 5th George S. Prugh Lecture

Shortly after Joseph Holt's character was added in post-production in Robert Redford's film *The Conspirator* I was contacted by Fred L. Borch, retired Colonel and Regimental Historian and Archivist for the Judge Advocate General's Legal Center and School, U.S. Army. Charlottesville, Virginia.

The introduction was by E-mail. Fred Borch said he had been given my contact information by one of his students, Todd Wayne, who knew me well. Fred began by saying he had a copy of *Lincoln's Advocate* and was planning to do a review of it for the "Military Law Review." But stated that was not the reason for writing. He invited me to be the speaker at the Fifth Annual George S. Prugh Lecture in Military Legal History on Wednesday, April 27, 2011. Stating it was a year away but it was not too early for him to think about a speaker since this year's lecture was tomorrow. Their speaker was Chief Andrew S. Effron, the Chief Judge of the US Court of Appeals for the Armed Forces.)

Fred began by saying, "the Prugh Lecture is unique in America—the only lecture at an American Bar Association accredited law school (The JAG School) that focuses solely on military legal history—and since Joe Holt is such an important figure in the military legal history of the Civil War period, your talking about him would be a real treat for us.

The offer was the JAG School would pay my way (by air) and pay for my hotel and meals. The speech would be Wednesday, April 27, 2011 at 10:00 a.m. They would want me to speak about Joe Holt and his place in military legal history for about an hour. Then they would have a question and answer period. About 11:30 they would adjourn for a luncheon in my honor, then they would take me back to the airport to return home."

John W. Miller II, Brigadier General, U.S. Army, Commander, Susan Dyer, and Retired Col. Fred Borch

This was a lot to consider, delivering the lecture. I was asked to respond at my convenience. Having the background of a middle school teacher and understanding the significance of this speech it was much to consider. After two days of waiting without an answer another E-mail was sent from retired Colonel Borch. It simply said, "Did you receive this E-mail?" Realizing that a decision must be made I called Kentucky State Representative Dwight D. Butler who has been instrumental in supporting the efforts to save the Holt Home and was the first person I contacted to begin a grass root effort to save Judge Holt's Kentucky home.

Representative Dwight D. Butler told me this was a unique opportunity, an honor to be asked to deliver the lecture and it could bring wonderful opportunities for our small, rural community. Representative Butler encouraged me to accept the offer.

After much thought, I replied to the request from Fred Borch. He thanked me for the letter and told me to consider myself a "go" for the lecture next year.

Patt Prugh, youngest daughter, Susan Dyer, and Stephanie Prugh Beach, eldest daughter

I was told to please call the Colonel "Fred". I had requested my husband, Eddie to accompany me and was told that was fine but he would need to come up with his airfare.

I was told that since I was a retired schoolteacher he was certain that I was the right selection for them. Fred also said there are many smart people in the world, but he really wanted a good speaker. Not someone who reads a speech that was boring! The challenge of a life time now confronted me as Fred told me he was one of the historical advisors on the new Robert Redford movie, *The Conspirator*—the story of Mary Surratt—that he knew much about Joe Holt and advised the actor playing Holt (Danny Huston, son of John Huston the director). I was told we had something in common.

Unbelievable work began as I met with an historian, Mr. John P. Behen of Elizabethtown who had assisted me with the beginning of the book on Joseph Holt. Mr. Behen told me that this was a most wonderful opportunity and that I had better prepare well. His wife, Mrs. Behen told me that this was nothing less than an opportunity for a nervous break down to satisfy the JAG School. However, courage and determination to give only the best to my community, the entire summer was spent reading everything I could find about the Civil War and Holt and restudying all the research I had done for twelve years with the writing of the book as well as information used for grant writing, programs for the Holt Home Community Day, the web site for the Holt Home and every speech I had given about Joseph Holt.

Once again, I called Dr. James C. Klotter, Kentucky State Historian and Professor of History at Georgetown College, my mentor who guided and edited *Lincoln's Advocate: The Life of Judge Joseph Holt*. Dr. Klotter said he would be glad to look over my speech and make suggestions. The work began. Reading daily and composing the speech I began practicing the lecture. I was first told I would speak an hour and then later told the lecture needed to be forty minutes, so the lawyers could question me after delivering the speech. From January through April the lecture was given once daily, sometimes twice. It simply was a work of love to put so much in to this lecture, but the goal was to try and enhance the JAG School hopefully to get them involved with saving Judge Holt's home.

The lecture was written then edited twice by Dr. Klotter and then sent to my own publisher Doug Sikes who personally read the lecture, made suggestions and told me I needed to add some of my stories with the lecture. The tedious undertaking continued until the stories were polished. Once again, the lecture was sent to Doug Sikes. Finally, with only a few weeks remaining the lecture became something I was very proud of and looked forward to delivering to the 59th Graduating Class at the JAG School.

What happened next will forever be pressed in my heart. Little did I know I would be treated like Cinderella upon arrival at the JAG School. Before leaving home, I practiced the lecture one last time in the sanctuary of the Harned United Methodist Church where Pastor Janet Carden listened. My requested prayer from three churches including my own was to do my best, not to have a back attack and to enhance the JAG School. A priest named Father Greg Trawick encouraged me to wear flats instead of heels because speaking in high heels can cause back attacks.

Leaving on Easter Sunday, Eddie and I placed flowers on Joseph Holt's first wife, Mary Harrison's grave in Bardstown on the way to Charlottesville, VA. This was a very different Easter since we are both very active in our church. The date was April 24, 2011 the wedding anniversary of Joseph and Mary Harrison Holt.

We traveled a few days early, so I would be well rested and energized for the lecture. I wrote in my journal that I now know how Cinderella felt as I was treated as royalty at Charlottesville, VA.

These are only the highlights:

*Retired Colonel Fred L. Borch III, Regimental Historian and Archivist at the Judge Advocate General's Corps United States Army treated me to a tour of the grounds at the University of Virginia, had a dinner in my honor at a very fine restaurant on April 26th where I had the opportunity to meet eight wonderful people closely connected with the Annual George S. Pugh Lecture. One gentleman named Charlie Singer, a lawyer from Manhattan asked me numerous questions about my book and Judge Holt. Fred told me personally that Charlie donates yearly to a high-profile grant for preservation. Charlie Singer asked for my business card and told me he would send information about the grant.

Next morning Fred picked us up at the hotel, treated us to breakfast, and we went directly to the JAG School. Upon entrance Fred took me to see the big screen that had my picture and information about the 2011 Pugh Lecturer. Then we toured the entire JAG School and met Brigadier General John W. Miller.

Fred had told me earlier that I would have the opportunity to meet Brigadier General John W. Miller II, Commander of the Judge Advocate General's Legal Center and School United States Army. Told me I would spend about ten minutes there. Upon entering the room Brigadier General Miller shook my hand and told me he had read my book and thanked me for bringing back Judge Holt's legacy, said he was so proud of me. Brigadier General Miller told me he attended high school at Fort Knox and played sports against Breckinridge County. He then asked me to view a large table filled with medals. Said he buys them himself and gives them to soldiers to honor them. Told me that he wanted me to have one because of all the work I have done for Judge Holt's legacy and to save his home. As the medal was placed in my hand I thought I was dreaming. The Brigadier General, the same rank as Joseph Holt is handing me a medal. Many times that morning the General thanked me repeatedly. I asked him to please come to Kentucky and view Judge Holt's home and grave. I was given a promise by the Commander of the JAG School.

COL Borch wanted us to leave but the General insisted we had more time and he wanted to continue talking to me. Finally, Fred Borch got permission to head to the preparation room. Instructions were given to me by the Brigadier General and Retired Colonel Fred Borch. I was told how to walk out on the stage, where to sit, where to stand after the lecture as the audience questioned me. Then we all came back in the preparation room where a lady from the Army connected the microphone and equipment to my clothes.

In this room, Fred told me I would receive a gift from the JAG School. He took a beautiful

Clippings from the Media

DEPARTMENT OF THE ARMY
THE JUDGE ADVOCATE GENERAL'S LEGAL CENTER AND SCHOOL
600 MASSIE ROAD
CHARLOTTESVILLE, VIRGINIA 22903-1781

REPLY TO
ATTENTION OF:

January 7, 2011

Ms. Susan B. Dyer
4557 Highway 1401
Harned, Kentucky 40144

Dear Ms. Dyer:

Thank you for agreeing to deliver the 5th Annual Major General George S. Prugh Annual Lecture in Military Legal History on Wednesday, April 27, 2011. The audience will consist of military and civilian personnel from The Judge Advocate General's Legal Center and School, the University of Virginia, and the local community. Mr. Fred Borch, our Regimental Historian and Archivist, informed me that you are working on a presentation about the life of Brigadier General Joseph Holt, who served as The Judge Advocate General during the Civil War. We look forward to this lecture.

Thanks again for graciously affording us your valuable time. I hope you will enjoy your visit to Charlottesville.

Sincerely,

John W. Miller II
Brigadier General, US Army
Commanding

Letter from Brigadier General Miller

silver bowl out of the box and showed me. He told me it would be given out after the lecture. It was engraved:

Fifth George Prugh Lecture
April 27, 2011
Susan Dyer

From the cameras in the control room I could see all the audience filing in Decker Auditorium. I had to sign papers the day before giving permission to record my speech and publish my remarks in their Military Law Review. The audience was filled as Fred told me it would be. The audience was all lawyers, 95 percent military, and most career soldiers but there were some Navy, Air Force, Marine Corps and Coast Guard. Just before exiting the preparation room Fred looked at me as if to say, "Are you ready?" I answered, "I am not afraid." Fred said, "I knew you wouldn't be." Finally, the chance of a lifetime for Kentucky and Judge Holt's legacy.

Mr. Fred Borch III introduced me to the audience and told them that he was going to try and have as much passion for Brigadier General Miller as I had for Judge Holt. Told the audience that Ms. Dyer was the authority of Judge Holt across the nation. After all the kind words, I approached the lectern and gave the lecture that had been researched and practiced for a year. Dr. Klotter had edited the lecture twice and Doug Sikes, my publisher had also edited the lecture. The audience was so quiet you could hear a pin drop. A photographer took pictures during the lecture. And the daughters of George S. Prugh flew there from California to hear the 5th George S. Prugh Lecture that their father had given money to begin back in 2006. Upon finishing the lecture, I received a standing ovation. Then Fred Borch began the question and answer session. All questions were answered. Finally, closing remarks were made by Lieutenant General Dana K. Chipman, 38th Judge Advocate General of the United States Army, 3 Star General who flew in from Washington D.C. He told the crowd that if they wanted something done Susan Dyer was the lady to get it accomplished.

Then pictures were made with many people including me on the stage. The Prugh daughters made many pictures and afterwards a luncheon was held in a beautiful location close to the JAG School. The conversation at the luncheon was wonderful as the Hon. Andrew S. Effron, Judge of the Appeals Court for the United States Army, and last year's speaker gave me his card, and told me the lecture was perfect. The lawyer, named Charlie Singer told me all we needed was the jury, that my lecture was fantastic.

Fred Borch the historian who coached Danny Huston told me I did great and that people had already told him they loved the lecture. Once again, all the Generals thanked me, and the daughters of George S. Prugh hugged my neck and gave me many wonderful compliments.

This was my first time to be paid for travel and lodging. I made a personal slide show for Fred Borch and he watched it in our hotel room as he took my husband and me back after all the activities. Fred personally asked me if we had written to the American Film Company and I told him yes both the Governor and I had written but have not ever received an answer.

Fred told me he would try to get the American Film Company involved. He told me he had spent many hours on the phone with Danny Huston coaching him to portray Joseph Holt. I made a slide show for Fred to view the past two community days for the Holt Home. He fell in love with the Holt Home and upon saying goodbye told me he would visit the home and asked if he could have a hug! He was given a nice HUG and I thanked him once again for the opportunity.

Fred told me he would be contacting me soon, would send several DVD's of the lecture, and pictures that were taken.

I donated a book to the JAG Library as was requested.

My heart was given once again for Judge Holt's legacy and his home. I truly believe the JAG School was enhanced but only by having the faith that God was leading me, three churches praying for me, along with friends, and numerous ministers including a priest who advised me to wear flats instead of heels, which I did.

At the luncheon, Lieutenant, General Dana K. Chipman asked me again how the project started, and I explained to him I told that during the lecture. He said, "Please tell me again" and I said, "God put it on my heart." The General said, "I am glad you told us that."

Fred Borch told me the lecture would be published in the United States Military Law Review in 2012.

The Fifth Annual George S. Prugh Lecture in Military History: Joseph Holt: Lincoln's Judge Advocate General was published in the Spring of 2012 by the Military Law Review and is housed in the Library of Congress.

Twenty-two windows were broken during an ice storm.

The back side of the Holt Home on Appraisal Day.

Taken and used in a PowerPoint presentation for the Kentucky Lincoln Bicentennial Commission, shortly after the Breckinridge County Fiscal Court received $7,500 for stabilization of the home.

Stair tower view before the SAT grant.

With downspouts missing, rain ran down the historic brick exterior.

The East side of spiral staircases before the Holt Home was purchased with two combined Kentucky Lincoln Bicentennial grants.

East twin door entrance.

A medallion still hangs in the parlor room from Joseph Holt's era, where three gas chandeliers hung.

Beautiful hand carved moldings on the stairs.

A detailed view showing the proud craftsmanship of the past.

One grate remains in the Holt Home and will be used as the pattern for reconstruction for the other needed fireplaces.

Gorgeous staircase railings in the Holt Home.

West spiral staircase. (Note: it was unique to have two spiral staircases in one home!)

Free standing spiral staircase.

Remains of one of the six fireplaces in the home that was heated by coal.

The East staircase was walked many times by Holt.

Craftsmanship with pride graces the Holt mansion.

Twelve foot-high doors grace the rooms!

Original wallpaper in the progress of historical documentation.

Research about wall finishes tells how the Holt Mansion was furnished during Holt's era.

The six fireplaces granted warmth to the home.

Historic hinges from Holt's era will be beautifully restored.

The blue border in one of the 2nd floor bedrooms has been documented by Kevin Herford, a specialist in restoration of wall coverings and flooring.

Oil cloth was a sign of wealth during the Holt era. Kevin Herford, a specialist in wallpaper and floor coverings, has identified this in the Holt Home.

The eagle atop Judge Holt's monument is the symbol of America!

Beginning restoration of the dormers.

Judge Holt's stately monument welcomes visitors! Judge Holt is buried on the Holt grounds.

Repair work and restoration of the dormers.

First line of defense in helping preserve this structure was removal and replacement of the existing roof.

Over decades while the home was unoccupied, the original lead coated metal roof began to deteriorate, allowing water into the home and gutters and down spouts failed allowing water to wash down the brick removing fragile mortar in the process. (Jon Rollins, GRW)

Note: Many interesting things have occurred during the restoration. The side view (back of the home) was not part of the original design to the Holt mansion and was demolished. When the add-on room was removed it became apparent that during Holt's era a porch went across the back section of the home to connect with the stairs on the west side. (Jon Rollins, GRW architects, Lexington, Kentucky.)

Dormers were taken off site to a shop, and Stuart, the Forman for Lanham Brothers, did the work. (Jon Rollins, GRW)

Eighty percent (80%) of the tile from the kitchen was taken off, cleaned, and reused, and 20% purchased to retile the kitchen. Note: roof tiles on the east side are ALL original, while tiles on the west side facing the stair tower are a blend of original and added tiles.

Restoration of the windows included replacing non-original 'flat' glass with period accurate 'wavy glass at the 1st floor, reattaching window balancing weights, restoration of window hardware and applying a new coat of paint. (Jon Rollins, GRW)

Kitchen roof (completely restored).

At the front elevation, notice the flat upper sash of first floor windows while the upper windows are curved to match the brick opening.

Restoring 2nd floor windows!

Bringing back unique windows.

This interior room was used as a classroom setting for the Indiana National Guard JAGS Professional Development and was the first new use of the home!

Shortly after complete restoration of the Holt Family Cemetery, the Holt Family Trust transferred the ownership to the Friends of the Holt Inc., a non-profit organization.

The Friends clean the home yearly for the annual Holt Home Community Day along with JAG events.

After the room not original to the house was removed. Note: This will be built back during another phase of restoration and will serve as a warming kitchen for events in the Holt Mansion.

Sketches and construction drawings of the phases have been carefully gathered and compiled by GRW architects of Lexington, Kentucky. This will enable the home to be brought back as close as possible to the period of Holt's national service to our nation.

Beautifying the Holt grounds with leadership by Charlie Corbett. (Funded by the Friends of the Holt Home, Inc.)

New Security System in place, thanks to a $10,000 grant from Blue grass Pipeline.

Original sidewalks unearthed by Charlie Corbett, funded by the Friends of the Holt Home, Inc.

Interpretation marker of the Lincoln Conspiracy Trial thanks to a grant written by the Kentucky Heritage Council, lifetime partners

Decorative woodwork and trim below the eaves is original to the home.

Each original piece put back helps enlighten the home. New wood elements consist with 'flat' woodwork at the soffits as well as an exact reproduction of the crown molding. All of this has been painted gray, the color matched to the existing example that was hidden from the elements. (Jon Rollins, GRW)

Charlie Corbett, one of the directors of the Friends organization, and architect Jon Rollins inspecting work.

Window restoration

Front view of one of the twin entrances.

Historic Holt fence restored thanks to the Brown-Forman grant.

Byron Crawford's Friendship

Meeting Byron Crawford was such a blessing to me personally and the Holt Project. It was such an unexpected pleasure from someone so well known across Kentucky. Not many writers would be as humble and as interested in others as Mr. Crawford. For numerous years he wrote about the lives of interesting Kentuckians and his articles appeared in one of the most favored columns in the Louisville-Courier Journal.

My remembrance is strong about the occurrence of that Saturday in November of 2008. The dreary day was unwelcomed to most to even attempt to get out and do something. However, a strong feeling presented itself that it would be wise to drive to Frankfort and visit and chat with mentor Dr. James C. Klotter who was attending the 27th Annual Kentucky Book Fair with his latest book.

Always busy, aisles filled as anxious readers searched for the greatest reads as anticipation grew of patrons supporting Kentucky authors. After chatting with Dr. Klotter and purchasing his latest book, time was spent talking with other writers and enjoying the enthusiastic environment of voices with a busy hustle. Walking down the aisles of the narrow passages between the rows of authors suddenly I felt a touch on my right shoulder. Turning around to greet the person, I was surprised to encounter Doug Sikes, Publisher from Acclaim Press. He invited both future author and my husband to find a seat in the Frankfort Convention Center and talk. The discussion was as always about the progress of grant writing as he continued to wait patiently for *Lincoln Advocate* to be completed.

Briefed about the continued work and progress of the Holt project Mr. Sikes seemed very excited and asked once again, "When is the book going to be finished." My reply was, "Work is continu-

Well-known Kentucky newspaper columnist and television personality Byron Crawford introduced by Susan Dyer

ing between meetings in Frankfort and completing the research for several more chapters." That seemed to satisfy the publisher but he could not wait forever. He needed closure and work continued around the clock. With a smile he said, "Next year you will be here! "Imagine that, being at the 28th Kentucky Book Fair, the dream of dreams for a writer! Mr. Sikes' requested, "Call me when you are finished with the book. Almost in a trance and dreaming for an instance, I thought, this is really going to happen. All the work of research and writing for twelve years is coming together. The feelings given for the anticipation of the finished product, gave insight into the drive, the labored enthusiasm of completing the work and knowing you had labored your hardest on it all!

One last walk was taken through the Convention Center imagining what it would be like next year, to be present, to experience the new life of writing. Once again confronted by Doug Sikes who called out my name. I turned to see standing with Doug Sikes a person whom I thought I had seen numerous times in the *Courier-Journal.* Mr. Sikes said, "There is someone I want to introduce you to - this is Byron Crawford." Wow! To meet such a gentleman who had written so many wonderful stories about Kentuckians. Mr. Sikes continued with his story, sharing that a biography would soon be completed about Joseph Holt and how Acclaim Press was going to publish it. Doug Sikes explained how the spearheader of the project had worked diligently, had written numerous grants as a volunteer for the county government for the Holt Home, and how he had waited patiently for over a year for this lady to complete the grants first and then finish her book. Surprisingly, Mr. Sikes said, "Byron Crawford is going to write a story about you."

And it happened! Byron Crawford asked if he could call and have an interview over the phone the next week or two. Reality came unexpected and the voice I recognized as Kentucky's storyteller was on the phone! And he was going to interview a middle school teacher. Being a gentleman, he asked if he could record the interview. Mr. Crawford began with saying this story would be on the front page of the Courier-Journal; Section B. The first question he asked was, "How did this project begin, what caused you to be intrigued?" The answers flowed easily as my love of saving history was shared, and how God put this on my heart. As the years have passed the repeating question continues…with all new partners, foundations, the Army, and interested persons.

The featured story was admired by many patrons with compliments keeping the phone lines busy. This was the beginning of numerous invitations of engagements to speak about saving the Holt Home and *Lincoln's Advocate*. Being included in the Kentucky Humanities Council Catalog of featured speakers, and the article presented numerous invitations from organization from across Kentucky as I shared the journey of writing the book, researching, speech giving and grant writing before the publishing of *Lincoln's Advocate* in 2009. People across the Commonwealth read Kentucky's own storyteller Byron Crawford's story about the Holt Home, the effort to save it and the first biography ever written about Joseph Holt.

After the article appeared Mr. Crawford and I became friends. "One trait in the Holt project is once you are a friend I will not let you go! Friends, one of the strongest forces on Earth cause you to do more than you even expect of yourself!" The friendship grew and the work continued diligently.

Later in 2010 upon receiving the Ida Willis Memorial Foundation Award for Preservation at the Governor's Mansion in Frankfort our paths would cross again. And when the Friends of the Holt Home had four months in 2012 to raise money for the Phase 2 TE match we needed a celebrity to come and speak at the closure of the county-wide based project.

Once again Bryon Crawford came to lend his talent as a wonderful storyteller. I made a call and said, "We need a celebrity to help with the final night of fundraising for the Holt Home and you are the only celebrity I personally know." Mr. Crawford said, "If I am the only celebrity you know you are in trouble." Because of the illness of one of Mr. Crawford's acquaintances it was not certain that he would be able to come and speak. However, understanding the request behind the special cause Mr. Crawford said he would certainly do his very best to attend and speak to the crowd."

Out of the three events of the summer the Byron Crawford event brought in over $25,000.00 out of the $34,000 raised! Mr. Crawford was a big hit for Holt, and spoke so graciously about the preservation efforts and work of saving the Holt Home, and how it is such a treasure not only to Breckinridge County and Kentucky, but to our nation. And how preservation is not an easy task but one Breckinridge County will be proud of in future generations!

The Gheens Foundation

***Lincoln's Advocate* was** written to bring attention to the Judge Joseph Holt home and it has accomplished that many times over since 1997. In November of 2014 while attending a book event at Rough River State Park a reader of the book, Mr. James Rogers who had also given money earlier on a fund-raising effort in 2012 to match a Phase 2 Transportation Enhancement grant, stopped by to chat. The conservation conveyed progress of the Holt project and the pictures on display showed Phase 1 exterior renovation in progress.

Mr. Rogers had been intrigued when he began reading *Lincoln's Advocate* while in Washington D. C. and completed while flying home. He suggested contacting one of his good friends Carl Thomas, Executive Director and President of the Gheens Foundation. With research of the foundation's work and funding a phone call was made with a brief message. Afterwards Mr. Rogers was contacted to let him know that the encouraged phone call was made. A reply came and the realization that Mr. Thomas was in Florida on vacation and would not be back until the following week.

With many duties as volunteer President of the Friends of the Holt Home, Inc. one of the jobs is to keep in touch with interested patrons and acquaintances made since 1997 when the grass roots effort of saving the Holt Home began.

Throughout the years one of the strong mentors, former Representative Dwight D. Butler, has taught if you do not stay in touch with people they will forget you and what you are working toward.

Case in point: On a deeply busy afternoon the phone rang and surprisingly it was Mr. Carl Thomas from the Gheens Foundation. The conversation was interesting as both parties talked about Brigadier General Joseph Holt and his legacy. Mr. Thomas confessed he had never heard of Joseph Holt but after the interesting chat he wanted to learn more. I explained I would love to come and meet in person to share Holt's legacy. The invitation was extended to choose a selection of possible dates that would work for us both. The choice was made and the Kentucky Heritage Council/ State Preservation Office/ Partner for life of the Judge Joseph Holt home was invited as well. Craig Potts, Exec. Director and the Kentucky State Preservation Officer could not attend and sent Diane Comer, PR at the Kentucky Heritage Council State/ Preservation Office where she has been involved with the Holt project since its beginning.

Planning began for what the December 15th, 2014 meeting would be - what questions would be asked and what preparation would be made. After thinking carefully, and considering what would you personally want to know about a historic treasure you had never heard of or seen or studied if you were the foundation? The decision was made to be personal, be myself. And when asked the question, "How did this project start?" The response was, "On a Sunday afternoon drive Holt's advocate asked her husband to stop the car as she stood in the middle of Highway 144 viewing the Holt Home in very grave condition. And that day God put it on a heart to save the home. *Lincoln's Advocate* was written to bring attention to the home and to get the community involved to save Judge Holt's home and bring back his legacy that had been suppressed for almost 150 years.

So, the story was told once again of how God put this project on my heart and how everything started happening at the same time.

The sharing of how the Holt Home Steering Commission with state partners began and the Friends of Holt Home, Inc. along with every single grant written as a volunteer for Breckinridge

County Fiscal Court and the Holt home since 2007. Major grants were shared with amounts, dates and how they all came about, along with the history of how the Holt Home became an official Kentucky Lincoln site, and Legacy project of the Kentucky Lincoln Bicentennial and how the Holt project was one of the greatest saves of the entire Lincoln Bicentennial! The conversation continued telling how the home gained three state agencies as partners and how after the 5th George S. Prugh Lecture was given in Charlottesville, VA the JAG School is now partnering. COL Robert Cotell, the first staff judge advocate at Fort Knox to partner with a wreath laying ceremony, made it a tradition for the Fort Knox Judge Advocate's Office to honor Judge Holt at the Holt Home Community Day with a wreath-laying ceremony because of all the hard work and success of the project.

The meeting was wonderful as the drama of the project was shared with all the blood, sweat, and tears, and continued work of 18 years - how the community of Breckinridge County had raised $34,000 over a five-month period with three fundraisers with leaders from magisterial districts assisting on this community-based project, and the grand finale was having renowned Courier-Journal writer and Kentucky story teller Byron Crawford coming to speak about saving the Holt Home.

Mr. Thomas invited the Gheens' grant administrator to be present at the meeting. Both Kathy Knotts and Mr. Thomas showed great interest with a project so massive for a rural community to undertake. I shared that education is the main basic for preservation! "You must teach your community what is so special about their heritage. And how important it is to save your history."

Friends of the Holt Home, Inc. were invited to write and submit an application to the Gheens Foundation. Much effort with personal narratives were put into the grant application! Calls made, notes sent, along with amazing support letters telling the story for the grant application; Senators, Representatives, the JAG School's Historian and Archivist, Fred Borch and Ret. Judge Advocate General Dana K. Chipman were asked to help along with other influential people.

After the most wonderful meeting Mr. Thomas and Kathy Knotts were both invited for a private tour of Judge Joseph Holt's home. Mr. Thomas said he would check his schedule after Christmas and would schedule a tour. Several weeks passed and Mr. Thomas was contacted once again inviting him for a private tour. He accepted and came to view Holt's beloved home. Standing in front of Judge Holt's home places the viewer in a different state of mind. It lets them imagine life in the 19th century. Mr. Carl Thomas could picture what the Holt Home was during Holt's era, and the grand estate surrounding the home with history at every corner. After touring the home, the grounds and the Holt Family Cemetery he said, "You were right. A picture cannot do justice for the home. It was worth the trip here!"

Holt being Lincoln's Advocate, history is calling.

On President Abraham Lincoln's birthday, February 12, 2015 the Gheens Foundation application was submitted on line. After submitting the grant on line that day, the same thing occurred as had occurred two times earlier that week. When driving to town on three different days all at different times "The Impossible Dream" was played on the Escape Channel on Sirius radio. Yes, it really happened!

Now came the waiting until March 17, 2015 for the winners of the grant. Will the Friends of the Holt Home become a winner? Will they receive $40,000? If they do they will also complete the 50-50 match required on the 2009 Save America's Treasures grant of $150,000 that was written three times, three years in a row, twice alone as a volunteer. Finally, with the help of Congressman Brett Guthrie, Senator Mitch McConnell, Diane Comer PR from the Kentucky Heritage Council, and Dana Beth Lyddan, former Executive Director for the Hardin County Heritage Council - that grant was won!

In a rural area without much industry we have had to match numerous grants and in a short while. However, since 2009 the 50-50 match has been mostly made by volunteer time. Winning this grant will completely restore the front porch of iron works that is so majestic, bringing the home back to life. And this rebirth will catch the eye of all who behold it.

A few weeks later I received a call from Kathy Knotts from the Gheens Foundation saying she was so sorry to say the Board of Directors went with the Portland project. But wanted me to know the grant application was perfect, it could not have been any better. The Friends of the Holt Home, Inc. were very disappointed about not receiving the funding. However, not receiving the funding gives you more confidence to know you could not have written a better grant or have done a greater deed for your community. It is easy to say we got the grant. And sometimes when all the work has been submitted and you have done the best possible job and not received compliments for writing the grant locally it gives inner strength that helps you meet with future foundations, because you know how better to present yourself — how to be yourself and the effort gives your organization a very professional and leadership quality required to pursue and receive funding – even when you are not chosen.

With encouragement from Former President of the Gheens Foundations Carl Thomas I went back to the Gheens Foundation in December of 2015 as I am not a quitter. I updated the new President Barry Allen about all the numerous achievements of the Friends of the Holt Home, Inc. from 2015 where the Holt Home received another $500,000 TE grant from Kentucky and a $199,000 tax credits from the Kentucky Heritage Council/ State Preservation Office. Both Mr. Allen and Kathy Knotts were very gracious and were amazed with the enormous accomplishments since the year before. I shared that Mrs. Gheens lived in a historical home in the East end of Louisville and she was also interested in Centre College where Holt attended and hopefully, someday the Foundation will want to be a part of this wonderful Kentucky legacy! And the Friends of the Holt Home, Inc. will welcome an invitation in the future when the timing is right to submit another grant when the Board of Directors are ready for preservation with some distance from Louisville.

The Friends of the Holt Home, Inc. have secured a wonderful historic part of American history where travelers throughout the U.S. will come to visit. And recently in the spring of 2016 the Friends of the Holt Home, Inc. have completed the match for the $150,000 Save America's Treasures grant from mostly volunteer time. All volunteer tasks cannot be counted. For numerous years I was told that I could only be counted for minimum wage hourly rate to match the grant. I would not give up. And after speaking with Dr. James C. Klotter, Kentucky's State Historian he said, "You are worth more than minimum wage with three college degrees. Don't give up on asking for more." Finally, Kathina Bell, the Breckinridge County Judge Assistant asked Joshua Wilks with the SAT grant if my time could be counted as hourly wage as a Kentucky retired teacher. And he said yes.

With persistence a rural community saved the SAT grant. It is the last in the United States to be administrated and will fund the tearing down of the rear porch, tearing out the old hand cement base and rebuilding a replica of the porch with stairs, renovate all the back windows and doors before the September 1, 2016 deadline.

The Friends of the Holt Home, wanted to use the SAT grant to complete the iron works front porch instead of the back of the Holt Home. However, Transportation of Kentucky who granted the Phase II grant of $500,000 on September 26, 2105 ruled that the SAT had to be used on the back of the home and approved the work could begin as the Transportation grant would be used to complete renovation on the front porch and begin restoration on the interior probably in 2017.

When a grant is submitted, you do not always win the grant. And sometimes individuals give up on grant writing, which separates the strong from the weak. For not receiving grants helps you become a better grant writer and helps you work harder. And the foundations you have the pleasure of meeting gives you more courage and more people come to know of your work. The Gheens Foundation know of the Judge Joseph Holt home and we look forward to being invited again to submit a grant for preservation for one of the most important homes in America today.

Valet and Companion to General Joseph Holt

This narrative was told to Dorothy Dowell Ramsey when she was seven years old by her grandfather Charles Foster Jasper, valet and companion to General Joseph Holt before he married. Later in life Ms. Ramsey recorded memories of long ago that never left her heart and always brought a tear!

"Our family had plenty to eat, and a warm comfortable home full of love. I had never been in a home so gorgeous until Grandfather took me with him once to visit Sam, an old slave very ill who lived with the Holts.

Our family lived in Holt's Bottom, and the huge white mansion that was General Holt's home, with its thick red carpeting and the beautiful rich red draperies meant a great deal to a seven-year-old girl whose home was a very modest cottage.

"My grandfather spent most of his evenings in the winter sitting around the fire place, living in the past, telling our family stories of the days when he was valet and companion to Joseph "Wash" Holt, a nickname General Holt acquired while in Washington.

I always knew from my earliest recollections General Holt had been surrounded by a terrible misery even though I was a child.

Grandfather's story began…Wash was a very prominent man in Washington. Born and reared right here in Holt's Bottom. Being wide-eyed I hung on to every word he said. And thought no one could tell stories like Grandfather.

I had never seen Joseph Holt because he died before my birth in 1901." However, I learned he had served in high positions for two presidents in Washington. And had his own graveyard and built the church that stood on the Holt plantation. Joseph Holt was well on his way to become the president of the United States when a twist of fate sent his hopes and plans crushing to the ground.

At this point in the story grandfather would stop and ask Bess, his wife, my grandmother, if there were any apples around? And she would answer, "Yes father," and she would take the old lantern down from the shelf and light it. Then she and my father would go to the cellar for apples and potatoes to eat and cider to drink.

I would run to the shed kitchen for a string of popcorn ears and on returning grandfather would wrap potatoes in brown paper and cover heavily with ashes right in the fireplace. Then he would call, "bring the salt Kitten." Then grandfather would resume his story as we ate roasted potatoes with fresh cow's butter, apples and popcorn. A cozy scene.

He told how the General was a bright national figure just before and during the Civil War, in which my grandfather also served. Grandfather had been a prisoner of war at Andersonville serving the Union. Grandfather shared the many experiences and adventures of General Holt.

During the administration of James Buchanan, the General served in two cabinet positions, that of Postmaster General and Secretary of War. Then grandfather would laugh, shake his head and say, "That Wash, meaning (Joseph Holt), "He was sure something, you know he wouldn't let me go home." If grandfather went home and stayed more than two or three days General Holt would send one of his servants with an extra horse for him to ride back, with the instructions that he would not take no for an answer. Needless to say, grandfather went back with the servant every time to care for Judge Holt.

In the fall before winter sat in when I was a little girl grandfather would hitch the horses to the surrey and take me on what seemed to be the longest buggy rides down through Holt's Bottom, to the old General store. This was the only place he could find a certain kind of, molasses (New Orleans) of which he never ran low.

On our way back home we passed the old Holt mansion. And as we traveled along the dusty dirt road Grandfather would say, "Kitten there is where Joseph Holt lived a long time ago, and I lived with the Holts for years before I was married to your grandmother. General Holt was the best friend I ever had."

Just after we passed the homestead there was the Holt Cemetery off to the right of the home. Grandfather always turned in at the cemetery road. We got out of the surrey and he took my hand as we walked over to the grave side and grandfather took off his hat, and bowed his head while holding on to my hand telling me to be very quiet.

We stood there for quite a while and then walked to the surrey and continued our way home without either of us speaking. Grandfather reminisced about long ago.

One evening several weeks after this drive we heard a knock at the door. When grandfather answered it, he stood in great and happy surprise as it was Dr. Kincheloe from Louisville, Kentucky. He had come down on the morning train. He was a friend of my family and General Holt.

Grandfather called, "Bess come see what just dropped in from nowhere!" Mother came running. They shook hands, completed greetings, and all went into the living room. Mother excused herself, and I knew from past experiences there would be a lot of talk of General Holt's adventures. So, I stuck close by as not to miss anything.

Grandfather would not talk of General Holt's tragedies to anyone but Doctor Kincheloe, and I felt I might be in for something good if they would only let me stay up and listen to their stories.

My father was a carpenter, and part time farmer. Mother's two younger sisters lived with us along with grandfather. Our family granted great affection for one another. Father would come in from work, clean up as everyone else tided themselves as we prepared for supper, where mother always received numerous compliments.

As shadows were falling, we settled down for another wonderful evening along the fireplace. I could hardly wait for the stories to begin.

Grandfather began.... "Ed, do you remember when Wash first became ill? How he would not let me leave him to get a drink of water, and how he called old Sam every once in a while to bring me a drink of water or something else to keep me by his side?"

Then grandfather would laugh and his blue eyes would twinkle, and then get just as sad as he quickly thought of how the General had suffered through the months, and even years when he was so unjustly defeated. My family one by one retired for the evening leaving only my mother and me to listen to stories about General Holt.

I asked to sleep on the sofa and my mother flatly refused. Begging and crying and putting up an awful howl mother gave in when grandfather said, "Oh Bess, let her sleep in here. She will soon be asleep and I will carry her to bed." However, sleep did not come quickly for I listened into the night as grandfather shared the story with the doctor.

It seemed Grandfather sat with the General through long days and nights, when he became ill and a semi invalid. Grandfather read volumes of books and page after page of other literature, and tried to comfort him in any way he could.

Grandfather was a school teacher and no one else in Holt's Bottom could read the kind of literature the General was interested in hearing. General Holt would plead with Grandfather. "Charles, you have stayed with me this long you can't leave me now." Grandfather would always answer, "No Wash I won't leave you. I have no intentions of leaving you, so rest assured I will be here, whatever happens."

The General would then seem to be satisfied for a short time. Grandfather never left the General's side when he was with Holt until his death. Joseph Holt died in Washington.

Even though Holt was a great man, and will always be in the hearts and memories of all who knew him best, and numerous others who did not know him personally, his success was not simple. He had a difficult struggle within himself that most people did not know. But his struggle was not in vain as he was very strong willed and dependable.

It must have been fate for he was almost overcome with the anguish and disappointment when President Abraham Lincoln made him Judge Advocate of the Union Army during the Civil War. It was in that later office his star hit an unexpected barrier as Judge Advocate General Joseph Holt's duty was to prosecute the people involved with John Wilkes Booth assassination of President Lincoln.

Holt was the leading figure in a crucial time in our nation's history. In addition to the positions named he held other offices. With stories completed my grandfather carried me to bed in the wee hours of the morning. The years have passed but grandfather's memoirs told as a young man serving General Holt are as clear today as it had been last evening.

The doctor left the next night on the evening train and I do not remember ever seeing Dr. Kincheloe again. I visited the old homestead a few weeks ago and there has been talk of the General's home becoming a shrine. It is located six miles from Highway U.S. 60, close to Cloverport. The land received by Judge Holt's grandfather was payment for his services in the Revolutionary War. The precious land was sold off into small parcels until it became a small farm.

As the Holt's died off, little by little the Holt plantation was sold as most of the family were not interested in farming or the plantation. When Judge Holt died in August of 1894, a military funeral was held in the Nation's Capital before the private funeral in Holt's Memorial Chapel of which Grandfather attended. Burial was in the Holt Family Cemetery. Judge Holt was a prized statesman, an outstanding orator and gave the greatest service to his nation.

If any man deserved to have a shrine dedicated in his honor it should be Judge Holt. I am sure it would please my grandfather immensely, if he could only know."

Footnote... *Story told by Dorothy Ramsey, Tobinsport Road, Tobinsport, IN, 1901-1981. Gloria Shepard of Cannelton, Indiana gave permission to the author to use both memoirs of her great grandfather, Charles Foster Jasper, Valet and Companion to Judge Holt and her mother, Dorothy Dowell Ramsey who heard the stories as a child and viewed the Holt mansion while in ownership of the Holt family.*

Renovation for the Jewel

A heart felt vision inspires others! It motivates doubts, turns negatives into positives, and paints the final portrait of the *Joseph Holt Mansion.* But not without persistence, work of almost two decades, speech giving and motivating talented resources to partnership.

For all visitors who have stopped to imagine what life was like at Judge Holt's home, the legacy has been reborn. For the memories there of life are being brought back. But not without the leadership and guidance of God, who in 1997 put the dream on my heart, sent the resources, the people, the grants, the timing of the Lincoln Bicentennial, and the continuous work of learning how to preserve the, "only home in America today that tells the complete story of the Lincoln Conspiracy Trail."

What a journey! What trials! And especially without any resources and funding in the beginning. However, as shared in numerous speeches across Kentucky and beyond, if God is leading you anything is possible.

To do something like this Dr. James C. Klotter has stated, "You must have a heart like a lion and a stomach like a goat to do this kind of work. And when I first met with Dr. Klotter at the Joseph–Beth Bookstore in Lexington, Kentucky and shared the dream of saving the Holt Home he said, "You don't really think you can do both, write a book on Joseph Holt and save his home." My reply was, "I don't have a choice."

I could not get peace even while still teaching at Breckinridge County Middle School. For every day facing me was a portrait drawn by local artist, Donna Sebastian of the Joseph Holt Home.

After the drive in 1997 when I stopped and stared on this most beautiful home, God put it on my heart to save the Holt home. And I could not get the home or Holt off my mind. Late at night I would be up searching the web trying to learn about Joseph Holt, not getting much sleep and having to teach school the next morning. But there was not much to be found on the internet then. I even searched the local library and found only a small vertical file with few things.

New Look for Holt Home!!!

However, as I mentioned, when returning later to make some copies someone had taken everything. And research began across the state as my husband went along as I searched through the dust, files and records to find anything on Holt.

After not being satisfied I contacted the Library of Congress and hired three researchers to assist. This helped provide the necessary information needed for grants I would write as a volunteer and letter writing seeking assistance with the research shared with state partners. And so, the journey began with a home.

I asked Ms. Sebastian to go to the Holt Home, stand in the road as I had done, take some pictures of the home and draw a large pencil sketch to hang on my classroom wall. Every day it got harder to face this picture as I continued to think. "Something must be done soon or there will just be a sign that reads, "This is where the

Reworked and painted wood dormers on the back of the Holt Home

Brick-tuck pointing done by Volunteer Joe Hobbs

With trim replaced and dormers completed from restoration the next step is the new roof!

East view of Holt Home (Beginning of new roof) Back view of kitchen (80% of old tile cleaned and reused!)

Save America's Treasures grant at work on the historic Holt Home!!!

SAT grant restores back stair tower and back historic windows!!!

Judge Joseph Holt home use to be." This enormous framed picture was taken everywhere I was invited in the efforts to bring attention to the Holt home.

The pencil sketch made guest appearances across Kentucky including the Kentucky Lincoln Bicentennial Commission meetings where I was asked to speak often about what was happening with the Holt home by another mentor and friend, Judge Tommy Turner, Co. Chair of the Kentucky Lincoln Bicentennial who was on the National Lincoln Bicentennial Committee also. At numerous meetings Judge Turner teasingly would say, "We will now hear from Mrs. Holt today." Sometimes, I would speak knowing in advance, sometimes on the spot and sometimes with joint efforts of Warren Greer, Becky Shipp, and numerous others. Friendships were made there that helped save the Holt home.

I attended every single meeting during the Kentucky Lincoln Bicentennial. And was approached by many — professors, historians, directors of Lincoln sites, employees of the Kentucky Historical Society, Preservation Kentucky, the Kentucky Heritage Council, senators, representatives and many walks of life. My own future publisher heard me speak not knowing I was writing a biography of Holt because I never mentioned my work but only the work for our community and how the Holt home needed help. Speaking from my heart I caught the attention of Kent Whitworth, the director of the Kentucky Historical Society. He privately told me and my husband that it was wonderful to put your heart into working to save a national treasure. And he told me someday when the home started getting attention and grants and recognition many would come to assist and want to be a part of it.

A gentleman named Mr. White who was a volunteer from Farmington spoke to me before one of the Kentucky Lincoln Bicentennial meetings and said, "You are a volunteer, you come to every meeting, you are not getting paid, but you still come to learn - and people like that," He told me, "you will gain many friends and they will help you, and remember your dedication for your community."

Once Judge Ray Powers, the Breckinridge County Judge Executive was present for a meeting and spoke briefly about me. He said, "All communities need someone like Susan. She won't give up and she will ask until someone helps her. My own Kentucky Representative, Dwight D. Butler once told me, "Susan, you remind me of the woman in the Bible who kept going to the judge to ask for help and he would not help her. Finally, after tremendous effort of asking the judge to assist he said, 'Give this woman whatever she wants.' "

Senator Carroll Gibson, at a meeting for the Holt home held in my home, invited me to the Lincoln Bicentennial Commission meetings and he thought he could get me on the commission because of my strong devotion and empathy for Holt and his legacy but that did not materialize. However, I was invited to attend the meetings and even though I was not on the commission I gained the respect from every person who attended the meetings from 2007-2010. And on the book cover of the first biography ever written about Joseph Holt, Kent Whitworth, Director, Kentucky Historical Society wrote a quote, "Saving the Joseph Holt House and its marvelous story are among the most significant legacy projects of the entire Lincoln Bicentennial! Our congratulations and deepest thanks go to Susan Dyer for championing this most important cause."

One day I was invited to sit at the table at the Lincoln site meetings prior to the Kentucky Lincoln Bicentennial meetings since I represented the Joseph Holt home that had been identified as a site of importance during the Lincoln Bicentennial. At the beginning of each meeting all sites shared what was happening as they introduced themselves. All were directors of their organization but I felt welcomed as I introduced myself. "I am Susan Dyer, volunteer for the Joseph Holt home in rural Breckinridge County."

A dear friend, author, and former public relations of Berea College, Edward Ford, asked me to write the story of how the Holt home has been saved the week after the home received a $500,000.00 Transportation Enhancement Grant for Phase 1 Exterior renovation.

Note* Judge Holt's home was fortunate in the research I did to have had Holt's father, John W. Holt to be the Surveyor of Roads in early Breckinridge County, along with having a strong history of the Ohio River, behind the home, the railroad passing through the Holt property and at an earlier time had had a depot there on the Holt grounds and the road in front of the Holt home had been Highway 64 before Interstate 64 was built when the name was changed to Kentucky Highway 144.

In the very beginning of the Holt project, hours were spent on the internet trying to discover all that has ever been written about Joseph Holt. But in 1997 not all public records could be obtained on the internet from the Library of Congress and numerous other sources. I did not have grants to pay for research used on Joseph Holt's life and home to assist county government with the grants they received. There were not volunteers to help, it was done ALL ALONE.

And there was not any funding to pay for assistants. I did not have any experience in grant writing except for one grant previously written for the Breckinridge County School System placed on my desk with two days until the deadline. I completed the grant for the school system alone and the school received $7,500.00 for a multicultural grant.

My husband Eddie paused from farming whenever there was a preservation conference in the state or a Kentucky Lincoln Bicentennial Commission meeting I had been invited to attend. Numerous days were spent on the road. After all the meetings I would always phone Representative Dwight Butler to give him updates and I followed up with county government and Senator Carroll Gibson.

The trips to Frankfort were expensive as hundreds of dollars were spent on gas, lodging, conferences, research, traveling, phone bills, and three Dell printers worn out on grant writing for the Breckinridge County Fiscal Court. Twelve grants along with requests have been written for the Holt home. As a volunteer grant writer or any grant writer on salary there is never a guarantee you will receive the grants you write.

In the beginning, I wrote all the grants for the Breckinridge County Fiscal Court for the Holt home as a volunteer before they even owned the home. I put in requests with all the senator's offices for funding yearly. Preservation is slow as another mentor and friend, retired Dana K. Chipman, the 38th Judge Advocate General of the United States Army shared with me, who has come to Breckinridge County as a guest speaker and spoke at the 5th Annual Holt Home Community Day on September 28, 2013 as he promised he would after meeting me at the JAG School when I was there to deliver the 5th George S. Prugh Lecture in 2011.

Since the county did not own the home I followed advice from the Kentucky Heritage Council State Preservation Officer, and Executive Director, David L. Morgan in 2006 who shortly retired and moved to Washington D.C. He is now a Resource of the Judge Joseph Holt Home and friend.

But it was even a struggle to get David's attention in the beginning. The Holt home had been recognized as a strong connection to Lincoln at the beginning of the Kentucky Lincoln Bicentennial because Holt was Lincoln's JAG during the Civil War. Upon the advice from the Department of the Interior in Washington D. C. I wrote for help and was advised to seek the Kentucky Heritage Council/State Preservation Office. The Kentucky Heritage Council State Preservation Office have numerous responsibilities and a steady stream of people just like me calling daily and asking for help.

With the home saved, and restoration at full swing, occasionally my thoughts linger back to the first public meeting where David Morgan and I spoke. Still today, this speech is remembered as smiles came across the room that evening, and numerous times, throughout I looked at David Morgan as he smiled. The memory is strong after completing the speech as all applauded when I introduced the person who is still a key resource for the Judge Joseph Holt Home. David Morgan's last project as Executive Director at the Kentucky Heritage Council was the Holt Home project.

After the trim work is completed the new roof will make this historical home in America reflect its personality of greatness !!!

Laying roof panels on Judge Holt's home!

The people will come once renovated!

Holt Home Phase 1 renovation enlightening historical jewel!

Renovation is slow. However, guidance of the Kentucky Heritage Council / State Preservation Office helps the community do renovation the proper way.

The beautiful turnings are being renovated. And some reconstructed as they have been damaged over the past four decades the home sat silent.

Holt Home historic sidewalks uncovered & Historic Holt fence removed for renovation!

Historic Holt Home fence provides the setting for the beautiful Holt grounds / Made possible through the Brown- Forman grant

Mr. Morgan gave insight for all possibilities and opportunities for the community to get involved to work with guidance from the Kentucky Heritage Council, who guides communities seeking to save their history, and now a lifetime partner with the Joseph Holt home because of the acquisition grant through the Kentucky Lincoln Bicentennial for the purchase that was a Kentucky Lincoln Bicentennial Commission Legacy project.

Hopefully, our community appreciates the drive it has taken to endure what has been overcome as someone from the audience that evening stated, "this community tried forty years ago to save the home and after Mr. Bill Thompson worked diligently to get the Holt home on the National Register of Historic Places the owners were not interested in any further help from the community."

Also, an individual in the crowd stated that this was a great idea, but it could not be done. However, with God guiding I did not listen to comments that the Holt home could not be saved since the county did not own the home, did not have any money to purchase the home, and had not ever written a grant for preservation to save the home. But daily I worked, calling, visiting with senators, representatives, and anyone who would listen while continuing teaching middle school.

Friends of the Holt Home, Inc., a non-profit organization today works in a cooperative- agreement with the Breckinridge County Fiscal Court. The Holt project began as a grassroots effort in 1997 through my volunteer work. The Friends seek to bring attention to Joseph Holt's life and contributions to our Commonwealth and nation through saving his Kentucky home.

When the Kentucky General Assembly announced plans to form a Kentucky Abraham Lincoln Bicentennial Commission, Holt's home was identified as a site to be included in the planning because of Holt's strong connection to Lincoln.

Wide view of new gutters and downspouts matching the style and installation method as used in the original

Representatives from Breckinridge County were invited to commission meetings from the fall of 2006 through 2009, during which time I and others advocated preserving the home, which had been vacant since 1969 but was still structurally viable. Numerous presentations were given by me before the commission and other groups across the state where I was also an invited speaker at the 2006 Kentucky Historic Preservation Conference. I published a biography about Holt, wrote grants and worked closely with the county and others to help create momentum for rehabilitating the home and restoring it to service for the community.

The house and surrounding 19.5 acres were acquired by Breckinridge County Fiscal Court in December 2008 for $158,000 through a Kentucky Heritage Council Lincoln Preservation Grant, funded through the Lincoln Bicentennial Commission, which also designated restoration of the home a Legacy Project of the bicentennial. As a condition of the grant, the Kentucky Heritage Council holds a preservation easement on the property. In addition to creating a visitor center with interpretive exhibits and a repository of Holt memorabilia, fiscal court and the community have expressed a desire to use the home as a community center and site for events, which would provide income to be reinvested back into the property and allow the home and grounds to be maintained in perpetuity.

Following purchase, a steering committee was formed and has met regularly, including the state historic preservation officer and representatives of the Kentucky Heritage Council, Kentucky Historical Society, Preservation Kentucky Inc., Kentucky Lincoln Bicentennial Commission, and the Kentucky Tourism, Arts and Heritage Cabinet in addition to local leaders and elected officials, volunteers and advocates. A volunteer support group, Friends of the Holt Home, subsequently formed under the umbrella of the Breckinridge County Historical Society until 2013 when the Friends group applied to become a 501(c) 3 to be eligible to apply for grants as a nonprofit organization. Presently, Friends of the Holt Home, Inc., is partnering with Breckinridge County Fiscal Court to work collaboratively on raising funds and rehabilitating the home. The group is also working to secure the home's status as a viable and treasured historical landmark and bring together all interested people, organizations, state and federal agencies toward its preservation and long-term operation.

Today this community-based project has a corps of volunteers who, among other activities, stage an annual Holt Home Community Day, which has drawn hundreds to tour the home and learn more about the project and Judge Holt. This group also has worked closely with Breckinridge County schools actively to involve young local citizens, who have assisted with tours, developed a web site, presented period music during community day, and assisted with various other tasks.

Americans can continue the journey every step of the way as they can see the last official Kentucky Lincoln site in the Commonwealth restored by visiting the Holt Home Community Day yearly on the 4th Saturday in September, and can view updates by going to www.jholt-houseky.org.

The 7th Annual Holt Home Community Day

It is hard to believe it takes an entire year to plan a successful event. Year after year thoughts go into how can we make the event better? What do people like? How do you keep the excitement? And how does it all fall in place? The key answer is vision. You must think beyond the year in planning. It is like plotting out several years in advance. And thinking how can the beginning event of one violin, house tours, free refreshments of lemonade and cookies and the premier book signing of *Lincoln's Advocate* empower citizens to be excited, stay excited and return.

It is easier for a small group to work together, to know each other's talents and what each individual can bring to the group. You need organization, people who are willing to take chances on new things. You must think of how the yearly event can bring out the best of your organization's goals, and work to change all the negatives. It will be a challenge but if you want the best, and work diligently you can make it happen. "There is nothing stronger than the heart of a volunteer." Many will want to help but few will see it through.

On the morning of September 26, 2015, the gray sky looked like rain could consume the day! As the Friends' non-profit arrived early on site the wind howled, the trees blew and skies seemed to bring the promise of rain. As WXBC radio station set up their live feed and the cars began to fill the parking area thoughts go to "Will the people come?"

As always in the month of July the writing begins on press releases, calling editors of magazines and newspapers and contacting the media. For advertising the event is essential for success. When your event becomes well known and the public wants to be present the media will come to view the event. But first you must prove the event is worthy. And always you will have competition with events in the region.

Finally, the day came. The period music filled the Holt Home, the smell of food being grilled floated through the grounds. People strolled and were amazed with the beautiful trees and specimens, some from Holt's era. Different this year the grounds began coming back as the partnership of the county government and the Friends' organization opened the area that had been entangled with overgrown trees and a fencerow for many decades. A backfield that had not been walked upon for years entertained the crowd with the first Civil War Baseball game to ever be played at an official Kentucky Lincoln site, the last in the Commonwealth to be restored. What a hit the baseball game was! Individuals came that had never had an interest before in the Holt Home. However, the interest of a baseball game brought them to Holt Field.

The 113th Army Band, quintet always gets the crowd motivated as the quintet sounds like an entire band. The atmosphere is created for visitors to feel the strong feelings for patriotism. Hearing the music of America reminds us that freedom is precious and on that day Bob Bell from the 12 Regimental Colored Heavy Artillery told the public we need to remember Holt for not just being the prosecuting judge of the Lincoln Conspiracy Trial but for developing the idea for slaves to become Union soldiers that Lincoln and Congress signed into law that gave freedom not only to the slaves that became soldiers but also gave freedom to their families. Thus, giving tribute to Joseph Holt who helped set people free and for the last era of his life diligently worked for the freedom of all people.

The organ grinder kept the rhythm of music going. When bands or singers were briefly silent

Pictured left to right: Dean Schamore, KY State Representative; Susan Dyer, President of the Friends of the Holt Home; Maurice Lucas, Breckinridge County Judge Executive; Shannon Tivitt, former Deputy Chief of Staff for former Governor Steven Beshear. Holt Home received second $500,000 TE grant from Governor Steve Beshear's administration. Photo courtesy of Glenn Arnold, Arnold Studios & more, Garfield, KY. Website: www.arnoldstudio.com

he played a jig, or brought in a tune for the baseball game.

Having Judge Holt portrayed enlightens visitors as does President Lincoln and the First Lady since Holt was Lincoln's Advocate. The feel of ambiance presents itself as you feel you stepped back in time to the 1860's. Why do you feel this way? The costumes of the period, the smiles of conversations, the grandness of the Holt mansion, and yes, it is a true southern lady. Why? Look at the architecture? Have you ever seen anything like it in Kentucky?

Behind the scenes of preparing, cleaning the home, caring for trees, working long afternoons on the ball field, growing species to sell, grooming the grounds, preparing programs, and the checklist of the three pages of items to do and redo yearly! Collecting all items for the event and storing, attending meetings locally and across the state, and writing at least 1-2 grants for the past 10 years in a row! And having patience of saints when you are told, "You have to have fundraising to make the matches," "Fund raise and make the match for Phase 2." Submit grant after grant, find the contacts, and rewrite the grants you do not receive. Hold your head high when you don't receive the grant but were told it could not be any better and do two grants at the same time if it is needed.

The 14 Kentucky Light Artillery cannon fired throughout the day building momentum of remembrance of past days when cannons fired in a battle between the states! And young men played the beginning of baseball that developed into America's favorite past time. However, baseball was quite different in the early 1860's as players rolled up their socks for balls and used sticks for bats, playing the beloved game in between skirmishes. And not knowing if they would live or die in the next battle fought.

Watching the faces in awe as they felt the presence of Judge Holt's spirit. Anticipating what it was like here one hundred and fifty-five years ago. Viewing the freestanding spiral stairs cases that are as sound today as when Holt walked them! Gazing in the restored wavy glass and viewing their own reflections on a tour of a national treasure saved by Holt's own community!

Speakers sharing thoughts about Civil War baseball, the vision of the restoration, the letters written by Holt and family sharing the stories of his life, his home, the sorrows the war caused, and the triumph of his legacy coming back are being honored today in 2015! Most would have given up when it seemed hopeless for restoration and now the reuse of Joseph Holt's home for the future is occurring! That is when the heart ruled the brain and God led the bold!

A colonel shared and praised Judge Holt's work under President Lincoln and gave the gift of General Orders NO. 100 to the Friends organization that the Judge Advocates Generals Legal Center and School introduced with the 2nd Regimental print and this one concerns Joseph Holt and the Lieber Code. Following a tribute given to Holt by one of his own, the Judge Advocate's office in Fort Knox which continues to partner with the yearly event in the wreath-laying ceremony begun by COL Robert Cotell making it tradition.

The yearly event continues to teach visitors that education is the strongest element in restoration! Visitors are learning that to continue successfully and have a prized, classic event for an historic home, it is all because of the person who lived and made the legacy for the nation, Lincoln, self, community and state. A wreath was carefully placed, giving honor and praise of a lifetime of work that was never recognized or praised while he lived. And then came the sound of Taps being played giving honor to a deserving Kentuckian, a nationally famous lawyer who served both President James Buchanan and President Abraham Lincoln.

It is amazing what faith can do! And courage makes people master seemingly undefeatable foes! Tackling every imaginable task! Only working with a positive attitude. Encouraging when others doubted! Praising all, and using the word "I" sparingly. Because God is the leader of the Holt Project! God sends the people. And when you ask for wisdom and truly give your best you will succeed!

Getting Kentucky, the Governor, four state agencies along with local, region, state and beyond, including the Army to work in harmony, and numerous behind the scene heroes, advocates, and individuals is truly a miracle. And our cause was honored and supported. The Friends of the Holt Home, Inc. and the Breckinridge County Fiscal Court received Phase 2 Transportation Enhancement grant of $500,000.00 from Kentucky and Governor Beshear and $199,000.00 in tax credits(same as cash) from the Kentucky Heritage Council/ State Preservation Office for restoration of the Judge Joseph Holt Home on September 26, 2015.

This blessing will forever be pressed in the hearts of those who gave their best! And those who never quit, never tired, never complained, only worked to make it happen when others said it could not be done!

Indiana National Guard JAGS Onsite Training in Historic Holt Home

Roger Wilson, Legal Administrator for the 38th Division of the Indiana National Guard contacted the Friends of the Holt Home, Inc. by E-mail. He wanted information on how to purchase the Second Regimental Print from the Judge Advocate General's Legal Center and School. The contact information was given for the Judge Advocate General's Corps and contact with Retired COL Fred Borch, Top Historian and Archivist at the Judge Advocate General's Legal Center and School. The print he wanted depicted Joseph Holt, President Lincoln, and the Lieber Code, an early attempt to regulate the conduct of hostilities on the battlefield.

The Indiana National Guard had built a new building located on South Holt Road, Indianapolis, IN and they wanted a print of Holt to hang there. After receiving the information along with several phone calls and numerous E-mails Mr. Wilson shared how COL Daniel Kozlowski had a quest to bring the Indiana National Guard JAGS to view Judge Holt's home. The JAGS realized the Holt Home was under extensive restoration on the exterior and how the interior had not begun yet. A request was made from Roger Wilson to come and tour the home and report back to the Senior Staff Judge Advocate COL Daniel Kozlowski. They were told how the Friends of the Holt Home Inc. could provide a tour of the home, grounds, and Holt family cemetery. Information was given on local lodging, how they could hold their training locally and then come for a tour with sandwiches, cakes and drinks provided. Later in October of 2015 Roger Wilson requested a private tour to see the grounds so he could report back to COL Kozlowski for his consideration for the JAGS to take up my offer as President of the organization for the JAGS to come to Holt.

Chief Roger Wilson and his daughter

The communications continued with Roger Wilson and me. Judge Executive Maurice Lucas and I gave the private tour on Friday, October 22, 2015. Shortly following Mr. Wilson E-mailed saying COL Kozlowski was elated to hear that the Holt Home would host their Onsite. They were currently looking at March 5 or March 19. They were looking to confirm the date with aviation.

On November 10, 2015 Roger Wilson confirmed the Onsite Training for 35 JAGS on March 5 and sent an agenda of the schedule for the four training sessions. The JAGS realized the historic home of Brigadier General Joseph Holt had not had interior restoration yet. However, they wanted to be present.

In conversations prior to the tour of the home, updates of the organization were given along with grants, and the journey as a dream is now reality. A letter was written and mailed explaining the Holt project and the massive work behind it for complete restoration along with the vision to bring back Judge Holt's legacy and home that I began back in 1997 as the spearheader of the Holt project.

The highlights of the project were shared, one being the Friends' organization had written yet another grant and won it in February 2015 from the National Trust of Historic Preservation for a site use plan of what the Holt Home will become once completely restored.

Since the home is listed on the National Register of Historic Places in three areas of national significance in politics, history and architect, Holt's local community realized the home will support local, state, and national new uses. The historic Holt Home holds a special place in the History of the JAG Corps and because of that I have diligently worked to get the United States Army to partner with the home. I have encouraged the local nonprofit organization to make our goal for the Judge Joseph Holt home to become a National meeting place for all the Army JAGS across America.

In communicating with Fred Borch, the Top Historian and Archivist at the JAG School, the Army does not have a national meeting place. I reminded him that when President Abraham Lincoln and Congress created the Office of Judge Advocate in 1862, Holt was appointed Judge Advocate and served as Lincoln's JAG during the Civil War and became the first Judge Advocate to hold general's rank. Holt still holds the record today for serving the longest tern from 1862- 1875 where he retired upon his own request.

COL Edmond Bowen at Fort Knox has shared they are working to help the regions get together. And Roger Wilson has stated the Indiana National Guard wants to assist in this worthy endeavor to help with the Holt Home becoming a National meeting place for all the Army JAGS across America.

Much preparation was done to host the Indiana National Guard JAGS. Friends of the Holt Home and the Lions Club did a thorough cleaning of the home. A classroom setting was designed that also was suitable as a dining room for a luncheon given in honor of the JAGS. Two small heaters were ordered and funded by the Breckinridge County Chamber of Commerce, Tourism, Director Veronica Ent and they also covered the expense of the meal.

White linens helped beautify the decorated tables adorned with patriotic centerpieces. A large America flag kept watch on the cozy setting. In the foyer, General Orders No. 100, a print of Holt standing over President Lincoln as he signed into law the etiquette on how troops treated each other on the battlefield greeted the JAGS upon entrance to the historic home. A guest registry recorded the history of the 26 attending JAGS including the Indiana Supreme Court Justice, Stephen David.

The day will long be remembered as it began at 4:00 a.m. Traveling to the Holt Home it seemed quite amazing to know three Blackhawk helicopters were flying here from Indianapolis. But this didn't happen overnight at the spur of the moment. Partnering does not occur instantly. An organization must first prove itself. And be deserving. Work honoring one of their own, Joseph Holt was studied (his legacy and the importance of saving and restoring his home) and surveyed long before the decision was made to come here. In fact, a letter was written to Roger Wilson, Legal Administrator telling the history of the spearheading, the grants, the journey, the state organizations, the partnering, and how a rural community have worked their hearts out to convey to their own community what the importance of this piece of American history is to the nation, state and world! And the publishing of *Lincoln's Advocate* and the massive, countless hours of volunteering week after week and year after year.

The morning ascended with heavy fog! The press began arriving at 7:00 a.m. for the 7:30 a.m. landing. But time passed and there were no helicopters. Those waiting began hearing sounds of geese flying, tugboats passing down the Ohio River, and the constant humming that became a passing freight train. Some even questioned the

The Indiana National Guard JAGS (Judge Advocates) held its Onsite Training in the Judge Joseph Holt Home March 5, the first new reuse for the historical home. Photo courtesy of Tiffany Cashman, Breckinridge County Herald News.

JAGS coming. However, I told the Friends the JAGS will be here! The Army does what it says! Newspaper reporters waited patiently and retreated to their vehicles numerous times because of the nipping breeze. After waiting over two hours a text message was received from Roger Wilson stating the JAGS had landed in Bloomington, Indiana because of the heavy fog. And they hoped it would lift soon so they could continue to the Holt Home. After a quite lengthy wait I texted Roger Wilson and discovered the JAGS were having part of their training at Bloomington since they were grounded. As the hours continued the Friends watched the sky, waiting, and anticipated the landing of the Blackhawk helicopters that had cleared aviation to land in Holt Field, behind the historic home where the first ever Civil War Baseball Game was played at the 7th Annual Holt Home Community Day on September 26, 2015.

Finally, a little before 12:00 noon I sent another text message to say… "We are still waiting, and lunch is ready." Soon an answer was sent, "You should see us soon!" And how the people stirred when everyone present saw history being made. The landing of three Blackhawk helicopters was truly amazing! The landing was smooth, and the force of the helicopters were blowing leaves majestically, like confetti. Most of the reporters had long since gone. However, WAVE 3's Rick Brown, Production Manager, weathered the bitter cold morning and stayed in Holt Field for the long, exhausting wait. Now the reward was clear! As Mr. Brown captured the first ever new reuse for the Judge Joseph Holt Home. The planned agenda was revised. The prepared welcome from Breckinridge County Judge Executive Maurice Lucas was skipped because of the caucuses that day. And I welcomed the JAGS. We had the pledge to the flag, spontaneously, and grace was said by a volunteer JAG.

The faces of all those present were amazed. The JAGS were so delighted with how they were welcomed into a classroom that was very inviting and warm that also served as their luncheon. They definitely were not expecting home cooked food. And later that day the Friends were told, "We

Tent set up for the JAGS

Rick Brown, WAVE 3 TV, former production manager.

Black Hawks landing in Holt field.

JAGS ascending on the Holt grounds

Eddie Dyer and Paul Joseph O'Donoghue. A happy day.

Indiana Supreme Court Justice David photographing Black Hawks and Sherry Stith, Friends Secretary & Treasurer

Blackhawk helicopters returning for the JAGS!

expected a boxed lunch with sandwiches. Roger Wilson shared "the Indiana National Guard JAGS have never received such a warm welcome and Southern hospitality." We were told the JAGS would give a donation and they would be back!

After the JAGS enjoyed their luncheon and had a brief meeting Roger Wilson asked me to give the JAGS a personal tour of the Holt Home. While giving a short interlude of the history of the home the judge advocates' eyes searched the west spiral stairs, intrigued by the remaining spider web wall paper which Frasier Museum had told me was from President James Buchanan's era, along with the unique features of soon to be renovated interior. Thoughts were…. "One of their own walked theses stairs, and now finally one hundred and fifty years later the Army dressed in camouflage are standing in the home entrance of the foyer where Holt himself appeared time after time.

Continuing to the Holt Family Cemetery the twenty-six scattered, some lingering along the grounds to admire the trees, some remaining in the home to take second looks enjoying every room, and all sights! About fifteen JAGS continued to the cemetery.

I requested the JAGS have their picture made holding the welcome banner on the front steps of the Holt Home.

COL Daniel Kozlowski, the Senior Judge Advocate referred to as COL K, could not attend the highly-anticipated event he had so determined to bring the Indiana JAGS here. At the last minute his General had requested he would have to be present at another Army event so during the day COL Kozlowski phoned numerous times to check on what was occurring. He relayed that no matter how late it was the Army JAGS would go to Judge Holt's home and land. And no matter what time it was he said, "Susan Dyer will still be there waiting, even if it is with a flashlight."

The replacing COL said, "We like passion. And I want you to know Holt is smiling down upon us."

The Indiana Supreme Court Justice David said, "I will definitely be back but I'll never find this place." He said "everything was amazing!"

Speeches Given from the Grassroots Effort

The first speech I gave was a request from David L. Morgan who came to Hardinsburg to explain the possibilities of how the Holt Home had been identified beginning with the process of the Kentucky Lincoln Bicentennial Commission and how it could be saved. After this it became non-stop speaking. I received a phone call one morning from Diane Comer PR at the KY Heritage Council/ State Preservation Office. She called to see if I would be willing to accept to be one of the speakers at the Kentucky Historic Preservation Conference held September 28-30, 2006 in Covington, KY. The conference was a milestone as the 10th Kentucky Historic Preservation Conference marked the 40th anniversary of both Kentucky's state historic preservation program and the passage of the National Historic Preservation Act. The Kentucky Heritage Council, Preservation Kentucky, Inc. and Renaissance Covington, Inc. collaborated to develop a program to be useful to advance their preservation efforts through the Commonwealth.

I did not give Diane an answer at first as much thought went into this. I was not afraid to speak. However, I knew I was not an expert nor had I a degree in preservation and I was to address the groups of people who might join in for the session on the Grass Root efforts of saving the Holt Home. And in 2016 I had been told by many that true preservationists are not always the ones who have degrees in preservation but the ones who have the heart for ALL that accompanies the process. I explained I would call Diane back in a few days. Thinking about being a presenter in a statewide preservation conference was somewhat intimidating. However, I accepted and explained this was a wonderful opportunity to address the public about the work and effort of spearheading to save the Holt Home. I explained I would present a slide show that showed pictures of the work and progress.

Owensboro/Davies County Remembers: The Civil War, with a lecture and book signing by Susan Dyer

My husband and I made reservations at the Marriott at River Center and requested the historic preservation conference rate of $150.000 a night. It was reassuring to know Joyce and Thomas Wheatley of Cloverport (my husband's aunt) would also be attending the convention as they were there to learn more about the Main Street program for Cloverport. The Wheatleys had diligently worked to make the Main Street program happen for numerous storefronts of the historic town, which were restored and renovated giving Cloverport a most beautiful Ohio River view about ten miles from the Holt Home.

This was also a great opportunity to meet again and spend time with my mentor David Morgan who when asked at our Holt House Steering Committee meetings who was going to write the grants for the Holt home — his calm answer was, "you are." It will be really simple. So many questions and ideas were thought of and how to meet and get acquainted with all the necessary connections with preservation in Kentucky. Most often meeting the people and having luncheons with them are utterly important. Some of the planning, and ideas for numerous projects occur when people are meeting and greeting and socializing.

When we arrived, the hotel was quite grand, and the atmosphere was very nice and inviting. I can remember it as if it were yesterday that the bed was one of the best sleeps I have ever had. The opening night reception at the Baker Hunt Art & Cultural Center on Greenup Street was very nice with a great atmosphere of wonderful Kentuckians. The night passed quickly and the next morning was very exciting as the opportunity was available to share with the Kentuckians who chose to come to the session about the Kentucky Lincoln Bicentennial and the following session about saving the Holt Home.

Warren Greer, the Coordinator of the Kentucky Lincoln Bicentennial Commission spoke first and did a power point presentation acquainting the audience with the Kentucky Lincoln Bicentennial. It was interesting to learn about all that was to begin with the Lincoln connection in Kentucky.

Diane Comer introduced me and the talk began… I had been asked to give a perspective of my work and interest with Judge Joseph Holt's home and share Lincoln ties and grassroots efforts to preserve the Holt Home. The slide show began with pictures of the road sign, Holt's monument, and pictures of the home. I began with…Do you believe in fate? I do. After being introduced I explained I was writing a biography on Judge Holt trying to rescue his home located in Breckinridge County. I told the story of how I became intrigued with the Holt Home, how the home became an important part of my life, how my students also became fond of the historic home that had been neglected. I shared with the audience my heart had been touched by this massive mission and I retired from 27 years of teaching in Kentucky with the desire to bring attention to this unique, irreplaceable home that could be possibly lost forever if I did not work hard, get involved, and try to convince others about the shrine sitting gravely neglected by historians for over fifty years.

I shared how I had attended a conference, met a publisher named Etta Wilson at a Christian conference who connected me with well know author John Egerton of Nashville who helped connect me with Dr. James C. Klotter, had Rep. Dwight D. Butler to assist, how I had met with Congressmen, Field Representatives, and had written letters to the Department of the Interior. Then highlights of the first meeting for the Holt Home in February of 2006 were shared and how a few individuals worked from February to June of 2006 beginning the Holt House Commission following the guidelines of the Kentucky Heritage Council/ State Preservation Office. My talk was to hopefully, inspire others about their possible connections or ties with Lincoln and to encourage them that one person can generate interest by being an active participant, trying to save historical homes with history that needs to be secured for Kentucky while preserving and protecting heritage for the next generation of school children.

For the remaining drama I summarized the main ideas and points. For starters, did the audience know who Joseph Holt was? Most people had never heard the name. They were informed on Holt's dedication of service and duty to our nation, always a man of honor who had served two presidents and had been grievously neglected and forgotten by historians and writers of the past. The words spoken were from the heart, "If the home can be secured, we can dream even more!" The speech told of Holt's life, his offices under two Presidents, and how now was the time for Kentucky to recognize Holt's work, and rescue his home, sharing rich history and the untold story of Judge Holt's personal life and work, dedicated to the 16th President, Abraham Lincoln. Continuing with the talk the audience was spell bound as I shared the Holt Home has seen much, and as you walk through it you understand the home has a story to tell. The pictures of the inside of the home were shown including the free-standing stairwells unique to Kentucky, windows, doors, and fourteen rooms that had been stripped of grace and righteousness.

The audience was asked to look and see that there is a story unfinished, but one we hope has a happy ending. In conjunction with Kentucky preparing for the Kentucky Lincoln Bicentennial Celebration it is the hope of many that this historical mansion can be restored, bringing back its dignity begging to return to its glorious days when it entertained the most distinguished people in America. The accomplishments were shared …The biography was 2/3 complete, The Holt Home had been selected on the 2006 Preservation Kentucky's Most Endangered List of Historical Places; three meetings had been successful in Breckinridge County trying to save the Holt Home; a proposal letter had been sent to the private owners of the Holt Home in regards of the county and state working together in trying to purchase Judge Holt's home through grants available through the Kentucky Lincoln Bicentennial Celebration. And with public interest now generated, lots of hard work, phone calls, determination, and the historical home of Judge Holt had senators, representatives, judges, the local historical society, the public, and the Kentucky Heritage Council joining forces to save history.

When the session ended, people did not want to leave. They lingered, and asked question after question. All were amazed and they had been touched with this true historical encounter of the Holt home in South Central Kentucky. The audience wanted business cards and longed for more information. However, the next session was to begin in 15 minutes. And the people still refused to leave. They were told numerous times by Diane Comer we must clear the room for the next speaker.

At the beginning of the presentation the computer would not work correctly and the slides would not advance to the next one. However, I did not stop and continued to speak and asked if someone from the audience could please assist me as the computer was not working correctly. Warren Greer came to my rescue and finally got the slides to work correctly. The pictures dramatically added insight and impact to the words spoken about this heart felt project for Kentucky and the nation.

Upon leaving the room Warren Green came to me and said, "Mrs. Dyer if there is anything I can ever do to assist with the Holt home please call me." And he gave me his card. Since that day, Warren and I have continued to be good friends, to work together for preserving important Kentucky Lincoln connections. Warren would soon invite me to attend the Kentucky Lincoln Bicentennial Commission meetings and the Kentucky Lincoln site meetings where he now serves as the Kentucky Lincoln Heritage Trail Alliance Director and I serve as the President of the Friends of the Holt Home, Inc. and the Vice-Chair of the KLHTA in 2016. However, there is nothing stronger than a heart of a volunteer and my job is still VOLUNTEER!

The speeches have been numerous and continue across Kentucky and beyond. I go wherever I am invited; small or large audiences. Some of those speeches continue to bring in partnering. The people can contribute in many ways as more learn about Joseph Holt, his home, legacy, and the team behind the effort. Word of mouth is very important hand in hand with technology. Especially when people know you are for real, and the work is deserving for the people of our nation who will enjoy this magnificent home in the future and will bring their children and families to Holt House!

Premier Book Signing

Everything always happens at the same time it seems. During the summer of 2009 the Kentucky Heritage Trail was re-introduced and all official Kentucky Lincoln sites were spotlighted. The Holt Home became an official Kentucky Lincoln site on February 12, 2007 at an event at the Rotunda in Frankfort. The Holt Home was officially purchased through grants for the Breckinridge County Fiscal Court by funding placed in the Kentucky Heritage Council by the Kentucky Lincoln Bicentennial Commission. And a decision had to be made on the very last two choices available for the Holt Home to be spotlighted on the Kentucky Lincoln Heritage Trail; August or November? Knowing Kentucky weather, the decision was made by Breckinridge County Judge Executive Ray Powers and me to choose August 15, 2009 for the Holt Home to be spotlighted. Tremendous work was done by local volunteers, inmates were supervised and did a wonderful job in preparing the grounds and home to be opened to the public for the event.

The book that had been researched and written from 1997 to 2009 with guidance and editing beginning in 2005 with Dr. James C. Klotter had been sent to the publisher Doug Sikes from Acclaim Press. At a Holt House Steering Committee meeting with state partners, and local volunteers planning the open house for August 15, 2009, Doug Sikes was invited to the meeting. The first biography on Judge Joseph Holt was at the printers. The name of the book was changed after Doug Sikes spoke with my mentor Dr. James C. Klotter. Dr. Kotter's suggestion for a title was *Lincoln's Advocate: The Life of Judge Joseph Holt.* Because of the Holt Home being spotlighted and opened to the public since the county government became the owner on December 5, 2008, Mr. Sikes thought this would be a wonderful time for the unveiling of the first biography on Joseph Holt. He also saw the importance of printing *Lincoln's Advocate* earlier than expected. Flyers were made by Acclaim Press inviting the public to the premier book signin; invitations were ordered at Towne and Country Florist; a caterer, Becky Wethington from Cloverport was contacted; a former student and violinist, Scott Moore was contacted to see if he would perform at the event and two other former students were involved; Mark Buckles, owner of Heritage Media of Kentucky (WKHG, WMTL) in Leitchfield was the MC and Renee Allgood Wright spoke as well. The event was to be at the Community Building behind the Breckinridge County Extension Office. Much care was taken in the planning of the book event. Carol Hinton, Breckinridge County agent put my name, and date of the book signing on the marquee.

The invitation had a picture of what the new book would look like. Earlier I had asked Mr. Sikes if we could have a picture of both of Holt's wives on the cover and a young picture of Joseph as most often pictures of Joseph Holt were used that were taken only a few years before his death. Most people want to be remembered at their prime. I had designed a collage of the Holt Home in the background with both wives on each side of Holt with him holding onto the banister. You could see the Ohio River in the background and a picture of a slave. All were part of the story. However, the publisher changed the design and after speaking with Dr. Klotter the name of the book was changed as well. After the meeting in July, Doug Sikes took the print James L. Wimsatt's gave to me for my work on the Holt project and placed it on the ground in front of Judge Powers' office. He took his huge camera, stood over the picture and with a puff sound the image became part of the cover of the book.

Invitations were sent and I did get nervous since this was another first for our community - to have a book signing by a local author where numerous invitations were mailed. Day by day the RSVP's came. Mr. Sikes told me in twenty years I was his first author to send invitations to invite the community and friends. The anticipation of waiting for the product that had taken twelve years of my life while at the same time working as a volunteer for the Breckinridge Co. Fiscal Court writing grants, sending requests to offices across the state, speaking where invited and to that day in 2016 I had accepted invitations small and large, some very distinguished groups but always by invitation.

The attire was also considered for the book signing as the event would welcome some of Breckinridge County's finest citizens, three former principals, one the first to read the finished book, another who had encouraged me to do more and even where I had always given my best he still told me "You can do more.!" He had once placed a grant application on my desk forty-eight hours before the deadline while I was still teaching and asked me to complete it. It was the first grant I had ever written and I did not have a clue on what to do. However, he did get me help and we received $7,500.00 for our school. As a result we were able to have a Culture Fair with the funding. But thank goodness, this was the beginning of my grant writing experience with many more demands and challenging grants ahead to research and write.

The menu for the book signing was planned down to the hors d'oeuvres. I asked the local caterer if she and her girls would wear black and white. They purchased black pants and white blouses for a classic look.

Brief messages from political and civil leaders as well as the author welcomed the guests. The first person to believe in the project and the book was former Kentucky Representative Dwight D. Butler who could not be present. He wrote a short speech that was read by the Breckinridge County Circuit Judge Bruce T. Butler. The speech follows…"We are often faced with opportunities that are disguised as challenges that seem impossible to overcome. When this happens we usually quit and think about what might have been if we had not given up. Susan Dyer was faced with the challenge of saving the Joseph Holt home. The obstacles that she faced were enormous. I know that many times the project seemed to have come to the end of the road with no possible hope that it could continue."

"Susan never gave up because she had the dream of letting the world know about this great man. The memory of Joseph Holt has almost been lost with the passage of time. Most Americans do not know his story and contributions to our nation."

"Susan has been able to pull together many people and groups to begin the process of restoring Judge Holt's home. She has written her book about his life to preserve his memory and to show the true picture of this great statesman. What began as an impossible dream has become a reality. Susan has been an inspiration to me and has shown all of us you can accomplish anything if you truly believe in your dream." Signed, Dwight Butler State Representative 18th District

Violinist, Scott Moore performed and the evening was well received. And the people came!

Earlier that afternoon I received a call from Acclaim Press telling me Doug Sikes was on his way from Missouri loaded down with fresh-off-the-press copies of *Lincoln's Advocate*, and should arrive mid-afternoon. Several trips were made to the Breckinridge County extension office. All tables were decorated, a guest book was reserved for those who attended, a table prepared to place books, and everything organized. I wanted the book signing event to be something people would always remember, a special evening together, with classical music, good food, socializing and finally to be present to hear the distinguished speakers… Breckinridge County Judge Executive, Ray Powers, Co-Chair, Kentucky Abraham Lincoln Bicentennial Commission and National Abraham Lincoln Bicentennial Commission member, Judge Tommy Turner, State Senator and Kentucky Abraham Lincoln Bicentennial Commission member, Carroll Gibson, A letter from

Susan Dyer and Mark Buckles, Master of Ceremony

Premier book signing for Lincoln's Advocate

Representative Dwight D. Butler read by Bruce T. Butler, Circuit Judge, President/ CEO, Heritage Media of Kentucky, Inc. Mark Buckles, 5th Grade Teacher, Hodgenville Elementary School, Renee Wright, Publisher, Acclaim Press, Doug Sikes, and most surprised and humbled by it all, me, author and local volunteer, Susan Dyer.

Around 3:00 p.m. the publisher arrived. Entering the premises Doug Sikes looked around, smiled and said, "Very nice." I told him all we needed were the books. Then he handed me a copy of *Lincoln's Advocate.* It was as if someone had handed me twelve years of my life condensed into 255 pages. Finished at last!!! Completing a book that gets published makes the work worth all the effort, all the time it took to research it, write it, re-rewrite it, and even add another chapter that had to be researched only a few weeks before the publication.

With book in hand I returned home to prepare for the evening. Doug Sikes checked into a local motel for the evening to have a place after the event that night. He had been invited to stay in our home, but we had already opened our home to a dear friend for the weekend, Mary Jean from Frankfort. Mr. Sikes then traveled on to the Holt Home where Judge Ray Powers had given permission for anyone to take a tour of the home that was to be seen for the last time before anything began. Lee Stinnett went to the home in case someone came for a tour. No one came that afternoon. However, Breckinridge County came out to support the book event later that evening at 6:00 p.m.

The feelings of happiness and encouragement as people began entering the Community Building were visible on every face. Everyone wore a smile. The musician played beautifully as the guests were served from their tables.

A little before 6:00 p.m. Doug Sikes returned from the Holt Home and could not find a place to park. He had to walk a long distance almost from the highway as all parking space was filled. Mr. Sikes' face was beaming upon entering the building. He came to me and whispered, "I have never seen anything like this in my twenty years as a publisher."

The program began as all eyes were upon the large book cover that had been placed in an easel. A huge banner of the book cover hung behind the speaker's podium. Mr. Sikes said Mark Buckles being a radio broadcaster and former student of mine was a great idea. Mark not only kept things moving but entertained as well. One of his stories was about the author when she was a teacher at Caneyville Elementary School and Mark walked into class on the first day of school and truly thought his teacher was "Wonder Woman". He went home and told his mother "Wonder Woman was his first-grade teacher." This got great laughter from the crowd. Another touching remark that I will always be remember and appreciate was one comment made by Judge Tommy Turner, "He said, "Judge Powers did you notice the parking lot outside? You better hope Susan Dyer does not decide to run for Breckinridge County Judge Executive." The room laughed loud and long!

Later, after placing the few remaining programs in a container to save I discovered the program Mr. Sikes had used for his notes. The key points for his talk were written on the program that is included in this chapter as is the invitation to the event and a flyer of what the publisher first designed, then changed, along with a copy of the flyer posted in numerous locations inviting citizens to the book event.

After speaking briefly, I could not keep up with the people in line to purchase a book. Mr. Sikes helped, and took care of the money. I wanted to speak briefly to each person and sign something special for them. Being new at signing books and the publisher being a gentleman he did not want to tell me to hurry. I will always remember hearing a clicking of nails on the tabletops and thought to myself, "what is this annoying noise?" Later, I realized it was my publisher, as if encouraging me to write faster, and move. I finally realized the code and tried to moved things along.

Before and during the book event my husband along with Carol Hinton continued to carry additional chairs as the Community Building was filled. One person even mentioned, "I think we have gone beyond the safety for the fire regulations. Two of my principals were present. And my heart will remember those who came and supported the beginning of something that continues to encourage others to work to make their dreams become reality!

After the crowd dissipated Doug Sikes told me he had never seen anything like this before and was wondering what the next day would bring for the Open House for the Holt Home Spot Lighted on the Kentucky Heritage Trail with another book signing on August 15, 2016.

That day will forever be remembered not only by me but everyone who was present. Judge Tommy Turner, CO-Chair of the Kentucky Lincoln Bicentennial Commission told us that this event was one of the best in the Commonwealth for the Kentucky Lincoln Bicentennial events. People stood in line for hours to tour the Holt Home. I signed books until my hands ached and spoke with every single person who bought a book or wanted to talk with me.

Once during the day while I had to leave the book signing station to deliver a talk Mr. Sikes took over for me. Several times during the day he motioned for me to come back to the table. However, I had to talk with everyone and left briefly.

At the end of the day I could feel the sand in my teeth from the grounds on the hot August day. Throughout the day the publisher went back to his car numerous times for more books. He told my mother, "We may sell out of books." We only had a few left and Mr. Sikes had to bring more the next week.

The Kentucky Lincoln Bicentennial Commission and Advisory Commission believed in this project and invested their time, energy, and allotted funding placed in the Kentucky Heritage Council for the acquisition of the Holt Home. Nine years later in 2016 the Kentucky Lincoln Bicentennial Commission members and Advisory committee members were invited and numerous members came and were recognized and viewed how their investment and funding is now successful with the partnering of four state agencies as the Judge Joseph Holt Home is well under way to restoration. *Lincoln's Advocate* is still telling the story of Holt and the effort to restore his home. In 2012 I began compiling and writing this follow-up book on how the Holt Home has been saved, which will also be published with Acclaim Press.

The Little Black Book

Pressed within the pages of a little black book bought in 1997 at a local store are preserved part of the history of the Holt project and the beginning efforts still continuing in 2016.

The contents inside are simple but include the personal information gained from respect of very dedicated people in Kentucky and beyond have been instrumental in the circle of people somehow connected with each other. The names listed in this book were given to me with respect, confidence, confidentiality and the trust of many who have worked behind the scenes of this magnificent project.

Many things can be written that tell the story of the Judge Joseph Holt project and other happenings have occurred that only the people who made them happen know about. This is not to be secretive but honorable. For the love of history brings people together just like David Hayes, a local retired editor from the local newspaper who wrote a story after Byron Crawford's featured story in the Courier-Journal stated, "The Holt project is coming full circle." However, the key to it all as former Kentucky Representative Dwight D. Butler states is, "somehow the people involved have all been brought together." And this united team is doing remarkable things! Some of those individuals graduated college together, served together in offices, universities, attended conferences, met at social events, retirement parties, Kentucky Lincoln Bicentennial meetings, celebrations at the capital, book events and some local gatherings. It may be said it is fate, or the right timing. However, the truth is, God has sent his blessings on this project and he continues to send the people he wants! The people who have made impossible tasks successful have been sent like messengers. I met these people at casual settings, was introduced to the numerous dedicated people

The little black book.

who served on the Kentucky Lincoln Bicentennial Commission, and Advisory committee. In addition, opportunities presented themselves because of hard work, and persistence, when in the beginning many did not believe in this project or its success. It is easy to join in when things are working, when there is money, and when people can see for themselves the success of it all!

The little black book was used to include the names of those who did believe, who did assist, who returned calls, who wrote support letters, who listened and sometimes were even revisited after they had stated, "There is not a thing we can do, Contact the Kentucky Heritage Council, maybe they can help you." Being a "nice" lady and as Dr. James C. Klotter, Kentucky's State Historian has told me numerous times, "You must have a heart like a lion and a stomach like a goat to do this kind of work. Dr. Klotter asked these questions… Are you sure you want to try and save the Holt Home and write a book at the same times? My answer in 2005 to Dr. Klotter was - I don't have a choice. I cannot have any peace. At the time was up all hours of every night working, searching, researching, looking for anyone who would listen, and hopefully, support and get behind something that had never happened in Breckinridge County: Save our history linked between Joseph Holt and President Abraham Lincoln.

One afternoon in 2008 at the capital in Frankfort, Ken Whitworth told my husband and me something I will never forget… He said, "Susan the Holt Project is amazing!" And on the back cover of Lincoln's Advocate he stated, "Saving the Joseph Holt House and its marvelous story are among the most significant legacy projects of the entire Lincoln Bicentennial! Our congratulation and deepest thanks go to Susan Dyer for championing this most important cause." – Kent Whitworth, Director, Kentucky Historical Society. Mr. Whitworth told me someday after everything is completed, the home is saved, restored, and open to the public many will join the bandwagon; they will appear as if this project just happened. But Kent told me it takes many and those who never gave up and withstood ALL THE TRIALS AND TRIBULATIONS know they had the bravery to believe and give only the best to make the Holt project successful. Mr. Whitworth said, "Someday, that little black book will be placed in the archives at the Holt Home." Now new technology, flash drives, over seventy-five notebooks, and many computers contain the work it has taken for a deserving project to become known across Kentucky and the nation. Visitors will see the little book that I carried all across Kentucky with names of those who gave!

Now that reality has set in Mr. Whitworth's words ring in my ears each time someone says, "The Holt project is wonderful, we are amazed with it all." For those who realized the importance of saving their history that could not be seen in the beginning, this will be a testimony. For the Friends welcome all who want to be involved, who want to work, who want to give their talents, who want to continue this project in a professional manner, and other communities across Kentucky can use the Friends as a good example of what community spirit looks like. Joshua Wilks at the National Trust for Preservation said, "The Holt project would serve as a wonderful case study."

Success is often measured by the wisdom learned — wisdom like — working to compromise, to LISTEN, to follow the guidelines of state partners. Most of all it is a testimony for your community that you will do anything professional and right to save and restore special places in America's history that enables us to learn about our past so we can understand the present and face the challenges of the future! The Holt Home will be remembered as the project that came from the heart, was done professionally, by the book, using state guidelines, persisting with patience, efficiently attending to requests that were asked and staying on course to be there to see the final product that will remain as part of our strong American heritage in south central Kentucky. These are the wisdom, works and words the people have lived and spoken and why the home is now the people's home!

The Holt Home Cake

Holt Home Cake being mailed by former Harned post master, Sharon Wakefield.

Colonels, Generals, Governors, Preservation Officers, Tourism, Professors, Representatives, Senators, Art Councils, and others from many walks of life have been sent Holt Home cakes. This sweet practice started with David L. Morgan.

This all began when I wanted to give thanks for all the little things people do and need to receive thanks. People should be appreciated for their many acts of kindness. In the beginning work of the Holt project David L. Morgan retired as the Kentucky Heritage Council/ State Preservation Officer and Executive Director and moved to Washington D.C. During that time, we were in between a new Preservation Officer being named. There was an individual who did assist, Becky Shipp, at the Kentucky Heritage Council/ State Preservation Office. She was very instrumental in assisting with the acquisition grant, the extension of the grant and gave advice submitting the second grant to add together to make an appropriate offer to the private owner of the property. During the transition period, it was very important to take the correct direction, to do things the right way the first time.

I wanted to send a token of thanks for being kind enough to answer phone calls, to give encouragement, to ask if certain tasks would be acceptable. It gave confidence to begin and continue on the long exhausting journey continuing to today. Only God knows the trials and tribulations a volunteer can endure. In a conversation once with David Morgan I asked what kind of cake do you like? David's response was, "I love chocolate cake." And then he shared a story about a lady in Texas who was working to save an historic home there. If someone did something nice to help with the restoration of the home, she baked a cake and sent it. It was just a small token, but one that was well received as she actually took the time to bake a cake and send an appreciation for the kindness shown to help save the home.

The story blossomed into the idea: send David Morgan a cake to show how much his help is appreciated. An old-fashioned recipe for chocolate cake was used. It was frozen for several days, and wrapped in Reynolds wrap using numerous layers, then placed inside a cake container. The cake was taken to the Harned Post Office in Harned, Kentucky where Postmaster Sharon Wakefield helped package the first cake. Through the years Sharon and I wish we had counted every cake mailed to individuals doing good deeds for the Holt Home. The cake was sent priority mail to Washington, D.C. to David Morgan. However, David was not home when the cake arrived so the package was left under his porch. A few days later returning home David noticed there was something sticking out from his porch and he got closer and examined that it was a package. Upon opening the package there was a note enclosed stating the appreciation for assisting with the Holt project. Making it even more special, David found the cake on his birthday! The next time he spoke with me he said, "I believe that cake is the best cake I have ever eaten." He wanted to know the ingredients, which were shared.

After that day, continuous calls were made to learn more about preservation that you could not learn from going to a conference, and sometimes it was just a voice reassuring me I was on the right tract.

Numerous cakes continued to make their appearances such as, the Kentucky Lincoln Bicentennial Commission meetings, the Kentucky Heritage Council and people who gave a business card, a kind suggestion, a phone number of where to ask for help, tips on grant writing. Whenever important information was gained to help continue in a professional manner, always asking scholars, individuals with experience, and anyone who would help, they received a cake.

Replies have been, "No one has ever sent a cake. It was really appreciated." As the years multiplied so did the cakes. By 2016 we had been sending Holt Home cakes for ten years! It is just a small token for all people who do wonderful things for the preservation of the Holt Home. Giving thanks can be done in small ways. Even though it has become expensive as now the weight of the cakes cost over $18.00 to mail, they have arrived all across the nation — even to the Pentagon when finally, in 2013 I was told the 38th Judge Advocate General, Dana K. Chipman would finally get to eat a Holt cake. Because of security the first cake was destroyed. But when General Chipman flew from Washington D. C. to Louisville, rented a car and spent the week-end in Breckinridge Co. accompanied by COL Retired Fred Borch, the Top Historian and Archivist at the Judge Advocate General's Legal Center and School, he personally tasted a Holt cake and received one to take back home.

David Morgan said, "The Holt cake may help save this home. It could be auctioned off in the future." The recipe is very special, a very hard to make cake. Taking time in a busy world to give back by writing personal notes, most hand-written with a homemade cake to say, "Thank you, you are appreciated" shows the individual who has helped is remembered, and has contributed in a very positive way toward the restoration. It also communicates well, which is an essential element for success. Learning from the refined talents of many walks of life it takes to make preservation successful, continues to be a blessing with the Holt Home project! And for any person who has not given their talents yet there is still a chance you might receive a Holt cake!

The JAGS Gave All

Col. Borch and General Chipman visiting Holt's monument

Did you ever work on something for two years? Have you ever experienced unexpected pleasure? When a dream became reality were you numb? And when the dream was fulfilled will it forever be in your memory? To awaken each day with a dream to work and accomplish a goal and always do the right thing gives us courage and keeps us from running away from challenging, sometimes almost impossible dreams!

From 2011 through 2013 an effort was pursued until the answer was yes. What effort? The dramatic fullfillment of a promise made by Lt. General Dana K. Chipman, the 38th Judge Advocate General of the United States Army and retired COL Fred Borch, Historian and Archivist at The Judge Advocate General's Legal Center and School, that they would come to Kentucky and speak at a Holt Home Community Day to lend support for the restoration of Brigadier General Joseph Holt's home.

After being invited by Fred Borch to deliver the 5th George S. Prugh Lecture and the lecture published in the Military Law Review in 2012 the work continued with the request I gave while at the JAG school to the two powerful JAGS, General Chipman and COL Borch, upon realizing the importance of getting the Army behind the Holt Home Project in honoring one of their own, who holds a special place in the history of the JAG Corps.

It took courage, persistence, genuine interest, letter writing, numerous E-mails with updates of positive work, not simply asking for money but working to raise funds through grants that have provided ALL OF THE RESTORATION of the Holt Home. When an individual and a non-profit organization such as the Friends of the Holt Home, Inc. work in a cooperative agreement with county government who owns the home and grounds (through grants) it paints a vivid picture of what the community is about. Not self, not paid salaries but caring and loving their history, so much so that they give the priceless gift of themselves. That is why state partners got interested and that is why not giving up on a $150,000 Save America's Treasures grant 50-50 matching since 2009 with mostly volunteer time was completed in 2016. This was the last community and site to receive a Save America's Treasures grant from the National Trust.

Organizations, foundations, and the U.S. Army admire and wanted to help in some way to save a place that plays a significant role in history telling the story of the unheralded hero, Joseph

Holt, who had almost vanished from history and deserved to be remembered. This lends strength and lets the public understand that all the work is for the people's home and the legacy of Joseph Holt. Saving his home has been done without primarily asking or continuing to ask for money. The region and Kentucky are witnessing what a rural community with mostly agriculture and few industries can accomplish.

On April 27, 2011 the JAG School was introduced to an almost unbelievably successful project. After studying, viewing pictures, and reviewing the Holt project, Fred Borch along with General Chipman said yes, "We will come to the Holt Home and we will speak to lend help to restore this magnificent home celebrating Joseph Holt."

On September 27, 2013 the day began with the final preparations for Lt. General Dana K. Chipman and Ret. COL Fred Borch's arrival. A dear friend, Mary Jean Atchison from Frankfort came to assist. We had had an earlier conversation about taking the ferns and urns to the Holt Home that afternoon. The only way to get them there because of their enormous size was to haul them in a cattle trailer. I had to wait until my husband could drive the trailer to Holt. We would probably be there unloading when the General and Fred arrived.

General Chipman and Fred both purchased their own airline tickets and rented a car at the Louisville International Airport. When renting the car Fred was asked, 'Why would you want to go to Breckinridge Co.?" He responded with a mini history lesson on the importance of lending support to restore the home of Joseph Holt. Both General Chipman and Fred enjoyed the drive and scenery from Louisville to Breckinridge Co. They had been offered the courtesy of being picked up personally at the airport and then returned the following day. However, both men wanted to rent a car so they could leave the 5th Annual Holt Home Community Day after speaking around noon and greeting visitors to catch an early flight back to Virginia and Washington D.C.

I have always wondered at the feelings of "Fred" as he makes me call him and General Chipman when they arrived at our home in Harned. Mary Jean came early and was present awaiting the special guests and making sure things were in place. All the planning, cleaning, and two months' work went into welcoming the JAGS to make them feel at home, welcome and relaxed!

Mary Jean was walking through our home and saw Fred standing on the front porch with his hand above his brow looking in the living room. Mary Jean, the welcoming committee, opened the door and said, "Come on in, I'm the housekeeper."

She guided the gentlemen to the patio area by the pool. They all sat around the picnic table and talked and relaxed. Not long after settling down to hearing comforting sounds of the country so far removed from the fast pace of city life, one of the employees of WXBC radio, the local station, appeared for the final dress fitting for two historical dresses - one for my granddaughter and one for me for the next day's event.

Conversation was enjoyed with laughs and lifting the spirits of the group when I arrived home with my husband pulling a cattle trailer. I wondered at the thoughts of the COL and the General? Had they ever experienced being on a farm in the South?

A welcome with hugs was received! Terry and I continued into the house for the final fitting. She shared she had really enjoyed talking with our guests sitting on the back porch. I shared she had been personally speaking with the key speakers for tomorrow's Holt Home Community Day, a 3-star General and retired COL Borch and Top Historian at the JAG School along with Mary Jean who worked at Kentucky Tourisms, Arts, and Heritage Council. "WOW! I had no idea," were her words.

Soon after Terry's departure a tour of our home was given. I showed Fred and General Chipman the layout of the house. I took them to the upstairs bedrooms pointing out one that had recently been renovated with a master bath added after two tornadoes hit our home on July 13, 2004. Fred's reply was, "I guess General Chipman will be placed in that nice bed room and I will be stay-

The opening ceremonies, pictured left to right: Susan Dyer, Judge Executive Maurice Lucas, Alison Mattingly, and Judge Easton, Master of Ceremonies

Susan Dyer and granddaughter, Jaydyn, preparing for the fun day.

The Boy Scouts of America

12th United States Colored - Heavy Artillery

113th Army Band

Larry and Mary Elliott as Lincoln and Mary Todd

General Dana K. Chipman, one of the days keynote speakers, who promised Susan Dyer he would come to Kentucky to the Holt Home

Retired Col. Fred Borch, another of the days keynote speakers came to KY to speak at the Holt Home Community Day after being invited by Susan Dyer

Office of the Staff Judge Advocates in Fort Knox

Mr. James Wimsatt giving General Chipman pictures that he took of the Generals while stationed in Europe during World War II.

Kentucky Heritage Council unveiling Holt Home on the Kentucky Lincoln Heritage Trail

ing in the Palace Room with all the Barbie dolls". I apologized to Fred, saying, "sorry about all the Barbie dolls." "Fred replied, "I am used to Barbies - I have grand-daughters too!"

Amidst the excitement the luggage of both gentleman was brought in the home. On the final trip from the car General Chipman and Fred brought a gift to me for being the host. It was a bottle of Noble Wines 667 Pinot Noir 2012 that still remains in the refrigerator till 2016, and a container of Kentucky Bourbon Barrel Ati for dinner. The gift was much appreciated from the two nice Army JAGS.

Both gentleman came dressed for a fun-filled day in jeans. Our family was very busy in the tobacco fields with the migrant workers on that afternoon. However, after a brief discussion it was decided for General Chipman and Fred to have a private tour of the Holt Home before the Holt Community Day and upon returning Eddie would give a tour to both Fred and General Chipman of the farms while Mary Jean and I prepared supper for our guests.

Driving to Holt that day was memorable! I was thinking "Finally, the JAGS have come!" Upon arriving the grounds were so quiet. As the long-anticipated preparations were finished - cleaning the home, writing the press releases, all the work completed from September to September by requests, programs, mowing, tagging the trees. All final details by the Friends' organization had been completed. Now I took a few last moments to enjoy the beauty of the grounds before giving a tour. History was made as General Chipman and Fred Borch opened the doors to the Holt Home and walked through the foyer. They could see now in person the wonder of it all! We had hoped to begin the exterior restoration before the 5th Annual Holt Home Community Day but it didn't happen. Restoration would begin later that winter.

To have another Judge Advocate General in Holt's home and on the grounds was indeed history since General Chipman was the 2nd Judge Advocate General to walk the grounds and stroll through Joseph Holt's home. "The Father of the Judge Advocates" as Holt was known, serving when Lincoln and the Army established the office of Judge Advocate General and Holt was the first to serve with General's rank!

The tour was wonderful, and the trip will always be memorable for the JAGS that gave so much to make it happen. They came with commitment, paid their own way, lent their support to honor one of their own! The drive back home was short and upon arrival Eddie was preparing a tour of the farms in a Kubota.

Early that day some food had already been prepared. The menu for supper was baked Kentucky ham with a special recipe, hash brown casserole, cucumbers and onion salad, heavy tossed salad, rolls, and for desert blackberry cobbler with Breyers ice-cream, a coconut cream pie, chocolate pie and two prepared Holt cakes, one each for General Chipman and Fred to take back on the plane.

Mary Jean suggested I go on the tour of the farms and she would prepare the rest of the meal. It was a great idea as it was relaxing. What a friend in Mary Jean to complete the meal and have the table set beautifully upon returning. There was a small arrangement of fresh flowers with American flags for General Chipman and Fred. My mother told me later she prayed about the blackberry cobbler as she was afraid it might be too dry. However, there was not one bite left that evening. And mama told me "God must have been with me when I cooked that cobbler."

The time passed fast as the RTV took all four around to view the tobacco and cattle business of the farms. We toured the land, and Eddie explained how the farms were run. Fred Borch said, "Now we know what hard work is really like." Suppertime was close, so the tour was shortened and one of the remaining farms did not get visited.

Back at the house everyone cleaned up for supper. What an eventful night! The discussions were amazing! To see General Chipman and Fred on the couch in the Great Room having such a nice time will long be remembered. Time to eat! The prayer was said as General Chipman and Fred both had the honor of sitting at the head of each end of the table. Mary Jean, my mother, Eddie and I enjoyed Kentucky home cooking. We decided to serve the food cafeteria style, and everyone could choose what they wanted and return for more if they liked.

Fred and General Chipman had brought Kentucky Bourbon barrel Ati to drink for supper and as they were preparing their drinks they asked me if I would like some Kentucky Bourbon. Being honorable to our guests and showing gratitude for their long journey to Kentucky I said yes. You should have seen the look on the faces of my mother, Mary Jean, and my husband, as I do not drink and have never tasted bourbon in my life. Throughout supper the looks I received when taking a few drinks of the bourbon will be with me the rest of my life.

My thoughts were, "These honorable JAGS have brought a drink they like and they have asked me to join them for supper. Never having a drink in my entire life except for tasting a sip of whiskey when it was being used in a recipe for Christmas when I was a young girl, and once tasted of red wine, I knew this was not my character. However, for the respect of our guests and for the sacrifices they had given to come to Kentucky at their own expense and giving of themselves when they had already given so very much to our nation, then I could drink a small amount with them.

After supper I shared that my father had asked me numerous times, "When are the JAGS coming?" My reply always, was, Daddy I am working on it!" I only wish he could have seen the JAGS. We lost him three months earlier.

The evening was fun just talking and being together and appreciating what a wonderful opportunity it was to have the best of the United States Army in our community and to be present the following day at the 5th Annual Holt Home Community Day to give voice and support for what Joseph Holt meant to President Lincoln and to our nation, www.jholt-houseky.org. Events Courtesy of Wave 3 TV and Rick Brown, the Production Manager, came and recorded this memorable time. Thanks to them we will always have this historical event for visitors to view on the Holt website.

Discussions ended, deserts were enjoyed, and the day wound down. My mother assisted as host with Mary Jean. This gave General Chipman and Fred the entire upstairs for their privacy. I offered to prepare a home cooked breakfast for General Chipman and Fred. They both told me, "No" we will just have coffee and eat these wonderful deserts. I explained that I did not know how to make real coffee, that we always use instant coffee. Fred said, "I do not like instant coffee." I offered my apology.

The night was short. I awoke to a dark room down stairs in a bedroom designed and completed just one week before the weekend. I dressed in the historical purple dress and returning upstairs found General Chipman sitting in the Great Room and then shortly Fred appeared. General Chipman complemented on my historical costume and shared what a great time he had! I was told they both would dress and arrive at the Holt Home later that morning prior to their speeches to meet and greet the people.

My husband returned to dress for the event and found Fred and General Chipman enjoying the pies for breakfast. The small things we do are what is appreciated. The enjoyment of having homemade pies for breakfast was special to the JAGS! A promise for the next return of Fred and General Chipman which Fred has publicly stated, "You must be careful what you promise to Susan, because she will not forget." However, I have been told they both will return someday! And how that will be cherished! Just like the Army is always serving, wanting to work and to do the right thing, the Friends of the Holt Home, Inc. continue to carry the torch and teach others the joy it brings!

The Ida Willis Award

Susan Dyer being presented with the Ida Lee Willis Memorial Foundation Award – Service to Preservation of the Judge Joseph Holt Home

One spring day in 2010 I received a phone call from Diane Comer, PR at the Kentucky Heritage Council in Frankfort, Kentucky. Diane called to inform me that I had been nominated and was going to receive a Service to Preservation Award in recognition of my persistent advocating for the preservation of the Judge Joseph Holt home in rural Breckinridge County and for all I had done to educate others about his legacy and role in President Abraham Lincoln's administration.

Diane explained I could invite 10 people to be present for the 32nd Annual Ida Lee Willis Memorial Foundation Historic Awards honoring excellence in preserving Kentucky's historic places. This was quite overwhelming, and I was very excited to be honored at the Kentucky Governor's Executive Mansion at 2:00 p.m. on May 26, 2010, during National Historic Preservation Month, by the Ida Lee Willis Memorial Foundation and the Kentucky Heritage Council/ State Historic Preservation Office. Contributions I learned were through investment, advocacy, volunteerism, building partnerships, public involvement and a lifelong commitment or significant achievement.

A list of names was shared with Diane to invite. This was a very busy time for everyone. My minister at the time, Rev. Janet Carden and Mr. Tim Carden, were present as Janet has and continues to pray for the Holt project and for God to continue to lead me, send the wisdom and to guide the Friends during this dramatic project for complete restoration of the Holt Home. Also, attending were my mother Mrs. Aggie Butler, my husband Eddie Dyer, Mrs. Sheila Wayne from Evansville, IN, Ms. Mary Jean Atchison, from the Tourism, Arts, and Heritage Cabinet (Frankfort, Kentucky) and friend, Mr. Byron Crawford, a retired writer from the *Courier-Journal* who now writes for the "Kentucky Living" magazine and was currently completing a new resource entitled, "Kentucky Footnotes." And, of course, my publisher Doug Sikes and the owner of Acclaim Press from Missouri and President of Acclaim Press, Keith Steele. Mr. Sikes told me this was the first time he had ever had an author to get him into the Governor's mansion.

It was a beautiful day filled with enormous sunshine. With all the numerous trips to Frankfort for the Holt Home I never thought I would be honored at the Governor's mansion. Sheila

Aggie Butler, Sheila Wayne, Susan Dyer, Reverend Janet Carden

Eddie Dyer, Aggie Butler, and Susan Dyer

Susan Dyer and Steve Collins

Diane Comer, Susan Dyer and Mark Dennen, Executive Director of the Kentucky Heritage Council

Wayne a friend since childhood met my mother, Eddie and I outside along with Pastor Janet. We took pictures alongside the beautiful flowers in front of the Governor's Mansion.

Once inside I started meeting familiar faces such as Steve Collins, the Chair of the Ida Lee Willis Foundation and Mark Dennen, the Executive Director at the Kentucky Heritage Council/ State Preservation Office; Diane Comer, PR at the Kentucky Heritage Council; Marcheta Sparrow, Secretary, Kentucky Tourisms, Arts and Heritage Council; Lindy Casebier, Deputy Secretary of Kentucky Tourisms, Arts and Heritage Council, and Byron Crawford who walked in with a huge smile.

The Ida Lee Willis Award is named for the late Ida Lee Willis, who was appointed first executive director of the Kentucky Heritage Commission (now named the Kentucky Heritage Council) in 1966.

The call to order was given by Stephen L. Collins, Chairman, Ida Lee Willis Memorial Foundation.

Welcome was given by Marcheta Sparrow, Secretary Kentucky Tourism, Arts and Heritage Cabinet and Presentations of Ida Lee Willis Memorial Foundation Historic Preservation Awards were presented by Steve Collins and Chuck Parrish, and other board members of the Ida Lee Willis Memorial Foundation Board.

When my name was called it truly was an honor to accept the award for preservation of the Judge Joseph Holt Home. Not knowing if we would be asked to speak or not I prepared a short acceptance thank-you for all those present.

My speech for Ida Willis Service Award follows:

"Teamwork is the key to Success!! With a dream put on your heart by God the possibilities are unlimited! Always believe in your dreams! Empower yourself to be your finest, and work always to be positive even if it is the most challenging task in your life.

With mentors like Dr. James C. Klotter, David Morgan, Becky Shipp, and Mark Dennen along with a steadfast team of wonderful Kentuckians using their talents, and believing it possible to save irreplaceable history, this dream that started in 1997 on a Sunday afternoon drive in front of Judge Joseph Holt's home is now reality, touching hearts across the nation, even the JAG school in Virginia.

Our dreams continue as Joseph Holt has been portrayed this year by Danny Huston, the actor playing Holt in the Conspirator, the movie directed by Robert Redford and produced by the American Film Company.

With faith, hope and love of saving Kentucky's treasures, the Holt Home Team is excited about Judge Holt's legacy being brought back and also hoping the movie to bring attention to the Holt Home, and recruit more partners with the renovation.

Restored, people will come again to the showplace of Breckinridge County.

Voice has been given back once more to *Lincoln's Advocate*, Joseph Holt, the prosecuting judge of the Lincoln Conspiracy Trial through this empowering project with positive spirits, continued work, giving to the community and state, sharing grass roots efforts with big hearts, portraying the significance of Judge Holt's worthiness. I will continue to serve in a tireless effort always giving my best to Kentucky. I am honored to be here today showing other communities you can save history, by giving your heart. Thank you!"

My thoughts lingered while sitting there in the Governor's Mansion. Realizing that to get there much work had been done and others had recognized the importance of preservation on the most historical home in Breckinridge County.

Throughout the years Lindy Casebier has always told me to keep the faith. And through all the trials and tribulations in submitting, seeking grants and working diligently to get foundations to understand the importance of partnering with the Holt Home my reply has always been, "I have the faith, God put it on my heart to save the Holt Home." That day when I was introducing Reverend Janet Carden to Lindy Casebier I said, "Lindy, I brought my minster. You are always telling me to keep the faith, and I do. Today, my pastor is here, and she continues to pray for the Holt Project." Lindy just smiled.

Following the presentation and program, a reception was held in the Governor's Mansion to honor the recipients. This was enjoyed by all who attended and the others who also received awards that day. Cake was served and everyone enjoyed the fellowship following. It was another day to be treasured and remembered as the journey continues for our rural community.

After the event I received an inspiring letter congratulating me on receiving the award and encouraging the continuous work in my writing. This meant the world not only for everyone's presence that day, but also for Byron Crawford to take the time to write and congratulate me on the award and to encourage me to continue to write.

Friends are a wonderful gift as we encourage each other. Encouragement is a very strong force especially in the preservation of the Holt Home. Thinking you can positively be successful with preservation is one of the keys for success. You must first believe before you can hopefully encourage others to follow. When you do that then things start happening. However, it takes more time than you could ever imagine.

Three County Judges

I never dreamed of working with county judges as a volunteer. However, with preservation there are always unknown avenues to be taken in the pursuit of getting support locally.

The second meeting held in my home for saving the Holt Home was in 2006. The Holt Home Steering Committee was formed and in the beginning, it consisted of a few local volunteers, the Kentucky Heritage Council, an elected State Representative and State Senator including the Breckinridge County Judge Executive.

The meeting was led by David L. Morgan, the State Historic Preservation Officer and Executive Director of the Kentucky Heritage Council/ State Preservation Office. Mr. Morgan suggested getting Breckinridge County Judge Executive George Monarch III to write a letter to the guardian of the private owner of the Holt Home. It inquired about an interest to sell the home and enough acres to support the future of what the home could become. Judge Monarch wrote the letter and the Breckinridge County Fiscal Court received an answer within a month.

Following this meeting, an appraisal was planned for the purchase, including support for events and functions once the structure was restored. An initial appraisal was conducted that was too low, then revised with a higher appraisal.

It was decided the Breckinridge County Fiscal Court would be the entity to seek grants for the purchase of the home. Because Joseph Holt and his home had been identified with ties to Lincoln at the beginning of the Kentucky Lincoln Bicentennial, I was invited to attend the Bicentennial Commission meetings by David Morgan and Judge Tommy Turner. I attended every single meeting of the commission from 2007-2010 and also was invited to attend the Kentucky Lincoln site meetings.

Attending these meetings was a blessing as many individuals took me under their wings. I listened and learned and brought back important information to share with my community. In the beginning, no one thought the fruits of attending these meetings in Frankfort would materialize. The meetings took much time and patience with a costly amount of gas money and expenses. But attending the Bicentennial meetings was priceless.

Judge Monarch was very good to work with as the Appraisal Judge. He was professional, helped with taking people to see the home, attended the first meeting for the pubic, wrote the letter to the guardian and shared the return letter from the guardian so we could continue with the next phase. I became a go-between with the Kentucky Heritage Council and the Breckinridge County Fiscal Court. My work then and still today is without pay. I am honored to be called a volunteer as there is nothing stronger than the heart of a volunteer.

Shortly following the appraisal, Judge Monarch was defeated in the general election by Ray Powers. So then, I had a new Breckinridge County Judge Executive to work with and to familiarize with all that had been done for the Holt Home.

I shared all details about the importance of the Kentucky Lincoln Bicentennial and Judge Powers listened. I explained how this was our opportunity. How there was funding and how much the Commonwealth was competing for grants of the Kentucky Lincoln Bicentennial. I shared how we would submit a grant for the Breckinridge County Fiscal Court that I would write as a volunteer.

The first grant was written and won for the purchase of the home for $108,000, granted by the Kentucky Lincoln Bicentennial Commission placed in the Kentucky Heritage Council / State Preservation Office. The funding was held in the

Kentucky Heritage Council until the county government had the deed to the home and acreage. During this period, work was done preparing a suitable agreement (appraisal) for both parties – the guardian of the private owner of the Holt Home and the Breckinridge County Fiscal Court.

There were three appraisals conducted for the purchase of the Holt Home. Two were done by Maysville historical appraiser Claude Galloway. And the third was conducted by an individual the Guardian chose. The guardian also had an appraisal for a historical home in Louisville and wanted the appraisal value for the purchase of the Holt Home to be from the same source.

After speaking with Judge Powers, the Breckinridge County Fiscal Court did not have funding for the purchase of the home. As a volunteer, I submitted a grant request for Breckinridge County Fiscal Court with guidance from Becky Shipp at the Kentucky Heritage Council. But, after receiving $108,000 for the acquisition of the home it was not enough to offer the guardian. Time pasted as negotiations continued and the $108,000 grant was about to expire.

I called the Kentucky Heritage Council and spoke to Patrick Kennedy who suggested talking with Becky Shipp who assisted between Preservation Officers; as David Morgan had retired and moved to Washington D.C., Ms. Shipp suggested doing an extension on the grant to keep Breckinridge County Fiscal Court from losing the $108,000. Becky Shipp assisted me and the extension of the grant was completed. The $108,000 was saved! But it still was not enough for the purchase.

In preservation, you cannot be shy and you must ask people for help. If you quit everyone else also will. E-mails were sent, numerous phone calls were made. As I visited every Senator, and Representative — both nationally and state — I asked for help. Some helped and some told me good luck. However, I did not quit and in fact the one that told me good luck, later said, "We never thought you would get anywhere", and complimented me on the tremendous work and passion to continue. At that point, no one thought it was possible to purchase and get the deed for the Holt Home.

Breckinridge County should salute Ray Powers as he was the acquisition judge. He attended every court session for hearings about the purchase of the Home, as did Becky Shipp of the Kentucky Heritage Council. Being a volunteer I was not present. However, everything was shared with me and the massive work of completing the purchase of the home with two grants and an extension on the $108,000 grant made it possible to obtain the Holt Home for Breckinridge County Fiscal Court.

Judge Powers once told me, "I do not know who is more stubborn, you or me." My reply was, "You are determined and I am passionate for restoration." The judge was good to work with. He assisted on numerous tours, and together we gave a private tour to Judge Holt's great-great-great nieces and Dr. Elizabeth Leonard who came here on a cold January morning in 2009. It was soon after the county had the deed to the Holt Home on Dec. 5, 2008.

I will always remember the day Judge Powers phoned to say, "Susan, I wanted you to be the first to know that I have the deed to the Holt Home in my hand." It was truly providential to have the deed. Oddly enough, shortly after the county had the deed, the private owner died.

I invited Judge Powers to attend several meetings in Frankfort during the Kentucky Lincoln Bicentennial Commission. And he came and spoke. His words about my work will always be remembered as it is sometimes hard to be a prophet in your own home town. For all the times I asked Judge Powers for his help, he always came through. He came to Frankfort on President Lincoln's birthday where we were honored in the capitol for receiving the grant for acquisition and a grant for the appraisal. I matched the appraisal grant out of my own pocket. However, it was worth it!

In the beginning, we had much to prove. Not all citizens could see the vision of the Holt Home becoming a National Treasure, not all understood the definition of a grant, not all understood that a grant for preservation could not be used for road funds, and if Breckinridge County did not get a preservation grant it would go to someone else.

I will always remember the first discussion with Judge Powers about applying for a Save America's Treasures grant, and the work it took. Honestly, it took three months to write. And when completed, we had to have three copies of everything including pictures. Judge Powers told me to "go for it." Since the county did not then own the property, we had to do as the application instructed and get permission to write the grant.

What work, what worry, and how much was learned. It completely wore out my photo printer! A new computer had to be purchased to make the grants appear more professional. After months of work, months of waiting, we found out we did not get the grant. However, Judge Powers said, "Maybe we will get it next year." I almost got sick thinking of writing the grant again. However, the future was calling. I remembered the promise to the students of Breckinridge County who I told, "I will work until the Holt Home is saved and restored." At the same time, I remember my publisher, Doug Sikes saying, "When are you going to finish the biography on Holt?" My answer is still freshly in memory. As I told him, I still had two more grants to write for the Breckinridge County Fiscal Court before I can complete the book.

The Save America's Treasures grant was re-written and I sought help from experts. I phoned the National Trust, asked questions, and took advice and help from Diane Comer, Becky Shipp, Dana Beth Lyddan and anyone in grant writing I could find. The SAT grant was submitted online which meant learning many new things, and after working for months. When it was time to submit the grant, the program I was using would not save the SF 424 form.

With only a few hours before the deadline, I finally spoke with a young man at Save America's Treasures and told him after completing the grant there still was a simple information form to complete. However, the information would not save and would have to be typed all over again. I explained months of work had been done on the grant and I was not quitting if I had to type the eight pages of information at the beginning of the grant application 100 times! I had already typed it ten times.

The young man said, "Mrs. Dyer, I am not going to leave you, stay with me, we will submit it successfully. We did! But even the second Save America's Treasures grant was not won for the Holt home after all that was done.

Persistence takes courage and courage takes patience. Would I write the SAT grant again? Could we win the grant? This grant was very competitive as all states were in competition with each other. After continued thought and studying comments about the grant, it was decided to go for it again. This time we were in for the hunt! You cannot get tired; you cannot get weary. You must always think about the plan. Always be one step ahead. And think five to ten years ahead of what might be. We had to receive a large grant.

Diane Comer and Dana Beth Lyddan and I worked our hardest on different angles. The narratives were edited and improved, the picture selections chosen were heartwarming, telling the sad state the Holt Home was in after sitting empty for more than four decades. It is amazing what can be accomplished when you ask for help and diligently work with the experts to make it happen.

There is not anything magical about grants. They are hard work and many times not encouraging, so you must be your own booster if that is what it takes. When success comes, others will congratulate you. Be brave during the grants you do not receive as you may not even receive a thank-you for all the work behind the scenes. However, hard work pays off and finally the rewards come to the deserving ones.

On a summer afternoon, I received a phone call from Judge Powers, saying, "Susan, someone from the National Trust called and mentioned the Save America Treasures Grant. I believe we have won it for the Holt Home."

Wow! $150,000 for the Grand Lady as I call her. Judge Powers was so excited. And I was in shock! Most people would have given up after the first grant. However, grant writing is not for the weak or weary or people who complain. But for those who are brave, who are not afraid and will continue until they reach the goal. All my life, I have been taught to do work first and then play. There has been little time for leisure since 1997 with the beginning of research for the Holt Home.

The Save America's Treasures grant had the support of Representative Brett Guthrie and Senator Mitch McConnell as they both worked and got the grant approved through the House of Representatives and the Senate. On the first Holt Home Community Day, Aug. 15, 2009, we were very proud of this enormous accomplishment. Brett Guthrie was present and a crowd of 1,500 people attended the first Holt Home Community Day.

Since 2009, volunteers have put in hundreds of hours of planning the Holt Home Community Day, grant writing, meeting with foundations, attending conferences, writing letters, giving speeches and numerous other tasks. With the SAT grant, the back-stair tower was torn down and a replica built along with completing the back windows and restoring three back doors. The SAT grant was discontinued by President Obama. It is a miracle we saved this grant a month before it would expire. Thanks also goes to Kathina Bell for all the reports she did for the grant as Breckinridge County Judge Assistant. Many thanks go out for the hundreds of hours turned in by volunteers who made the match for the grant a reality.

Breckinridge County can be thankful Judge Powers labored for more than a month to make the Holt Home presentable for the first open house in August 2009. The judge and I only had two dates remaining to select a time and August was chosen as we both felt November would be too cold. It was a grand event as the Kentucky Lincoln Bicentennial was spotlighting official Kentucky Lincoln sites in the Commonwealth. To open the home that had not been lived in for four decades was a huge task.

I can remember wanting to help clean the home. However, the judge would not permit me to do this. There were truckloads of garbage hauled to the landfill. There was dust, dirt, debris, and unwanted items. For the cleanup, Judge Powers pulled together a team from the jail on work release and the men took much pride in their work. The completed cleanup had a remarkable finale as visitors could walk through the home and admire the beautiful stairways, hand crafted woodwork and architecture.

There has been widespread media interest in the home's preservation with stories to date in *Kentucky Monthly* and *Kentucky Living* magazines, a feature in the Owensboro *Messenger Enquirer* which got picked up by the Associated Press and distributed nationally. The book — *Lincoln's Advocate: The Life of Judge Joseph Holt* — written about Joseph Holt with assistance from Kentucky State Historian Dr. James C. Klotter also helped create awareness and interest.

Judge Powers was very supportive of the premier book signing of *Lincoln's Advocate* and spoke at the book signing. After passing the baton of Breckinridge County Judge Executive to Maurice Lucas, Judge Powers has donated items to assist with the Holt Home Community Day. Without him, the county would not own the Holt Home today.

Transitions are always interesting. Breckinridge County Judge Executive Maurice Lucas became the third judge for the Holt project. As always, there is much to learn, much to do. The first meeting with Judge Lucas was on a cold January morning. It looked as if we could get a snow blizzard. He called to say he would send someone out to drive me to his office as we had to have a conference call that morning with our state partners. I explained I could drive on snow.

Since that first conference call, Judge Lucas and I have worked together for almost eight years. Upon the advice of several mentors in 2012, the Friends of the Holt Home has had three fundraisers. However, Judge Lucas and I went personally to individuals in each of the magisterial districts. Our plan was to raise $ 40,000 to help make a match for Phase 2. This was not an easy task, but we worked diligently, and the community did not let us down. This was like raising a million dollars to obtain our

The great-great-great nieces of Joseph Holt and Dr. Elizabeth Leonard, Professor of History at Colby College, getting a tour from Ray Powers and Susan Dyer

goal in a small, rural community without much industry. It was the first of its kind and was the first community-based project where Breckinridge County worked together to save a historical jewel. In a three-month period, more than $34,000 was raised.

The finale was having television and newspaper luminary Byron Crawford speak at the final fund raiser and tell about the efforts to save and restore the historical Holt Home. He noted how the home would become a national treasure Breckinridge County would be proud of in the future. That event brought in another $25,000.

Restoration Judge is the title I personally have given Judge Lucas. His role has been essential as he is the Shepard with Fiscal Court. He has not had an easy role as he has worked with Fiscal Court members to explain how the county efforts support restoration of the Holt Home. Even with grants, it still has taken patience and understanding of how grants received for preservation must be used for restoration. He has always been positive and supportive of the cooperative agreement between the Friends of the Holt Home, Inc. and the Breckinridge County Fiscal Court.

Judge Lucas is on the board of the Friends, attends meetings, helps with preparing the Holt Home for visitors and makes sure the Holt grounds are well maintained. Judge Lucas always assists when private tours are requested to help seek partnering of interested foundations, organizations, the Judge Advocate Generals (JAGS) and interested individuals.

As I continue to share with all who are a part of the Holt project, it's obvious to me that God only sends the best. And for the Holt project, that's all three judges who have had important roles for the appraisal, acquisition and restoration!

Susan B. Dyer, author, at the Brandenburg Expo for Women.

Enjoying the opportunity of being present at the Kentucky Book Fair.

Numerous copies of Lincoln's Advocate were sold at the KY Book Fair.

Susan at the Hardin County Historical Society Dinner before delivering a talk on Lincoln's Advocate. Pictured l-r: Kenneth Tabb, former Hardin County Court Clerk, Susan B. Dyer, author, a member of the Hardin County Historical Society, and, seated, Aggie Butler, mother of the author

What a nice surprise to see your name on the marquee!

One of the numerous book signings at Barnes and Noble.

Susan with Vestal Rogers at a book signing at Lincoln Days in Hodgenville.

Guilderoy Byrne Band, a crowd favorite at the annual Holt Home Community Day.

Susan B. Dyer and Jaydyn Dyer (author's granddaughter), who has attended the annual Holt Home Community Day since an infant in costume.

Larry and Mary Elliott, who portray President Abraham Lincoln and Mary Todd Lincoln, at the annual Holt Home Community Day.

After all the day's excitement, author Susan Dyer takes time for a picture with her mother, Aggie Butler.

Vestal Rogers has been present and has helped support numerous Holt Home Community Days and assisted to get the Ninth Michigan Volunteer Infantry to participate and greet visitors at a campsite like they would have had during the Civil War era.

President Lincoln, portrayed by Larry Elliott, works diligently each year at Student Day where ALL 5th grade students in Breckinridge County are invited to encounter an educational field trip to explore the past at the historical Judge Joseph Holt Home.

Students eager to enter Judge Holt's beloved home.

Larry Elliott, portraying President Abraham Lincoln, inspiring and motivating pupils to observe and learn about President Lincoln's life, and Judge Joseph Holt, Lincoln's Judge Advocate General and his historical home.

Larry Elliott's presentation portraying the 16th president takes students back into the pages of history.

Students will soon come from across the Commonwealth and nation as they do now locally to encounter history alive at the Holt Home.

Elizabeth Parks, artist, drawing of the historical Holt Home.

The painting hangs today in the old Breckinridge County Court House in Hardinsburg, Kentucky.

February 12, 2007 was a special day for the historic Holt Home at the capitol building, where the Holt Home became an official Kentucky Lincoln site and a member of the Kentucky Lincoln Heritage Trail.

Former Breckinridge County Judge Executive Ray Powers, former Kentucky State Representative Dwight D. Butler, and Susan B. Dyer enjoyed the special day.

Officials hold a check representing the second grant written and won for the Breckinridge County Fiscal Court for the acquisition of the historic Holt Home. Pictured L-R: Former State Senator Carroll Gibson, Former State Representative Dwight D. Butler, Susan B. Dyer, and Former Kentucky Governor Ernie Fletcher.

Medal presented Given by General Flora D. Darpino, The Judge Advocate General (First female to become a TJAG.), 39th Judge Advocate General, U.S. Army.

Lt. COL Christopher Fredrikson, Staff Judge Advocate for the United States Command in Fort Knox gave this medal.

Medal given by COL Andras M. Marton from 101st Airborne Division (Air assault) Fort Campbell, Kentucky.

Medal presented by the Commanding General John W. Miller II, Brigadier General, U.S. Army, April 27th, 2011. Silver bowl given as a gift to the 5th George S. Prugh lecturer. Lecture published in the Military Law Review, Spring 2012.

Note: medals were given from the United States Army JAG Corps to Susan B. Dyer for her selfless service for Brigadier General Joseph Holt's legacy and the work with saving and restoring the Holt Home.

Holt Family Cemetery before $68,000 of restoration was completed by the Holt Family Trust.

Radar testing by Dr. Philip Mink, Professor at the University of Kentucky, reported that it is very likely Judge Holt was buried in a vault, very rare for the time. Funded by the Friends of the Holt Home, Inc. nonprofit organization.

10-year-old child buried in the Holt Family Cemetery. Researched by Charlie Corbett, the child lived on a very large farm next to the Holt property.

Picture of Thomas Holt, (Joseph Holt's brother) and wife, Rosina Board Holt's tombstone.

Joseph Holt's parents John and Eleanor Stephens Holt's tombstone.

Holt Family Cemetery was in grave condition before restoration.

Hundreds of trips have been made to the Holt Home and Judge Holt's monument.

Each year visitors take part in the stately wreath-laying ceremony at the Holt Family Cemetery (before restoration).

Throughout the years, volunteers place wreaths on Holt's grave and the gate to the Holt family cemetery (before restoration).

The large crevice was repaired. Presently, the Friends of the Holt Home are in the process of redoing the back wall, as it is in serious condition and will be restored again in 2018.

The cemetery walls were almost crumbling before restoration.

This visual marker located in the grass in front of the Holt family cemetery gives visitors a glimpse of Joseph Holt, Father of the Judge Advocates.

Grant Tips

The Holt Home has been saved by numerous grants, many of which have been very competitive. Through hard work, trial and error, blood, sweat and tears, you learn what might lead to success. Your best attempts don't always work. But there is a method, a route, a formula to follow. Here are some suggestions…

First of all, you must be passionate. Grant writers must totally know the project and must understand its history.

Grants are not easy to locate, but once you find a potential source, fully know the objectives of the granters. It may be the best grant available for your project, but your goal may not fit the objectives of the funding agency. Do your homework! Know the agency's history of grant funding. Do they give to organizations like yours? Does the grant have to be matched? Does it allow in-kind donations from private organizations, people or corporations? When you find an available grant, it is always better to be invited to submit the grant from the agency.

There are normally a specific number of grants available each year from organizations, and a time frame in which to submit an application. Often, it takes several submissions to be rewarded a grant.

Before submitting a grant, allow several months or more to work, research, write the narratives, and plan the budget. Once I had to redo the budget the night before submitting an SAT grant upon finding it didn't meet the requirements.

Have strong, clear photographs supporting the narratives and carefully study the grant questions. Answer them truthfully. Answer what you are asked.

Many grants will allow only so many words (word count). Do not worry about this in the beginning. First, answer the questions with strong narratives and then work diligently on deleting unimportant words. You will be surprised how many words you can delete. Diane Comer, public relations specialist at the Kentucky Heritage Council, is the best I know for taking a piece and condensing it to fewer words.

Answer the questions with the best possible answers. Then work on limiting the number of words. This can be a challenge, but will make your writing more powerful and less reading for the grant reviewer. Remember, the reviewer will not only be reading your grant, but many others as well.

Allow yourself several months to finalize and complete the application. Two or three hours a day should be the limit. By reviewing your writing the next day, you will see things that were not so obvious the day before. And if you begin reading the grant by taking the last sentence of the application first and reading the grant back to the beginning, you will also catch and notice items you did not notice earlier.

When your last draft is completed, put the application away for the night and the next morning begin again. I learned this from Dr. James C. Klotter, history professor and State Historian of Kentucky. The application will appear to be fresher, and you will see new editing and revisions you need to make. Learning by doing always provides insight for the next grant. The more you write the better you will get. Talk to individuals who have submitted the grant you are presently writing. Ask questions? Have a proofreader look over your work and have more than one proofreader. You must be willing to listen to others in grant writing to improve. Everyone was a novice at one time.

Attending meetings and socializing with others in your area of work and interest will assist in the knowledge of locating grants. Speak to your elected Representatives and Senators as they may be aware of grants.

After submitting a grant and not receiving it, determine how the grant could have been made stronger. See if it is possible to read the evaluation from the grant reviewer or grant administrator. If so, turn the weak areas into positive rewrites for the next cycle if you choose to write the grant application again. Many people will become discouraged especially if this is new or if they are inexperienced with grant writing. Put your heart into the grant. Yes, you may be discouraged for a while, but this separates the brave and strong from those who give up and quit.

Be willing to write the application numerous times if you need the grant.

Remember, you are submitting a grant for a worthy organization, and you are not a quitter, and not negative. Then, once you receive a grant send a letter of thanks.

Letter writing is almost a lost art. However, hundreds and hundreds of letters have been written and continue to be written for the Holt Home – some to provide updates and keep progress fresh. Keeping interested individuals updated is very important for your project. Grants are a very time worthy investment for future success.

You can learn from everyone. Learn what to do and what not to do. Your attitude, perseverance, compassion and work ethic, along with being yourself and always doing your best will take you far.

The Architect

The blueprints for the historic Holt Home were seen at one time in Margaret Smith's collection of historical papers in Cloverport.

That was the story I was told at one of the first Holt Home Community Days. The gentleman told me he had seen the prints.

This was exciting as the Kentucky Heritage Council/ State Preservation Office (lifetime partners) does not know who the historical architect was nor do they have a copy of the blueprints for the home.

During the past two decades, it has been a continued challenge to locate the original architect and blueprints. If the prints exist still today, they would provide a clearer picture about the home and its history. After hearing the visitor's story, I called numerous people involved with the history of Cloverport. I learned Margaret Smith had died many years ago and her family had left her historic papers to the Cloverport History Museum. After speaking with museum officials, they agreed to search through Margaret Smith's papers, but the blueprints were not there and they do not remember ever seeing them.

In 2010 while vacationing in Florida, I met a lady who had worked for the State Preservation Office in Alabama. After a conversation and her purchase of my biography, *Lincoln's Advocate,* she said, "Oh my goodness, the stairs in the Holt Home look like the ones in the Alabama State Capitol Building." Since we were seeking the name of the architect, I did additional research and contacted Elizabeth Brown with the Alabama Historical Commission. Ms. Brown was very kind and we talked numerous times on the phone and by e-mail. She even sent photos from the Library of Congress taken during the restoration of the spiral stairs in the Alabama state capitol restoration that began in the 1970's.

One of the unique stories Elizabeth Brown shared was one of Horace King, born a slave in 1807, who bought his freedom. King was famous across the South and the most respected bridge-builder in Alabama, Georgia and northeastern Mississippi during the mid-nineteenth century. King worked as partners with his master, John Godwin, on major construction projects, and, in 1860, was one of the wealthiest free blacks in Alabama. During this time, King traveled without any restrictions throughout the Deep South and later served as an Alabama legislator following the Civil War. His role as an engineer and contractor was unique during a period when few professional opportunities existed for African Americans. His legendary status enhanced as communities were eager to have their own Horace King covered bridge, warehouse, mill, courthouse, church, elaborate Gothic house, or staircase.

To my knowledge, there are not any other homes in Kentucky with two spiral free- standing staircases like the ones in the Holt Home.

Ms. Brown explained that the entrance and foyer of Alabama's Capitol Building were so large she doubted the stairs of a residence of 6,225 square feet would resemble each other.

You can now view on line Ms. Brown's photos at Historical American Building Survey at the Library of Congress. The pictures have been studied in much detail as the capitol stairs do look comparable with the Holt Home's stairs. Information and the photos were forwarded from Elizabeth Brown to Mark Dennen, State Preservation Officer and Executive Director at the Kentucky Heritage Council State Preservation Office at that time.

The stairs in the Alabama State Capitol were based on the same principles as the techniques to build bridges. The conversations with Elizabeth

Field Representative for Governor Matt Bevin, Isaac Myers; Craig Potts, Director of the Kentucky Heritage Council; Jon Rollins, GRW Architect for the Holt Home Project; Col. Daniel Kozlowski, Staff Judge Advocate for the Indiana National Guard JAGS.

Brown and Mark Dennen concerned questions such as - could King have come to Kentucky to build the Holt Home stairs and would he have traveled that far?

King was involved with many projects during the 1850s when the first section of the Holt Home was built. Was it possible for Horace King to have designed the stairs? And was it possible for him to have been the architect?

However, after carefully researching, and examining the places, the times and the distance, Dennen was of the opinion it was not possible for King to have come to Kentucky and designed and built the Holt Home staircases.

When composing this chapter, I thought back about Ms. Brown and remembered I had kept one of her phone messages on my answering machine. After checking, I found it was still there.

I called the Alabama Historical Commission and almost one hour later was happy to hear Ms. Brown's voice. She explained that she had retired, but someone at the Alabama Historical Commission knew her. We had a wonderful conversation.

Ms. Brown was updated with the 2016 accomplishments of the Friends of the Holt Home. She was truly amazed. We agreed, when time permits maybe the review of the more than 20,000 items in the collection of Holt's papers will provide the name of the architect along with the blueprints of the mansion.

Hopefully, someday we will have the blueprints, but, for now, the search continues.

Historical photos taken of the Holt home and fence were made in the late 1890s. It is remarkable they are of great quality. Some show deer tied to the historical fence and Vanna Holt standing on the historic brick sidewalk. The Friends of the Holt Home paid for and uncovered the sidewalks in early spring of 2016. As I was told by historical surveyor Claude Galloway, the sidewalks were there when he did the surveys back in 2007.

We were told homes like the Holt mansion were susceptible to lightning strikes, and when the new roof was added, lightning rods were included for the home. The surveyor showed me where the original lightning rods had been and said he guessed where the circle drive way was located.

Marguerite Bennett, one of the oldest living persons I interviewed, grew up in the Holt Home. She shared with me her father was a farmer and moved the fence and rearranged the circle driveway.

When I did research for the first Transportation Enhancement Grant, I learned much about the home and road leading to it. The road was relocated and a highway cut through part of the grounds. That is noticeable today as the home is very close to the road.

I remember another conversation about the virgin timber on the property that can be seen from the third floor. I learned that you cannot purchase lumber like this today as it just does not exist. But that lumber does exist in the Holt Home.

When a wooden structure not original to the home was torn down, architects shared how long ago a porch went across the back of the Holt Home and connected to the stair tower. It also was easy to see how the original red brick under the wooden-structured room was original to the home.

Even finding Holt graffiti was quite remarkable. In an e-mail from architect Jon Rollins in 2014, Jon said he had noticed a "Holt" marking on the east side third-floor pediment. It appears to read J.B. Holt. And Jon believes this was likely added when this element was being fabricated to identify who had ordered it.

The fun of the restoration is learning about the past and working to keep the history for the future. It is important to tell America's history well and Judge Holt's legacy is of great value to the scholars, students of history, the United States Army and visitors.

Judge Holt's home is a part of our culture, a time in our nation's history that wears massive scars. But to fully understand the strength of America and the men who helped make it great, we must examine the lives of the people who lived the history we now study and read.

As Americans, it is our responsibility to work, to teach appreciation, to save the stories of our nation, giving encouragement to the generations who follow the importance of preservation and respect for those who lived before us and who gave us the freedoms we enjoy today.

SS Joseph Holt

Through conversation with my dear friend Sheila Wayne of Evansville, I shared information about a postage stamp I had found of the SS *Joseph Holt* Liberty Ship of WW II on Ebay. We discussed how interesting it would be to locate one of the crewmembers from the Liberty Ship. Sheila did some research with the U.S. Navy and found an address of a gentleman who had spent decades locating pictures of U.S. Liberty Ships built at a remarkable fast pace during WWII.

S.S. Joseph Holt *liberty ship. Courtesy of: Bill Hultgreen from Erie, PA, who was in the 42nd infantry of the US Army during World War II.*

I picked up the phone the following day and called the number and spoke to a stranger. I introduced myself and explained how I had published a biography on Joseph Holt for whom the postage stamp was named along with the SS *Joseph Holt* Liberty Ship. Bill Hultgren was so nice on the phone. We both told stories and enjoyed the conversation. I also explained the continued efforts to save and restore the historic Holt Home in rural Breckinridge County. Mr. Hultgren was delighted to learn the home existed. He was such a great find as he explained he had spent sixty years locating pictures of Liberty Ships of WWII. And I was told that it would be possible for me to purchase a picture of the SS *Joseph Holt* Liberty Ship from him. However, it would take a few days to receive the copy as Mr. Hultgren was old-school and did not do the internet. And he would have to take the photo to town to get a copy made at his local drugstore.

It was worth the wait. I shared with Mr. Hultgren three articles about the Guinea Pig Squadron I had discovered. The articles included a picture of the crew of the SS *Joseph Holt* standing in the wheelhouse of their ship as they cruised Japanese bays and channels looking for "live" pressure mines hidden beneath the surface. Upon receiving the picture, the excitement was high as I wondered, "Is the ship still in existence? Would I be able to locate the crew?" If so, they would all be in their nineties. How wonderful to hear stories from the crew aboard the SS *Joseph Holt*.

This all happened in 2012 when I had begun writing *Joseph Holt Mansion.* Along with writing the new book, the work was the same as in 1997 when I was researching and writing *Lincoln's Advocate.* The work continued non-stop with meetings to attend, agendas to write, grants to complete, speaking engagements and lectures while still promoting *Lincoln's Advocate* and planning the annual Holt Home Community Day with the Friends of the Holt Home.

When asked in January of 2012 to submit an outline of the new book to my publisher, Doug Sikes, the SS *Joseph Holt* chapter was included. However, this chapter was not composed un-

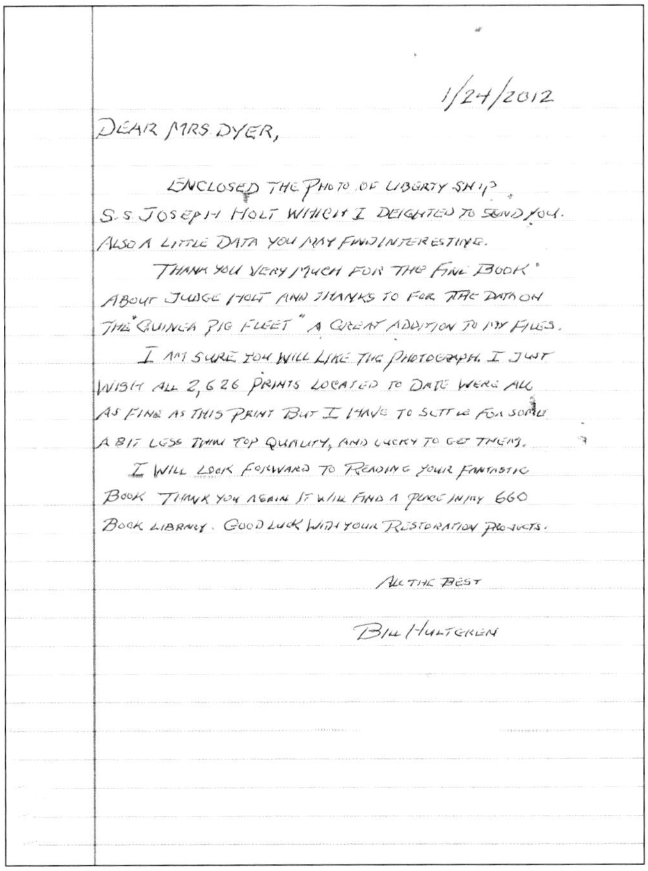

1/24/2012

DEAR MRS DYER,

ENCLOSED THE PHOTO OF LIBERTY SHIP S.S. JOSEPH HOLT WHICH I DEIGHTED TO SEND YOU. ALSO A LITTLE DATA YOU MAY FIND INTERESTING.

THANK YOU VERY MUCH FOR THE FINE BOOK" ABOUT JUDGE HOLT AND THANKS TO FOR THE DATA ON THE "GUINEA PIG FLEET" A GREAT ADDITION TO MY FILES.

I AM SURE YOU WILL LIKE THE PHOTOGRAPH. I JUST WISH ALL 2,626 PRINTS LOCATED TO DATE WERE ALL AS FINE AS THIS PRINT BUT I HAVE TO SETTLE FOR SOME A BIT LESS THAN TOP QUALITY, AND LUCKY TO GET THEM.

I WILL LOOK FORWARD TO READING YOUR FANTASTIC BOOK THANK YOU AGAIN IT WILL FIND A PLACE IN MY 660 BOOK LIBRARY. GOOD LUCK WITH YOUR RESTORATION PROJECTS.

ALL THE BEST

BILL HULTGREN

A letter from Bill Hultgreen.

til October 2017. On October 9, 2017 I had searched for several days to locate the letter Bill Hultgren had written me in January of 2012 after I had sent him a copy of *Lincoln's Advocate*. He had been so kind and helped me locate the photo of the SS *Joseph Holt*. Following this, I had sent him a book as a token of appreciation.

Five years later, I wondered if Mr. Hultgren was still located in Erie, Pa. Finally, after locating his letter from 2012, it was missing an address and telephone number so the hunt began for most of the day searching many resources. Finally, the much-wanted address and phone number was located in the little black book. I was nervous when I dialed the number. The voice on the answering machine was strong and that of a woman. I left a short message requesting Mr. Hultgren to return my call. I knew he was an elderly gentleman as he had served in WWII. And first my thoughts were, "Someone else has his number, and maybe he has passed away." After all, we lose many veterans of WWII each day.

As the day progressed I thought, "I will never hear his voice again!" In early evening the phone rang and it was from Erie, Pa. Saying hello, I prayed it was Mr. Hultgren. The distinct voice said, "Ms. Dyer this is Bill Hultgren, and you had asked me to call you." Being very excited I began thanking Mr. Hultgren for returning my call and he stopped me with the words…. "Ms. Dyer, I can't hear you. So, I took a deep breath and stated, "I can speak louder, can you hear me now?" His answer was, "yes". He said, "What do you want?" in a very firm voice. I continued saying I was completing a new book and was going to include a chapter about the SS *Joseph Holt* Liberty Ship and was going to include his photograph of the ship. I also shared that restoration of Judge Holt's home was continuing and the Army was getting involved after much work to obtain its partnership.

Mr. Hultgren responded that he had collected 2, 550 pictures of Liberty Ships that had taken 60 years to accomplish! He said he still had 81 more to find. I explained I would give him the photo credit and I was also going to include his letter in my book. Mr. Hultgren shared he was wearing hearing aids, could not hear well, and was 91 years old.

I told him I had called him back in hope of determining if he had been in the Navy as I could not remember from years earlier. He told me no! He was not in the Navy but was in the 42nd Infantry in the Army during WWII. As the short interview continued, I asked how he had begun collecting pictures of the Liberty Ships. Mr. Hultgren said it was because it was a challenge and that he had been collecting photographs for six decades of ships from the 1800s up to today's time. I gave him compliments for a life's work of collecting.

With the picture of the original SS *Joseph Holt* Liberty Ship, readers of *Joseph Holt Mansion: Saving and Restoring the Home of Lincoln's Judge Advocate General* should enjoy the story that this picture will bring. When war in Europe began in 1939, the merchant fleet was not prepared to withstand the massive sealift of war material. With continental Europe under German control and Great Britain under terrible air attacks, President Franklin Roosevelt made the decision to increase the production of standardized ships named the Liberty Ships in 1941.

Liberty Ships would fill the need for a simple, standardized cargo steamer. This ship could be mass produced inexpensively and converted to individualized military service. The U.S. named this new ship the EC2. E standing for emergency, C for cargo, and 2 for medium-sized ship that was between 400 and 450 feet at the waterline. The first of these new ships was launched on September 27, 1941. A group that raised $2 million dollars in War Bonds could suggest a name for a Liberty Ship. The ships were named after prominent deceased Americans, beginning with Patrick Henry, the first signers of the Declaration of Independence, patriots, heroes of the Revolutionary War, famous politicians, and scientists along with outstanding African-Americans, among others.

Liberty ships were more than 441 feet long and 57 feet wide. They used 2,500 horsepower steam engines to move them at around 12.5 miles per hour. The ships contained five cargo holds, three forward of the engine room and two aft in the rear portion of the ship. They could carry 10,800 deadweight tons. Crew quarters were in the middle part of the ship.

Numerous advances were made during this era. The steel cold-rolling process was developed to save steel in the making of lightweight cargo booms and new welding techniques were developed to produce the first all-welded ships. Prefabrication was perfected along with deckhouses, double-bottom sections, stern-frame assemblies and bow units. This expedited production to ships being built in 42 days. The crew was small, 38-62 civilian merchant sailors and 21-40 naval personnel to operate defensive guns and communication equipment. Liberty ships were produced from 1941-1945 and became the largest class of ships built worldwide.

The crew of the S.S. Joseph Holt stand in the wheelhouse of their ship as they cruise Japanese bays and channels looking for "live" pressure mines hidden beneath the surface. Courtesy of: Associated Press. Left to Right: William H. Hill, S2/C., 26 of Brooklyn, NY; Albin C. Scheppiner, QM2/C of Erie, PA; and Harvey L. Hunter, RM2/C, 21 of Vancouver, Washington. (US Navy Photo)

Lt. Commander E. G. Rifenburgh of New York, Skipper of the S.S. Joseph Holt stands beneath the eight-ball insignia on the ship's funnel. The eight ball indicated the vessel is part of Mine Division 9 of the Navy's Mine Force. The coat of arms is a guinea pig behind the eight ball.

The SS *Joseph Holt* was built for the Maritime Commission at yard No. 432 in 1942. The official number, 242587, was designed as an EC2-S-C1, a standard emergency cargo ship at the cost of $1 million. The keel was laid 15th of October 1942 and the SS *Joseph Holt* was launched the 20th of November 1942.

The SS *Joseph Holt* was one of three ghost-like ships of the United States Navy's "Guinea Pig Squadron." These ships were volunteer-manned seeking what all other ships were striving to avoid – deadly mines that lay beneath the waters of the bays and channels of Japan dropped by our B29s. The Liberty Ships were operated with only a few sailors and officers. Occasionally, foots steps could be heard echoing down long, dimly lit pathways as the ships steamed ahead through dangerous waters making sure the explosive-laden machines were no longer a threat to American ships.

During the height of the war, U.S. B-29 planes under Navy Mine-layer direction flew low over the waters dropping new mines. The mines stayed silent resting on the bottom of harbors and in shipping lanes until a ship of 8,000 to 10,000 tons passed over them. When this happened, a change of water pressure surrounding the mine caused them to explode with the passing of large ships. The plan was developed with the anticipation of the invasion of Japan. The mines were set to neutralize themselves after a certain length of time.

However, the only way to make sure the mines were no longer a threat was for large ships to steam over them. The "Guinea Pig Squadron" did this work using battered ships that had been damaged in battle or in storms; all ships were manned by volunteer crews. For protection, the crew of the SS *Joseph Holt* stood with padded mattresses below their feet and above their heads and wore tank helmets in case they encountered an explosion.

Rear Admiral Arthur D. Struble, USN Commander of Minecraft, Pacific Fleet, directed the Guinea Pigs over Nagoya and Bongo Suido waters, then moved to sweep the Hiro Wan and Kure areas of Japan's Inland Sea. Luck was with the crews and no mines exploded during their missions.

Approximately 22 men made the runs as the remaining crews stayed in port awaiting their turn. The engines and boilers were controlled from the main deck and a flying bridge thanks to remote controls. Utilizing compartment below could have resulted in steam-filled death traps in the event of a mine explosion.

The Guinea Pig Squadron consisted of three ships –the USS Marathon (the flagship which led the vessels), the SS Pratt Victory and the SS *Joseph Holt*.

Pigging consisted of three ships steaming about 150 yards apart with a fleet tug equipped with salvage gear following at around 1,500 yards. The ships checking for mines in the 40-mile channel from Hiro to Kure, made 30 trips. It took four hours each way for more than six days. Minesweeping was very boring until something happened.

Daily, the caravan of the three ships passed by half-sunk hulls of the Japanese Navy and Merchant Marine. Many had exploded a mine. Clouds with icy mist made it challenging to travel among the numerous small islands of the Inland Sea despite marker buoys planted by the fleet of smaller minesweepers.

The ships faced many challenges. The Marathon was torpedoed in Buckner Bay, Okinawa on the early morning of 22nd July 1945 losing 37 crewmembers. The torpedo damage caused a gaping hole in the vessel's port side, which was patched and the ship was put back in service. During the operations with the Guinea Pig squadron, the Marathon caused a mine to explode while sweeping the Kobe Channel. However, the explosion did minor damage.

The second ship, the *Pratt Victory*, was torpedoed on the starboard side in the No 2 hold almost a month before the war ceased. The gaping hole was partially closed with a metal plate extending to the water line. However, below the hold, it was open to the sea. This caused the ship to steam much slower as the sea poured into the open hold making a dangerous situation.

The third ship, the SS *Joseph Holt*, was pushed ashore in Buckner Bay during a dangerous typhoon. This caused her keel to bend but did not interfere with the ship's steaming ability.

Group Commander, Capt. Henry J. Arm strong, stated, "I'm proud of them. Their spirit has been excellent, and they appear to have had no thought of fear. The mere fact we have not hit a mine is not our fault. It's just good sweeping."

Ray Coll, Jr., of *The Honolulu Advertiser*, wrote about the *Joseph Holt* and its return from Japan where it was used as a "guinea-pig to detonate pressure mines sown by B-29s on Saturday morning, January 26, 1946." He noted that the *Joseph Holt* along with the Marathon and the Pratt Victory, were sent in to set off mines that were still armed until the month of February. This, of course, followed the surrender of Japan.

Cmdr. Rifenburgh told Coll as they sat in his cabin, "The quick surrender of the Japanese left the U.S. in a quandary because we have to use these waters. And someone came up with the idea of using 'guinea pig' ships to set off the mines."

Cmdr. Rifenburgh stated that because he had been in command of a high-octane tanker ship carrying fuel to Okinawa, he guessed the Navy thought he would not mind taking over this job. So, he volunteered and got a volunteer crew made up of men eligible for discharge. That had been in October 1946 when they were in Okinawa. His first ship assigned was the John Rawlins and they were just aboard when a typhoon hit the island and the ships were destroyed.

"Then I was given the *Joseph Holt*, which was still steaming nicely," he said. "The *Holt*, stripped down was drawing eight feet of water and by this time the crew was gladly awaiting to get out and start the guinea pig mission. The sailors preferred mines to typhoons and I agreed." The SS *Holt* got under way and headed for Japan and enroute the ship was turned into a regular padded cell. The crew lined all decks, bulkheads and overheads with mattresses and the group stated they knew they would wind up in a padded cell."

Next to be interviewed was the navigator, Lt. P.J. Martin of Lowell, Mass. Lt. Martin shared how The *Joseph Holt* worked for 10-12 hours in daylight daily, traveling fast through waters never tread before. The Liberty Ship crashed into numerous lighthouses and buoy markers and the worst hazard was the Japanese fishing junks and sampans.

"The Japanese seemed to believe we could surpass them," he said. "However, we always had a skeleton crew and operated by remote control so when we passed over a mine it would be set off and we hoped because of the seep we would only receive small damage. Our crew learned we could scare the fishing junks by firing a rifle across their bow and they would get out of the way."

"With over 300 missions, the Holt never set off a mine, but managed to shoot at a floating mine. Our machine gun shot a mine however, it exploded, and the mine did not. Most of the mines were destroyed by the typhoons that struck them before we arrived."

"The Japanese helped as well," he continued, "as they moved through these waters and many mines were destroyed. Later, after the war, we brought Japanese navy men as observers and they later took over the jobs using their ships."

The crews were recommended for awards. However, since no one was killed on the *Joseph Holt*, Cmdr. Rifenburgh thought the job might not have been considered hazardous. The only casualty was the ship's mascot, a dog who fell down a hatch, went loco and had to be shot. The mascot was buried at sea with honors.

The only memento given to the crew was by Capt. Henry J. Armstrong, Commodore of the Guinea Pig Fleet. They each received a fancy scroll stating their name and how they served as volunteer members of the Guinea Pig Fleet Squadron engaging in checking mined channels of the Japanese Empire waters during occupation by the United States.

Liberty Ships were made to last five years. However, many served long after and many were put in storage and then, finally in the 1960s, most were sold for scrap. The fate of the SS *Joseph Holt* was to be sold and scrapped in 1961. After researching and trying to locate the crew of the SS *Joseph Holt*, no one could be found. However, what they did, with such gallant spirits can be celebrated today as one of the greatest generations of all time. And now the people who will explore the history of Joseph Holt will know for whom the ship was named and those who served on the SS *Joseph Holt*.

Note: *Any family members of the crew on the SS* Joseph Holt *are encouraged to contact the author as she welcomes any memoirs or journals the crew might have written during their time on the SS* Joseph Holt.

Discovering Rose: Judge Holt's Great Niece

It's happened again! The past wants its story told. Many years ago, descendants of Judge Joseph Holt, came to Breckinridge County on a very cold frosty morn. The first time they had ever visited the home place of their beloved g-g-g-uncle. Two sisters were amazed with the landscape and quite concerned over the appearance of the Holt Family Cemetery, which was in grave condition (restored shortly after by the Holt Family Trust and ownership transferred to the Friends of the Holt Home, Inc.) that had been in a trust for years.

Rose Holt, great niece of Joseph Holt, lived in the Holt home in the 1890's. Photo courtesy of Margaret Rose Badger (g-g-g- niece of Judge Joseph Holt.)

Judge Powers, Breckinridge County Judge Executive called me and said, "We have descendants of Joseph Holt who would like a tour. I thought you would like to be there." The ladies were very nice and enjoyed touring the home and grounds. They had heard numerous stories about the home their entire life but had never visited. Both were elderly ladies and shared how excited they were about the work I was doing to find partners, write grants and get the community involved and how the county had purchased the property and grounds through grants. One of the sisters, Margaret Rose Badger gave me her contact information and she showed both Judge Powers and me pictures from the past.

A short while after the visit that day Ms. Badger e-mailed me for the names of all owners of the Holt Home since it was sold from the Holt family in 1910 when Vanna Holt moved to California shortly a few years after the death of Washington D. Holt, who was Judge Holt's nephew and son of Thomas Holt. We corresponded several times after their visit. Ms. Badger gave me photos from the 1890's of the historic home. She told me to use them for preservation and they could be put to the best possible uses. When restoration began on the Holt Home in the late fall of 2013 pictures were shared with GRW architects from Lexington. The Friends of the Holt Home, Inc. wanted the restoration to be as close as possible to what our state partners for life, the Kentucky Heritage Council, had approved for each phase of the restoration. The 1890's photos are the oldest known photographs existing that give insight to what life was like during the last of the 19th Century at the Holt Home.

Over the years, the photos have been kept in place waiting for restoration to occur step-by-step the right way, approved by the Kentucky Heritage Council who also has copies of the photos. With the upcoming book, *Joseph Holt Mansion: Saving and Restoring the Home of Lincoln's Judge Advocate General* I thought this would be the right place to share the photographs that were given to make sure the home is brought back as close as possible to its original glory. That day lingers in my memory clearly as Margaret told me, "This is a picture of Rose Holt." Through the years many have asked for pictures of the inside of the Holt Home during the Holt era while still in ownership. I have responded always, "they are being shared with the architects and will be in the upcoming book on how the Holt Home was saved."

Since 2012 numerous journals, notes, pictures, E-mails, letters, and many items have been studied, re-examined, read, and sorted through the 19-year collection including grants and proposals made from my home as a volunteer. During the summer of 2016 I completed and revised the chapter, Finding Mr. James L. Wimsatt, (artist who did the Holt print in 1972) for which he gave a written agreement for me to use in any upcoming books, the Holt website, programs and for the Friends of the Holt Home, Inc. to use including reproduction of his Holt print in the future.

Sketch drawn by artist James Wimsatt when he came to do the Holt home print in 1972.

Last summer I called Mr. Wimsatt once again to ask the same question, "What was it like when you came here to draw the Holt print? And do you have any sketches left of when you did the print?" Mr. Wimsatt's answer was, "that was 43 years ago and I believe they are gone." However, after searching for a few days what he discovered will reward the future.

Mr. Wimsatt mailed me the collection of sketches! The collection has been kept with the chapter that shows the turnings and also the image he sensed while having difficulty trying to get the turnings perfect. Finally, after giving in, setting down and drawing what he could feel was present, he completed the drawing of a woman. Mr. Wimsatt never spoke of this happening until 2015 when he told it to me. He explained that after taking time to draw the image he could feel someone present; the sketches came easy and he completed them and the print soon after. The sketches were put away for 43 years until our conversation in 2015. And after receiving the sketches to include in my book I thought… this drawing reminds me of the Statue of Liberty. Who is this? Why are they present?

On July 6, 2016 Kim Nyberg, Consultant for the site use plan from the National Trust grant asked me if I had any photos of the inside of the Holt Home and I told her, yes, they are going to be in the new book. I have shared them with the KY Heritage Council and GRW architects for restoration and preservation of the Holt Home. She wanted copies of interior pictures to assist with wallpaper interpretation and the interior coming up in Phase III.

On the morning of our monthly meeting I was looking in my manuscript for the picture of the interior of the home where I noticed the picture of the image of the woman Mr. Wimsatt had drawn. Somehow it had been placed next to Rose's picture sitting in a chair at the Holt Home. To my surprise and delight, I realized the image of the woman Mr. Wimsatt had drawn 43 years ago, was Rose Holt! He had never seen the picture taken in the 1890's of Rose or did not know it existed. Wow! Another spirit from the past is here to give approval! For the picture of Rose in the Holt Home has a sad look but the look Mr. Wimsatt captured in his drawing is that of a warm heart with a smile as if someone is here to care!

Anticipating the find and excitement after the meeting with the Friends of the Holt Home, we were off to the Holt Home to look at wallpaper once again which we will soon have analyzed. During our conversation I could not wait to show Kim and John the discovery.

Once on-site Kim used her tablet to copy the historic pictures of the interior of the home. And the tablet enlarged the photo. We could see luxury items in the room and examine them more closely. Both Kim and John said, "This is Rose!" I have never experienced anything like this. And as the journey moves forward, people continue to be sent to help tell this great American story for the future to preserve. For it is important to know the lives of the people who lived before us. This "appearance" of Rose Holt cannot be explained. However, it is truly a blessing, a kind spirit is with us as the love of history continues in rural Breckinridge Co, KY. We know Rose has given us a clue. And what fun it was to take the tablet and search to find Rose's room. Yes, it is here in the historic, Holt Home. And if you come we will share what Rose shared with us. We will do everything possible to bring Rose's room back to the time she was here. It is for you, and for all who will travel here in the future to hear the story.

A Memorable Day for the Fort Knox JAGS

The Fort Knox Judge Advocate General unit (JAG) spent a memorable day at the home of one of their own, Judge Joseph Holt on April 20, 2017! COL James Bagwell, Staff Judge Advocate brought his entire JAG team and invited legal community from the Army Cadet Command and Fort Knox for a historical professional development and field trip!

The breezy day filled with brilliant sunshine was enjoyed by all the JAGS, media, and host of the event, The Friends of the Holt Home. Breckinridge County Judge Executive Maurice Lucas welcomed the team of JAGS and briefly shared how Holt is remembered for the Prosecuting Judge of the Lincoln Conspiracy Trial. Judge Lucas introduced me as the spearheader of the Holt project and President of the Friends of the Holt Home. I gave a warm reception to the deserving JAGS, praising their work for our great nation and thanked them for their service! Refreshments were served upon arrival beginning at 9:30 a.m. This was the first Kentucky group of JAGS to view the historical Judge Joseph Holt mansion under extensive restoration and the Holt Family Cemetery recently restored by the Holt Family Trust who graciously granted and transferred ownership to the Friends of the Holt Home.

The day was planned by SSG Robert Love who came and toured the historical facility of national significance prior to the JAGS visit requested by COL James Bagwell, who continues to partner with the Friends for the yearly wreath-laying ceremony. The Judge Advocate's Office is making it a tradition for the Fort Knox JAGS to come to the annual Holt Home Community Day giving honor to Joseph Holt! COL Bagwell is also devising other ideas to partner as he is working to bring different regions of the Army together.

Fort Knox JAGS and the Friends of the Holt Home. Photo courtesy of: Tiffany Cashman.

Col. Bagwell addressing the JAGS

Beginning at 10:00 a.m. SSG Love directed everyone to walk to the front of the Holt Home where two soldiers stood proud and bravely as they briefed the group on Judge Holt's life. Private First Class Christian Arbec and Specialist Caroline Bedoy each spoke. They had studied Holt well and did a wonderful presentation giving the JAGS insight into Holt's amazing career. Following the presentations, SSG Love and COL Bagwell made comments that gave praise to Holt's tireless effort and work during a crucial time in our nation's history where he was dedicated to President Abraham Lincoln as the top legal advisor and lawyer for the U.S Army, spending hours upon hours working with the President in the White House on critical issues during the Civil War.

COL Bagwell encouraged his JAG Team to visualize how today's Army was compared to Judge Holt's era. After the 20 minutes of bringing important history alive, I gave the requested home tour beginning on the front lawn of the grounds. I pointed out what now remains of the once 10,000-acre plantation received from the Revolutionary War by Holt's maternal grandfather, Richard Stephens who served George Washington.

Explaining only 19.5 acres remain today! The private side of Holt was shared with some stories taken from his personal letters from the Library of Congress.

Information about ongoing restoration was shared with plans in place to begin the next phase with the 2nd Transportation Enhancement Grant to complete exterior restoration and begin on the interior in 2017. The JAGS were amazed by everything — the teamwork, state partners, perseverance, and the numerous grants to make the restoration reality!

The Fort Knox JAGS brought lunch and enjoyed sitting under trees of Judge Holt's era with a modern-day Army learning about the "Father of the Judge Advocates", and how they can learn of his life, his effort, his tireless work, and that Holt was Lincoln's right-hand man. The ongoing work and hope to make the Holt Home a National meeting place for all the Army JAG across the nation was voiced numerous times throughout the day!

High lights of the day were watching the JAGS view the historic jewel, take pictures, learn about the variety of trees on the Holt grounds, touch the banisters made of walnut, hear the stories told of how five rooms have original wall paper from the 1850's, with wall paper analysis documented in the summer of 2015 by Kevin Herford, a specialist. We received many compliments from the soldiers to the Friends saying thank-you for saving this home. One soldier from Texas stated seeing Judge Holt's home was a highlight of his Army career.

The JAGS loved the atmosphere, the peacefulness, the beauty gracing the remarkable restoration and realizing the remarkable home belongs to the people, to everyone as it tells the complete story of the Lincoln Conspiracy Trial and much more. The young JAGS learned Judge Holt has a special place in the heart of every Judge Advocate.

The JAGS gave complete attentiveness to the beautiful monument of Holt where his honorable offices are engraved in which he diligently gave his heart to President Buchanan and President Lincoln.

The smiles, respect, and the gracefulness of JAGS everywhere on the Holt grounds bring to life the continued work of restoration for the Holt Home where once again all the Army and public will know the name Joseph Holt, as the nation did during the Civil War.

After the media left, COL Bagwell gave closing remarks about the day at the historic Holt Home. He asked his JAGS for comparisons of today's Army and how the Army was in Holt's era.

The Friends of the Holt Home, Inc. received a plaque of appreciation that will hang in the Holt Home. Then COL Bagwell introduced Master Sergeant Konrad Nikolao to give a brief talk of appreciation for the work of the Holt Home. To my surprise, I was given a Certificate of Appreciation for outstanding selfless service while serving as the President of the Friends of the Holt Home, Inc.

An additional amazing surprise came as The Fort Knox JAGS office communicated with the TJAGS at the Pentagon about my service and duty for the past 20 years with the Holt project,

Susan Dyer received a metal from General Flora Darpino, 39th Judge Advocate General from the Pentagon and a plaque from the Office of the Staff Judge Advocate in Fort Knox.

Holt's legacy and the restoration of his home. Being humble I shared that it takes a team! As I received a coin medal For Excellence from LTG Flora D. Darpino, the 39 Judge Advocate General of the United States Army. Asked to say something I replied, "This means the world to me." And I thanked the Army JAGS and praised them for their service to our great nation.

The Friends appreciate the Fort Knox JAGS' dedication and work they do daily advising the legal aspects of the Army.

The Fort Knox JAGS continue to partner with the Friends of the Holt Home, the rebirth of Judge Holt's legacy, and all efforts with restoration and new re-uses of the home for the local community, Kentucky, the nation, and the U.S. Army.

With each new restoration phase, continuing grants, and positive work, visitors are viewing, "preservation at its best!" The Friends of the Holt Home remain inspired and are taking actions to preserve and protect Judge Holt's legacy and home! The heart of this important effort is saving a National Treasure in rural Breckinridge County!

For the Fort Knox JAGS, and all of us so closely involved, "It was a memorable day!"

Journey to Georgia

The last of April I received a phone call from Janet Wheatley of Duluth, Georgia. She called to share her Dad, Tom Wheatley formally the Mayor of Cloverport had passed away and the family wanted to donate an entire Victorian bedroom suit to the Holt Home. She had sent a photo earlier of the Lincoln bed and explained the furniture was in storage and it would remain there for one month. Janet asked if the Friends of the Holt Home wanted the furniture, saying it was museum quality.

I told her I would speak with Breckinridge County-Judge Executive Maurice Lucas and call her back. I phoned Judge Lucas and told him about the great news! He said that was wonderful, that we would think about it but the county did not have any way to get it here. Judge Lucas said he would ask around and see if someone would volunteer to go and bring it home. This was also shared by e-mail to the Friends' organization, state partners and those who have been working with us on the Holt project.

After two weeks, we received one reply from Warren Greer the volunteer Director of the KLH-TA. Warren stated he would try and find someone to bring the furniture back to Kentucky. Without any more responses and time running out my husband said, "Let's go to Georgia during the weekend before the upcoming Washington D.C. Trip." The farm pick-up truck was cleaned and our youngest son Justin brought a topper from the junk pile he used for camping and it was scrubbed and cleaned and put on the truck in case of rain.

Sunday morning, April 29 we left early and began the journey of 884 miles round trip, filled up the truck with 35 gallons of diesel and loaded with all the blankets and covers to be found, borrowing many from my mother to wrap and protect the furniture.

The day was pleasant with a soft rain from Bowling Green through heavy traffic in Nashville and GA. About 2 and ½ hours from Atlanta we drove into a traffic jam completely shutting down the entire south side of the freeway for an hour and a half.

We called the Wheatleys explaining we were trapped without any movement. They asked, "where are you? Maybe you can exit and get out of the traffic." All that could be seen was huge semi-trucks, and pine trees. No one moved for ninety minutes! Finally, a small movement began as it took over thirty minutes to get moving at a normal speed. Dark was soon approaching and the traffic was thick, the signs hard to read and the GPS took us over multiple roads, interchanging to connect with the home address of Janet Wheatley.

The family was cooking dinner for us and we were almost two and a half hours late. Finally, we arrived exhausted, tired and hungry since it had been a long time since lunch. Getting into the gated community was a memorable experience. Janet forgot to mention they lived in a gated community. However, she had given security our names. I was driving the nice looking pick-up truck with a not so nice-looking topper. It was embarrassing for me. There were two lines, one for residence and one for visitors. I did not notice I had pulled in the residence line. When we did Eddie said we will never get through here. The security guard was talking with a guest and he looked at me and I smiled. Then he raised the gate and motioned for us to go through. Viewing the prestigious homes in Duluth was amazing. Something like you see in movies. It was now dark and difficult to see the numbers on the mailboxes. We watched carefully and finally saw the anticipated numbers and pulled in the driveway.

It was relaxing to sit down with the family and have a wonderful dinner. Eddie is first cousins to Janet and Glenda, the daughters of Tom and Joyce Wheatley. A lot of reminiscing was done as it had been years since the cousins have spent time together. Fun and conversation continued until all were ready to retire. Janet's home was beautiful and very relaxing for anyone who might be a guest. The night passed like a flash and I awoke to see Eddie had already gone down stairs. We had a light breakfast with continued conversation and Janet was so kind to share the family had more items they wanted to donate. A chest of drawers and a set of china from the period the historic Holt Home will be restored from Joseph Holt's important national service time. However, this would have to be a different trip since there was not any more space for these items.

The skies looked as if it could rain at any moment. How wise to have put the topper on the truck for the trip to Georgia. Glenda and her husband went with Eddie and me to the storage unit about 15 miles away. Once we arrived it was amazing to see the items in the storage unit. Numerous pictures were taken of the donated treasures to grace the halls of the Holt Home once the interior has been completely restored. How amazing for the Wheatleys, who at one time lived just a few miles down the road in the river town of Cloverport, to partner and give such a nice gift. Hopefully, their generosity will encourage others to give items so all can enjoy, view and help furnish the Holt Home for future visitors!

Once everyone was inside the storage unit and we decided how all the furniture might be placed in a regular pickup truck, a torrential rain began. It rained for a prolonged time. Finally, the rain ended and the hard work of loading the furniture began. It was heavy and difficult to pack and place the furniture where it would fit and ride safely. The rain period had allowed plenty of time to carefully cover the furniture that had already been put in a protective plastic wrap. Glenda, her husband and Eddie loaded the furniture while I took pictures to record the work for readers and for future visitors to view the effort of getting the furniture back to Breckinridge County, KY and to Judge Holt's home. Thanks goes to the Wheatley family for opening their home to Eddie and me as we were going to stay in a hotel. However, they insisted and we accepted.

We all said good-by. Glenda wanted to know who cleaned the Holt Home for the annual Holt Home Community Day each year. I told her most of the time the Friends of the Holt Home do it. Glenda wanted me to contact her when we clean the home for the annual September event. She wants to help us because that is what preservation is all about - cleaning, restoring, championing, and finally enjoying the completed work. I explained the Friends will be honoring families and individuals whom have given gracious donations and we would love to have her family present this fall. She said she hoped they could be present.

Part of the bottom of the Lincoln bed

Bottom part of the marble dresser

Ready to load

Packed for safe travels

Now the journey back to Kentucky began and Glenda's husband told us we would hit the heavy traffic in Nashville because of the rain that had made us get a later start. He suggested stopping and eating twice and then maybe we would miss the rush hour traffic. With good intentions, we began driving with a loaded truck. We drove for a long while and stopped at a nice rest area to eat a snack, rest and change drivers. We decided to continue and for the next several hours we drove. We talked about many things along the way and enjoyed the weekend trip. Since we were wanting to drive through Nashville later we were watching for something to do for a short while. I spotted the outlet malls and Eddie said, "Oh, no!" but he stopped anyway, and we bought a few gifts and then continued. It always seems I get to drive through heavy traffic. And there is always construction in Nashville. The GPS did help as you cannot have too many eyes watching as you make your way through the city. And yes, there was so much traffic. However, I prayed, and we safely got through Nashville and continued and decided to stop in Bowling Green to have dinner. The drive from there was relaxed as we have traveled those roads so many times back during our college years at WKU.

Home was a happy sight as the truck was put in the shed and we both were glad to be home safely with treasures for the Holt Home that many will enjoy for the future. The following day all the furniture was unloaded and placed in a protective climate-controlled environment until the Holt Home and the Friends of the Holt Home will place each piece in a restored bedroom, welcoming visitors to Judge Holt's beloved home!

The Heart of the TJAGS!

A story was shared in 2013 with retired COL Fred Borch, Historian and Archivist at the Judge Advocate General's Legal Center and School about the effort in trying diligently to get First Ladies - Mrs. Laura Bush and Mrs. Michelle Obama to come, visit and speak at the historic Judge Joseph Holt Home, but without success. Mrs. Bush did answer but I never heard from Michelle Obama. Fred's reply was, "write and ask the first lady TJAG General Flora D. Darpino the 39th Judge Advocate General of the United States Army to be the key-note speaker for the Annual Holt Home Community Day." Fred advised me to write at least two years in advance. Upon Fred's advice, I wrote to Lt. General Darpino's executive officer, Francis P. King on February 16, 2016 sharing Fred Borch had given me his contact information and Fred and LT. General Chipman had been at the Holt Home a few years earlier. I received a reply the same day. The letter was very kind and I was thanked for the gracious invitation to LTG Darpino to participate as the keynote speaker in the 9th Annual Holt Home Community Day on 23 September 2017. The letter stated the TJAG would evaluate the request along with other travel and professional engagements for General Darpino.

COL King stated, "The Holt Home holds a special place in the JAG Corps' history" and they were working hard to support the request! I was told the TJAGS would be meeting soon and this would be discussed among various other requirements and they would let me know. Since the first letter of introduction with the Holt project, special requests along with numerous letters have been written to the TJAG. The letters have consisted of updates, along with restoration progress, grants, and partnering for the Holt project. The next executive officer was COL Sean McGarry who has been very gracious with his responses and always answered with positive remarks about success and hard work and how it is so very much appreciated. Along with the updates for the Friends of the Holt Home, Inc. in 2017, the List of Accomplishments of the Friends of the Holt Home, Inc. for 2016 were sent as well. COL King sent a reply in January of 2017 with kind words spoken for the effort of the work for the Holt Home. He shared the JAGS had recently featured a photograph of COL Jimmy Bagwell's wreath-laying ceremony in their Regimental Quill & Sword publication and that they continue to look forward to future updates from the Holt Home.

A picture of Col. Jeffrey Miller, Executive Officer for Flora Darpino, the 39th Judge Advocate General (retired).

Susan Dyer standing beside a portrait of Judge Joseph Holt. Anyone entering the TJAGS office in the Pentagon must pass Holt's portrait.

I shared about the planned trip to see the recently restored Lincoln Conspiracy Court Room at Grant Hall in May. COL McGarry requested when I had set the dates for May to let him know and he would schedule a Pentagon tour. He told me the Honor Guard does a really nice job and he thought I would enjoy the experience. He asked me once I knew of the date and time he would plan for a special escort after my official tour of the Pentagon to bring me by to meet everyone in the front office and to take a photo in front of the Holt portrait.

On April 24, 2017, I received an e-mail introduction from COL Jeffery A. Miller with greetings from the Pentagon! He wrote to introduce himself as he was replacing COL McGarry in the TJAG'S office as COL McGarry was preparing for an upcoming assignment and he would be my new point of contact for the upcoming visit to the Pentagon. COL Miller was tracking the time to be 12:00 on May 5. COL Miller told me he would meet me at the visitor's center at around 1:00 after my tour was complete and he would escort me to the TJAG'S office. When he told me LTG Darpino was looking forward to seeing me and sharing some of the Regiment's history I felt numb! Amazing things happen when you believe they can!

May 5th began with an early rise and a downpour of rain. The pounding made it difficult for my husband to steer safely as the visibility was so low driving to the airport in Louisville! And it was Derby weekend! We were second to arrive at Gate B2. Washington- D.C. American 4531 on the screen made it real. The flight was to be an hour and 10 minutes, however that changed with the Washington D.C. weather. Heavy rain caused our jet to fly twenty minutes circling the airport which turned into forty minutes more, and because of low fuel, flying to Pittsburg, PA to refuel and an additional 45-minute flight back to the Reagan National Airport. While the plane was refueling, passengers could use their cell phone. I called COL Miller at the TJAGS office and explained the status of not arriving on time, refueling and flying back to D.C had made me late for the scheduled Pentagon tour. I will admit my heart was somewhat faint after all that had been put into this trip. However, I tried to remain positive and explain I could not control the weather, and was so very disappointed I would not be able to make the Pentagon tour as planned. I asked the Colonel what he advised and his reply was, "Call me when you land in D.C. and we will make sure you get a Pentagon tour." I was told COL Miller would give the tour himself and I would still have the honor to meet with General Darpino and tour the TJAG office.

After landing in D.C. I called the Colonel and he asked me to call him once I had reached our hotel. When we called the prepaid shuttle to take us to the St. Regis all I could get was, "Punch 1 for this, punch 2 for…" and so on. No one was going to speak with me as our plane was three hours late landing. My husband and I took a taxi and were relieved to finally arrive safely at the hotel. After reaching our room it was so nice just to be off that plane! Another phone call was made and COL Miller told me to relax and meet him around 3:15 at the Welcome Center at the Pentagon.

Visiting Washington D.C. expect to have a large cash flow for taxies and food! However, the service was very good, and the food wonderful! Another taxi. Arriving at the Pentagon is quite overwhelming. Over 50,000 people work there. We walked to the visitor's center taking our time. I introduced myself to the police on duty at the visitor's center. The policeman's dog was a white lab named BOSS. I explained we were waiting for COL Miller. And asked if it was okay to stand close to him. He told us yes. I called COL Mill er and told him we were in front of the Visitor's Center. He said it would take ten minutes to get there. And it was time for the guard to change. The policeman told me the changing guard dogs knew each other and had been trained together. With the changing of the guard the dogs greeted one another with a welcome!

Watching for Army officers I wondered which one would be COL Miller. An officer came walking with a high stride and a smile. I knew it must be the Colonel. He walked over to my husband and me and told us we would have to go through security to get in the Pentagon. He walked through the doors with us pointing out the direction we needed to take. First, through screening and security. We needed two pictured IDs. We presented our driver's licenses and Passports. We handed them through a glass window and waited for the officer to check out our I.D. Then we typed in our S.S. numbers again. Following this we had to take off our jackets, belts, lay down small purses, go through a scanning machine, holding up arms, then we typed in social security numbers again and received an I.D. badge. And we still had to have an escort to enter the Pentagon after all the screening.

The Pentagon is like a city. All you might need is available, food, shopping, a haircut. It is amazing! COL Miller took us through the Pentagon Hall of Honor for different wars and the engraved names given for the causes of our history in America's War of conflicts. The medal of Honor in every war honoring soldiers is very moving and makes you think how special to appreciate the service of all our men and women in uniform in America today, as well as the past who gave their lives for our continued freedom. We must not take it for granted. Taking a tour makes you proud of what soldiers do and how they serve! Honoring their lives and work is amazing! Seeing the numerous pictures and displays and learning more about our military's history should make Americans be more aware of what is done for citizens daily!

After walking up and down corridors and experiencing the history on display at the Pentagon it was time to go the TJAG office. Walking and examining the portraits of all the TJAGS since the beginning is breathtaking. Upon entrance one of the highlights of the tour was the center roll of portraits where, who else's portrait but Joseph Holt, the First Judge Advocate to have General's rank greets you when making a right to enter the TJAG office. Holt, staring at you front and center, makes you proud for his legacy and the continued effort for the restoration of his Kentucky home, knowing every person who enters the TJAG office passes directly by Judge Holt every time they enter and exit the office. I had a flashback when standing by Judge Holt's portrait as I remembered General Dana K. Chipman, the 38th Judge Advocate General telling me, "I face Judge Holt every day I go to work."

COL Miller asked me to sit and wait a moment for General Darpino. Upon her entrance and introduction from COL Miller it was gratifying to meet General Darpino in person. How rewarding to know and to be able to share with readers and especially Holt's own community that today's TJAG knows and appreciates ALL that has been done in bringing back Judge Holt's legacy and his beloved home. What a remarkable time with General Darpino and COL Miller, her executive officer. What a fine lady, and wonderful lawyer! She shared important history of the TJAGS and explained the Regimental Prints, no.1. Of course, she knew I knew all about the Regimental Print no. 2 of General Orders No. 100, The Lieber Code with Holt standing over President Lincoln as he signed into law the etiquette of soldiers and how they were to treat each other on the battlefield, which was given to me by General Chipman in 2011 personally for my service for continued effort to preserve the legacy of a distinguished member of the JAG Corp.

Next came the history of the clock in the TJAG office. The clock was made in the 1800's. There is only one man living today the TJAGS know who can work on this kind of clock. The assistant to the Judge Advocate General has a most demanding job to make sure the clock is wound every 7 days. The theory is… if the clock stops the heart of the TJAG stops. For the clock's ticking is the heart of the TJAGS. Therefore, it must never stop. If the clock is to be moved it must be shut down correctly.

General Darpino shared a personal story when she gave my husband and me a tour of the Office of The Judge Advocate General's Executive Suite. She shared one of her responsibilities when she was an assistant and how she had to make sure the clock kept ticking. The TJAG clock was always wound on Friday. Several times General Darpino told me she would wake up during the night and wonder if she wound the clock. To make sure, sometimes the General would make a trip to the office to see if the clock was ticking. It was ALWAYS on her heart, that if the clock ticks the TJAG'S heart continues beating!

Another heartwarming story was that only a four-star general could have a private bathroom in their office so when the Pentagon was remodeled the bathroom was removed for the executive office. There are not a lot of 4 Star Generals today so this also made the office much larger! How presidential the office is! How organized, and structured! I asked if a president had ever visited her and she said, "No". My comment was, "They should." Holt visited Lincoln often.

General Darpino told of the 911 attack on the Pentagon and how the Judge Advocate General's Office was under restoration during the time. The executive suite was heavily damaged and no one was in the office during the time the plane hit the building.

When talking with General Darpino I told her I could tell she was inspired to do what she does daily and what an honor it was to have the opportunity to meet with her. I shared how the Holt project started with God putting the idea of saving the home on my heart and the work it took getting support for others to believe in the dream. I shared how we have four state partners, and now the Army. However, it has been a wonderful journey with non-stop work getting our community to believe this could happen and now they can believe in the dream by seeing the positive results.

When General Darpino first met me in her office she walked up to me and said, "I like what you are doing." I thanked her and told her it was an honor to meet her and I had heard so many wonderful things about her from General Chipman when he came to Kentucky, as General Chipman's wife had baby-sat for General Darpino.

I voiced that after General Darpino retires in September 2017 I knew she would still serve. She said, "Yes," I will still serve in a different role to continue to help others." What a remarkable lady, soldier, Judge Advocate General, and top lawyer! I expressed how she must be inspired and motivated to come to work each day. General Darpino told me she was inspired, and if she needed more inspiration she only must look out her window and gaze upon the home of General Lee at the top of the hill at Arlington National Cemetery. She shared what a brilliant lawyer General Lee was to win back his home after the Federal government took it because of taxes.

A framed plaque hangs proudly in the TJAG office to Joseph Holt from the Lincoln family for what Holt did as he had the tremendous job as the prosecuting judge of the Lincoln Conspiracy Trial to prosecute the conspirators who had slain the very president who appointed Holt as the Judge Advocate General. Joseph Holt's spirit should be happy to know how the TJAGS remember his legacy as he worked tirelessly for his country!

Another inspiration for General Darpino is her two daughters. When needed, the General faces their pictures and knows she will always give her best. I explained how Holt's community have worked their hardest with mountains of obstacles to overcome. And when we give of ourselves it is the greatest gift of all. I explained how we keep writing grants, and working to gain more partners. I shared the personal story of how I had written and corresponded with COL Francis King, COL Sean McGarry, and finally, COL Jeffery Miller, and sent updates for the past two years to try and get her to come and speak for the 9th Annual Holt Home Community Day on September 23, 2017. And what this means to Holt's own community. I shared the story of how we want to have an Honor Roll in the Holt Home for all the Judge Advocate Generals who come and speak at Judge Holt's home, and if she would come and speak she would be the third Judge Advocate General counting Holt.

General Flora Darpino did not know if her very demanding schedule would allow her to come and speak. However, she said, "The TJAGS will work on making it a tradition to send the Judge Advocate General to the Holt Home because of Holt and his leadership and what his legacy means to today's JAGS! COL Miller, General Darpino's executive officer stated they would begin work on this as the TJAGS base strong belief in Holt's work! This will complement the continued work of the Friends of the Holt Home to make the Holt Home a National meeting place for all the Army Judge Advocates. All good works take time and patience!

Toward the end of the tour and the wonderful experience that will always be appreciated, I shared with General Darpino that the coin medal she sent by COL Bagwell, Judge Advocate from Fort Knox for my service of Excellence for the Holt Home and Holt's legacy will be treasured and shared. And whenever I speak about Judge Holt, his legacy, and the massive effort continuing for complete restoration and reusing the historic Holt home I will always carry the coin medal given to me by the 39th Judge Advocate General of the United States Army, whom I was told only gives medals to soldiers. General Darpino said, "for a good luck charm?" I smiled and said, "No, it's more than that. It means the world to me and it is deeply appreciated!" I thanked General Darpino for her service and coming to work each day.

When you believe, something is possible it gives strength and causes others to join forces working together. The heart of the TAGS is beating strong as they work daily to serve and to be ready for our nation!

Their inspiration comes from within. To be a good soldier is to have a good heart. And with the beating of the hearts the clock continues for the generations of TJAGS to come and serve and give their best!

Before leaving the executive office, I asked General Darpino if it was okay to hug a General? She said, "Yes". That hug reminds me of the strength it takes to be the Judge Advocate General, and doing so with a smile shows the great character, and how even a General is humble when they love what they do with every heart beat and breath taken for the work of our nation to keep us safe and continue our freedom in America, just like the ticking clock continues for the work of the top lawyers of the Army who work tirelessly like the TJAGS clock that continues ticking - with purpose and plan!

Good byes, hugs, and handshakes were exchanged as General Darpino and COL Miller gave their best with encouraging words and works to follow concerning the continuing partnership with the TJAGS and Judge Holt's legacy and his Kentucky home. COL Francis King, his replacement COL Sean McGarry, and General Darpino's executive officer today, COL Jeffery A. Miller voiced the special quote the Friends of the Holt Home, Inc. continue to use, "The Holt Home holds a special place in the heart of the JAG Corps."

Walking through the exit from the TJAGS office COL Miller paused with his camera saying, "We want to get a picture of you standing by Judge Joseph Holt who faces every person entering the TJAGS' office." Visitors are not allowed to take any pictures inside the Pentagon. COL Jeffery Miller had to get permission from security to take the picture. To be given this opportunity to have your picture taken beside the legacy of the man, Joseph Holt whom the TJAGS respect with dignity, and honor as the Brigadier General who served Lincoln and in today's modern Army was a high honor. Holt's legacy still inspires the Judge Advocates serving, represent to all soldiers a man who stood up for what he believed, who helped hold our nation together during a crucial time. His career as the top lawyer inspires the United States Army today where he is remembered as, " The Father of the Judge Advocates."

With our continued escort through the Pentagon, COL Miller asked my husband and me if we would like to visit the Memorial for 911. We took a picture with COL Miller by the memorial. It will always be pressed deeply in our hearts! We will always remember this visitation with the beautiful benches graced with the names of those lives lost, with trees and sitting areas outside the Pentagon where the plane flew in and burst into flames on that sad day when terror stuck our nation. However, the bravery and courage of what Americans are made of took hold and after caring for the injured and those who lost their lives, the stars and stripes was soon flying, high draped over the building showing the world our flag was still there, our country still free, and we are "the home of the brave." And the heart of the TJAGS keeps ticking!

The Lincoln Conspiracy Trial Court Room Revisited

In fall of 2013 retired COL Fred Borch and the 38th Judge Advocate General Dana K. Chipman of the United States Army came to Kentucky to speak at the 5th Annual Holt Home Community Day in Breckinridge County, KY as keynote speakers. The JAGS came to lend support for the restoration of the historic Holt Home.

Fred Borch shared the evening before about the Lincoln Conspiracy Trial's Court Room being restored from 2009-2012 with renovation of Grant Hall, and how he had given the first tour. The courtroom was originally part of Washington's Penitentiary from 1829-1868. The third floor of the building was restored as it appeared during the 1865 trial. "The courtroom features were based on artistic drawings and written material with descriptions of court proceedings."

Some furnishings and artifacts on display today are on loan from the production company of the 2011 historical film "The Conspirator" directed by Robert Redford in which actor Danny Huston portrayed Joseph Holt. Retired COL Fred Borch did much coaching with Danny Huston, portraying Holt, prosecuting judge of the Lincoln Conspiracy Trial. Other artifacts and documentation from the courtroom are from the National Defense University Library.

Today the public is permitted to tour Grant Hall at Fort McNair in Washington D.C. four times a year. They can witness the courtroom as if they traveled back in time during the trial of Lincoln's assassins. The Lincoln Conspiracy Trial, which later concluded with the grim execution of Lincoln's assassins, was one of the darkest times in our nation's history.

"One hundred and fifty-two years later the conspirators are long forgotten and buried. Their names have no memories. However, in the Summer of 1865 theirs were the most spoken in the United States. The public wanted to know everything they could find out about the conspirators. The trial by Military Commission was ordered by the new president Andrew Johnson who ordered those who had conspired to kill the president to be prosecuted by a military commission." The Commission held its first session on May 9, 1865 with the trial beginning on May 12. The emotion of the Commission's first session are revived on the anniversary of 152 years ago today as I write about the Lincoln Conspiracy Court Room after visiting it in person May 6.

"To defend criticism President Johnson and Secretary Stanton requested the Attorney General James Speed of Kentucky prepare a formal legal opinion on the propriety of trying the assassins by a military commission." That opinion survives today in the form of a sixteen-page printed pamphlet. The assassination of President Lincoln and the attack on William H. Seward were acts of war during an armed rebellion against the lawful government. The legal opinion concluded, "Not only could the conspirators be tried by a military commission but they should be." On May 1, 1865, President Johnson issued the order to proceed.

Grant Hall, at Fort McNair's Building 20, is named after Ulysses S. Grant, general-in-chief of the Union Army during the Civil War and the 18th president of the United States, who served from 1869 to 1877. The defendants faced the court of nine judges, most being Army generals, none were lawyers. A simple majority vote would result in conviction. A two/thirds vote could impose the death sentence, and there was no right of appeal, as the verdicts and sentences of the commission would be final. The only possible appeal could be brought by the President of the United States.

This trial became the most dramatic series of events in the history of our nation! Rumors spread that the proceedings of the commission would not allow the public or press. If this occurred there would not be stories to write and newspapers to sell. Finally, the doors to the courtroom were opened to the public.

The historic courtroom located in Grant Hall, building 20 at Fort McNair had been quickly converted in a three-day period. The courtroom had not been quiet and solemn but was like a saloon with people coming and going during the trial. It became a popular entertainment for newlyweds. To witness the trial one had to gain a ticket. Many prominent officers, politicians and ladies enjoyed the gallery. Only a few were allowed inside the courtroom with the rest of the nation learning about what happened daily from reading the proceedings in major newspapers.

To reach Grant Hall you must go to the main entrance at Fort McNair, Washington D.C.-Joint Base Myer-Henderson Hall during the quarterly public Open House of Grant Hall's historic third-floor courtroom on the first Saturday of the second month of each quarter. It is located on the Fort McNair side of the Joint Base in southwest Washington D.C. The courtroom is the site of the military tribunal, held from May through June of 1865, of those thought responsible for the plot to assassinate President Abraham Lincoln.

Once reaching Fort McNair you must enter through the main gate on Second Street. At first you will meet the 1st security guard who will direct you to the 2nd, No. 66 Security check point and then visitors are completely checked out with a prior background check and two forms of pictured I.D. Some visitors will enter driving a car that is completely examined upon entrance to the base.

Arriving and viewing the exterior of Grant Hall Building NO. 20, the only remaining building today of the Old Penitentiary, makes it hard to imagine what the grounds were like when the Washington penitentiary became the center of national attention in 1865 when the trial and sentencing of those implicated in the assassination of President Lincoln was held on the third floor of the eastern wing of the building in a newly prepared courtroom.

Once inside Grant Hall my husband and I met Leah Rubalcaba, Community Relations Officer whom I had spoken with numerous times before the trip to Washington D.C. I had never met Leah. However, I knew her voice as I had heard it numerous times on the phone. We were greeted by volunteers with a sign in for the Open House. Leah shared the story of how the end interior wall of the room where guests signed the register was the end wall where soldiers stood armed with guns in hand on the day of execution. Looking straight ahead out the window the tennis courts can be seen today where the courtyard was in 1865. Dr. Paul Severance, Colonel (Ret.) U.S. Army Professor of Military Science, who was portraying General Hancock, a teacher at the National Defense University shared as he volunteers during the Open House how he personally painted the fence section to show where the scaffold was built where the assassins were hanged. He stated the condemned could see the fresh dug graves and the coffins as research shows. However, corrected information said they walked pass the gravesites. What a terror to see where you would be buried. At first after the execution the bodies were buried in the center of the outside wall where soldiers stood guard on that blistering, horrid day.

Many sad memories of the aftermath of the Civil War remain in our history. To understand our history helps us understand who we are as a nation. However, not knowing all facts and every detail helps history stay interesting for future scholars, historians and visitors to discover clues to the past and broaden the stories covered in the history books of those who lived and served, in the trial of the Lincoln Conspirators as well as those accused of murdering the president, and the four who lost their lives that day.

After getting permission from Leah Rubalcaba and Dr. Paul Severance I sat in Judge Holt's seat. It may seem strange however, I thought if I could sit in Judge Holt's chair I might experience something, and for years I thought about doing this.

Conspirators sat where the pictures are

The Military Commission and prosecuting team

The Military Commission, Judge Holt at far right

Susan Dyer standing where Judge Holt stood for the Lincoln Conspiracy Trial

Original items from the 1865 Lincoln Conspiracy Trial, including the gavel Holt used during the trial.

Finally, I carefully sat in Holt's seat with echoes of history ringing across the small courtroom. Yes, small courtroom. Good size for an office. However, for a courtroom it is much smaller that the historic drawings and lithographs depict.

Judge Holt's placement at the table of the Military Commission and the 3-member Prosecution team who conducted the trial was the end of the table on the right side. From where Holt sat he could see all the conspirators, 7 sitting to his right with a pot-belled stove close to the window, and in the left corner Mary Surratt.

After the first week of the trial the witness stand was moved between the tall pillars facing the tribunal (Commission) and Prosecution team. Mary Surratt was moved in the corner because of being a Victorian woman as it was not proper for her to be placed with the men. A lady was not to be without an escort.

The door leading from the courtroom went to the penitentiary. Today there are wire bars showing where the door was, as it is enclosed now. The courtroom was hot, small and had truly miserable heat conditions as research showed during the trial.

With visitors entering and exiting and portrayers talking with guests it was difficult to get a quiet time while sitting in Judge Holt's seat. I wanted to have the quiet time to feel the room and experience every possible angle. It took patience. Feelings, with echoes ringing of today's visitors made it somewhat like the time of the coming and going of those present at the trial.

Sitting in Judge Holt's chair will always be unforgettable! As a group of visitors descended the narrow stairs to the lower floors there was about five minutes of the time for what I had dreamed of experiencing. As I focused on the room, sounds, and the environment, thoughts of the sheer intensity of the trial came to me. I imagined the Old Penitentiary and the loss of it all except Grant Hall and how important it had been for a professor to plead with his Senator to help save Grant Hall in 1990. A grant was won to restore the courtroom. Without this effort visitors would not be able to experience the Lincoln Conspiracy Courtroom as I was visiting today!

Still seated in Judge Holt's chair, after a few minutes, an energy came to me, with a shaky feeling. While sitting in Judge Holt's chair immediately my right hand felt nervous, and when I looked down my right hand was shaking, unexplainable and memorable! My thoughts traveled back to 1865 to those days of the trial and the endurance of the prosecutors as well as everyone who lived in those moments, heard those words, and for the rest of their lives lived with the results of our government's actions!

Dr. Severance shared with me how on the first day of the trial the prisoners wore hoods except Dr. Mudd and Mary Surratt. That was entirely too unbearable for General Grant and he said, "NO MORE!". And never again did the prisoners wear the hoods while in the courtroom. During the trial the floors were covered in coco palm leaves rather thick to muffle the sounds of the metal pieces on the bottom of the men's shoes as the small courtroom had echoed every sound.

Today, May 6th, visitors examined history, and heard re-enactors of the period. All remaining today that is original are the walls, floors and pillars. On display, thanks to Robert Redford's film, *The Conspirator* in 2011, are displays borrowed from the movie props, Mary Surratt's costume, and numerous objects in cases under glass. There are a few authentic items from the trial, visitors can view under glass as well. The Lincoln Conspiracy Trial Courtroom was under restoration so therefore *The Conspirator* was not filmed on site at Grant Hall. However, today Dr. Severance who teaches at the Dwight D. Eisenhower School for National Security and Resource Strategy is working to produce a DVD for one day of the trial by re-enactors to sell and hopefully, generate funding to do continued work on the restoration.

I shared with Leah Rubalcaba, Public Affairs Officers, earlier and with Dr. Paul Severance in the wonderful conversations we had about the Holt project, Holt's legacy, the restoration of his home, the 20-year effort behind the project, and the state partnering and the wonderful team of people making the dream reality. Dr. Severance was glad to learn about the restoration of the

Judge Joseph Holt Home and said he would like to visit. He mentioned he had been to Kentucky to visit the Patton Museum at Fort Knox and had visited the Perryville Battlefield.

I asked numerous questions, one being what happened to the suit Danny Huston wore during the movie *The Conspirator*. Dr. Severance was not sure. However, he was going to check the status and see where the costume was. I explained Fred Borch had given me the e-mail of the American Film Company's contact and I had written asking if it might be possible for the American Film Company to donate the suit Danny Huston wore in the film to the Holt Home. Several attempts were made without an answer. I shared the suit should be on display just like Mary Surratt's dress is at Grant Hall today, and that if the whereabouts of the suit was located and Grant Hall did not want Holt's suit, the Holt Home would love to have it!

Footsteps continued moving on the floors where nine members of the Military Commission walked, sat and did their job! As visitors quietly walked in silence I grasped a few stolen moments still sitting in Holt's chair. People stared and wondered what I was doing sitting there. However, no one asked but simply watched my pen write the story for readers to experience. As I wrote this narrative, the wind blew a nice breeze through the window next to Holt's chair. The breeze lifted the pages of my notes as the sounds from outside filled the courtroom that remains today, where yesteryear our nation needed results, closure and healing.

The silence in a place of living history brings thoughts about how hearts felt during this very crucial time. Standing at the table similar from that day, in the same location designating where Holt was, I touched the table firmly. As I arose standing behind Holt's chair a warm feeling came to me as I stood silently stepping back and imagining the pressure Holt felt, the anguish he endured, and his history and legacy and how his life changed after the trial and for all the years there after he worked to prove that he DID indeed take the Clemency Papers to President Johnson, that they met in private and afterwards President Johnson denied ever seeing the Clemency papers. I shared with Dr. Severance how Holt delivered the Clemency Papers to the president and to the young actress on site portraying Mary Surratt. The young lady shared she had thoroughly studied Mary Surratt. Her comments were, "President Johnson had plenty of chances to help me as she spoke in first person. However, he did nothing to help save my life. She agreed at least Joseph Holt tried and she believed in the Clemency papers, which did not surface until a few years later when finally, John Surratt, Mary Surratt's son was apprehended and brought to trial in a downtown court room of Washington D.C where upon opening the court proceedings the Clemency Papers Joseph Holt had delivered to the President were among the other documents of the trial.

I also shared a researched story in my biography of *Lincoln's Advocate: The Life of Judge Joseph Holt* of the two senators, Preston King and James Lane who barred Anna Surratt from seeing President Johnson in hopes of getting a pardon for her mother. How Anna had wept on the White House stairs and later, two weeks after the execution of her mother both senators committed suicide. That occurrence has continued to make me think still today something was not right with this. The young actress agreed. however, did not know if the two suicides were connected somehow with Mary Surratt losing her life.

The young lady portraying Mary Surratt agreed Judge Holt had tried to lessen the sentence to life in prison. Ms. Surratt was dying and bleeding heavily as she had ovarian cancer, which 152 years ago the doctors called a diseased womb.

People came thoughout the day, as my visit lasted almost four hours. Questions have been repeated continuously for the past 152 years. Only the conspirators themselves and the Military Commission know exactly what happened. The court records have been examined for decades! However, truth eventually emerges from hiding. If documents surface that have never been examined and have proof to back up the writings, someday, this story of the Lincoln Conspiracy

Trial may have a new hearing about what happened behind the scenes when the government only had three days to prepare a courtroom.

Until then scholars will continue to study, the public will continue to question, and the knowledge that the Lincoln Conspiracy Court Room is now open to the public four times a year on the 1st Saturday in February, May, August and November will let Americans step back in history and imagine the roles of the conspirators, lawyers for the defense and the prosecutors for the government.

On May 6, all those on assignment in Grant Hall are volunteers. The sign-in table where you place your name is part of history continuing. After chatting with Leah Rubalcaba, Public Affairs Officer and seeing the wall that extended upward where the guards stood on watch, it takes courage to imagine what they saw and witnessed that gray day 152 years ago this July.

Walking down the hall on the first floor if you continue walking you would have been able to enter the OLD Penitentiary that no longer exists. Torn down in 1990, Grant Hall is all that exists today of the Old Penitentiary.

Feelings like no other came to me with each step of the narrow stairs to connect to the 2nd and 3rd floor and into the room where offices were until recently when renovation began to bring back the recreated Lincoln Conspiracy Court Room.

The walls hold the secrets of how life was during the trial. Mary Surratt's dress worn by Robin Wright in *The Conspirator* is on display along with some other props from the movie.

It is moving to gaze through the glass display cases and experience the newspaper clippings from the day (not all true stories) as the newspapers don't always tell the truth and get ALL the facts as they really were and as well as other important pieces from Robert Redford's movie in 2011.

Newspaper clippings placed on the table of the prosecutors today look as if any member could walk through the doorway from the stairs leading into the courtroom and pick up to read.

The sketches and lithographs make the courtroom appear much larger than the actual size. When you visit the Lincoln Conspiracy Courtroom, you will feel for the time your trip into the past gives a clearer picture of what terrific pressure there was, what important decisions were made here for closure of the ending of the first murder of a President in the history of our nation, beloved President Abraham Lincoln and all bound by duty to serve to find the proof justifying the action taken in response to that dreadful day when President Lincoln was shot and killed.

The aftermath lingers for 152 years. The people accused were tried, convicted and hanged with others barely escaping death and some that may have been involved who were never tried or captured.

Our nation experienced for the first time the death of a president by assassination. The court ruled and for the rest of the lives of all those present it would remain a dark and deep memory.

The Judge Advocate General's Legal Center and School's Partnership

Little did I realize the significence in partnering with the Judge Advocate General's Legal Center and School in Charlottesville, VA in 2011, that it would present wonderful opportunities as former Kentucky State Representative Dwight D. Butler shared with me when I called him for advice about delivering a lecture there on Judge Holt's career and life at Decker Auditorium.

Since delivering the 5th George S. Prugh lecture numerous doors have opened because of a partnering and friendship between the JAG School, COL Fred Borch, retired, and General Dana K. Chipman, the 38th Judge Advocate General whom I met while at the JAG School, and numerous other Army JAGS since then along with the partnering now at the TJAG Office at the Pentagon as all Judge Advocates know each other through the JAG School. These distinguished soldiers and lawyers have a great appreciation for one of their own, Brigadier General Joseph Holt as the JAGS refer to him. Locally we say Judge Holt.

The United States Army appreciates deep dedication, continued work and volunteering for a special cause without receiving a paycheck for doing the work. All Army JAGS relate to the Judge Advocate General's Legal Center and School, as it is one of the most distinguished law firms in America! Since 2011 continued communication with E-mails, updates, phone calls, and accomplishments, and the mountain of work has been shared with the U.S. Army.

All the Judge Advocates who have been stationed at Fort Knox since 2009 know of the Holt Home and the continued work here. It was not easy in the beginning to get the Judge Advocate's Office on board. The very first JA at Fort Knox to partner was COL Robert Cotell, now deceased, who came for a wreath-laying, said after much discussion how important it is for Fort Knox to partner with the Holt Home. He told me he, "wrote it in the books for his replacement to partner on the fourth Saturday of each September for a Wreath-Laying Ceremony at Judge Holt's monument during the Annual Holt Home Community Day." All the Staff JAGS since then continue to partner, which is amazing. They are volunteering on their day off without pay to drive to Breckinridge County to salute one of their own. And honoring Judge Holt is the reason for the celebration!

It is the small steps taken one at a time that turn into larger and better things. The Army appreciates hard work and determination and working to make things happen before asking for their help.

Meeting John W. Miller II Brigadier General, U.S. Army Commander in 2011 at the Judge Advocate General's Legal Center and School in his office before delivering the lecture also helped me listen to his words of much appreciated compliments. When the General told me of the medals he bought personally out of his own pocket and only gives to soldiers, he walked over to his desk and presented one to me. It was a day I will ALWAYS REMEMBER! It gave me a different outlook on the continued work and effort of restoration for the Holt Home.

Following the 5th George S. Prugh Lecture published in the Military Law Review in Spring of 2012 gave me much-needed confidence from this experience. This helped me to continue with passion and not to tire and to keep the quest new and fresh for those who find out about the Holt Home project.

Being the first non-Army woman to deliver the Prugh Lecture gave me the boost needed to continue as my role today is still to inspire and encourage others to assist in this most worthy project! Now, when the phone rings it continues to be exciting as it has always been. Being a volunteer has presented the opportunities to meet and work with the most distinguished citizens across our nation. I have met and am delighted to say these individuals know the Holt Project and they understand the work that caused the Holt Home to be saved for the ages!

First, I give all the credit to God because he is the leader. We just do the work. However, it takes more than work, and long hours, and lectures, and books written. It takes the people who can help to continue get the word out to foundations we are seeking, for private partnering, and continued grants, and for money in particular, which is always a challenge especially when our community is mostly agriculture. The Army's continued support is invaluable, with their kind words, presence and their support of bringing others to Judge Holt's home. We are looking forward to the day when the JAG School comes for a field trip to Judge Holt's home as it will be a beginning for a path for all the Army JAGs to follow - place all Army JAGS can call home. And what better place for a retreat, or professional development than the person who led the way for the future of the TJAGS.

Success is measured in the final product! The final product is the impact on our citizens historians, and the new uses for the historic Holt Home. In particular, one is to continue the efforts of making the Holt Home a National meeting place for all the Army JAGS across the nation. Yes, this is a big order. However, we must dream big here and with the continued partnering of the JAG school and all the JAGS who walk through the doors at The Judge Advocate General's Legal Center and School. We realize the JAGS have a place in their heart for Judge Holt. Hopefully, with all that has been done to bring back Judge Holt's legacy and his beloved home, the Army JAGS will continue to be an active part in assisting by being visible and returning to their beginning of one of the greatest JAGS in our nation's history who served President Lincoln.

Forever, I am grateful and thankful for the wonderful opportunity of bringing the JAGS to Kentucky to the home of one of their own and getting them involved with a very gratifying project that deserves the Army's presence. We salute the Army and are thankful for all they have done and continue to do. COL Fred Borch has been wonderful as he keeps the JAG School updated about what is happening in Breckinridge Co, KY. He has written numerous times in the Sword and Quill Publication. And special thanks to Captain Todd Wayne, a former student of COL Borch, for telling COL Borch about my book on Joseph Holt that became an invitation to deliver the lecture at the JAG School.

Delivering this lecture has given me more strength than I realized existed. However, God works in mysterious ways!

The Kentucky Heritage Council's Lifetime Partnership

The Kentucky Heritage Council/ State Preservation Office changes lives for communities that sometimes do not realize the treasures in their own back yard. They encourage local communities to take ownership and excel to preserve what is special to the locals.

Some of the citizens in Breckinridge County realized what a national treasure we had in the Judge Joseph Holt home. We just did not know how to begin the process, raise the money, get support, find the grants, write the grants, change the negatives to positives, get the community on board and interested, and get the word out across Kentucky and beyond!

Communities must take the initiative to contact the Kentucky Heritage Council to share their concerns, to ask for guidance, to seek help from the experts in preservation. Once doing this the long journey can begin. However, your community may encounter numerous rough bumps along the way like ours did, taking on a preservation project of saving the last official Kentucky Lincoln site in the Commonwealth. Don't expect the Kentucky Heritage Council to do the work for you! That is not their job. They guide you, encourage you, come to observe the situation you have whether it is getting your historical building on the National Register of Historical Places, or learning how to save what is special to you. They work with you and the process sometimes may be slower than you want it to be. However, taking time is necessary to restore your treasure the correct way the first time. This organization knows how the process works, and you will be glad to be guided by the best.

How did our community know what to do in the beginning? I asked questions, visited former Representative Dwight D. Butler, Senator

KY Heritage Council, State Preservation Office, on site. Diane Comer, P.R. and Mark Dennen, Executive Director.

Carroll Gibson, Congressman Ron Lewis' office, the office of Senator Mitch McConnell and attended preservation meetings across the state and held meeting in my home for all who would listen. This was not easy. After a visit from my local congressmen's field representative, Brittany Fausey, (now a lawyer) I was told to write The Department of the Interior with my concerns. After receiving my letter of concern about Judge Holt's home and expressing how this historical beauty was being neglected and left alone as the years passed, I received a reply from the department telling me to contact the Kentucky Heritage Council and speak with the Executive Director, David Morgan.

Letter writing has been a most important element in the Holt Project, and is almost a lost art today. It takes time to write letters. However, there is power is strong words spoken from the heart.

Judge Holt's home was on the National Register of Historical places thanks to a Breckinridge County teacher, Bill Thompson of McDaniel's, KY. Thompson worked diligently to get the

Friends open the Holt house for the Saturday Heritage Trail, 2 visitors, Paul Joseph O'Donoghue, Diane Comer, and Lee Stinnett.

Field visit to the Joseph Holt home by Friends members and the Kentucky Heritage Council. Pictures courtesy of the Kentucky Heritage Council, State Preservation Office.

home on the National Register in 1976. I did not realize that if a home is on the National Register it does not guarantee it will be taken care of in the future. In fact, the Holt Chapel built by Holt was torn down in 1986 because no one carried a torch to save it. I was not aware of this while I was in the middle of my teaching career and did not spearhead the Holt Project until 1997.

So much has been learned and much of it has been out of my comfort zone. Be assured all things done as a volunteer have been professional, lady like and sometimes very challenging.

The day David Morgan, Executive Director at the Kentucky Heritage Council phoned was an answer for help! Our community had never worked together to save a home and especially one of national significance. We had EVERYTHING to learn. I will always remember one of the first meetings held in my home, I asked David, "Who is going to purchase the home? "He said we will have to find an entity to do that." Next question was, "How are we going to purchase the home if the private owner will sell?" Mr. Morgan said "grants, it will be easy". Next question: who is going to write them? David said, "You are, it will be easy." And I believed every word.

To have someone listen to you and not turn you away gave me more courage and hope. With hope your faith gets stronger and the love you have for the project continues to grow. As the Bible states, faith, hope and love are the strongest things we have, but love is the strongest.

Love for the Holt Home has brought an unbelievable amount of work. However, when you love something so much it doesn't feel like work. It is therapy for your soul. To work with people who understand what preservation is, how it takes so much time makes the effort easier. And as former State Representative Dwight D. Butler has said, "money is always a problem."

The Kentucky Heritage Council not only became our number one source for help, but has guided our local community each step of the way. The advantages of having a lifetime partner is that you're doing restoration right the first time.

Sometimes in restoration the experts are not consulted and a home could be renovated but not be restored and brought back the way it was originally. And this is a sad occurrence. That is what can happen without the partnering of the state preservation office.

The Kentucky Heritage Council/ State Preservation Officer advised us to get an appraisal of the home, work on grants for stabilization, and for acquisition. An acquisition grant of $108,000 and another written for $50,000 made it possible for the Breckinridge County Fiscal Court to receive funds from the Kentucky Lincoln Bicentennial placed in the Kentucky Heritage Council/ Sate Preservation Office. The Holt home continued to be blessed by numerous sources in 2007. Preservation Kentucky helped get the Holt Home on the list of Most Endangered homes in Kentucky, and the Kentucky Lincoln Bicentennial Commission, another state partner, named the Holt Home a "Legacy Project of the Kentucky Lincoln Bicentennial." Both were powerful honors.

The Kentucky Historical Society, another state partner, also provided the Holt Home with an appraisal grant, and a stabilization grant. Kent Whitworth, the director, pointed out that "Saving the Joseph Holt House and its marvelous story are among the most significant legacy projects of the entire Lincoln Bicentennial!"

There are many people who have helped in some way with the project. However, without our state partners, Judge Holt's legacy with his restored Kentucky home would not have happened. With restoration doing things correctly is costly, sometimes twice the price! But when completed, we can be certain we did it right the first time.

During the appraisal for the Holt Home, Claude Galloway, historical appraiser, told and showed me where the Holt Home had original lightning rods. Galloway also pointed out where the Holt Home's circular drive way was before the construction of Highway 64, later changed to Kentucky Highway 144 when work began on Interstate I-64. During this process, the new road cut through the middle of the Holt grounds in the front of the home. What a shame!

All of this was shared with Executive Director, David Morgan. Not long after the appraisal and the appraisal grant, David moved to Washington D.C. My heart felt low as I wondered, "Could we do all that was in front of us? Could we do it without David's help?"

With David's retirement, I had him promise he would always help as a resource for the Holt Home and would not leave since this was HIS last project at the Kentucky Heritage Council as executive director. Because of his promise and efforts as a continuing resource, wonderful things continue happening for the Holt Home. Sometimes just an e-mail from him or to hear his voice of reassurance saying, "It will work out, we will find a way," really helps! "You are on the right path." He has been essential as he is a true friend of preservation, the Holt Home, and me. He is my mentor, and continues to send positive words when we need them the most!

With David's retirement, I would have to start all over again with someone new. But it is amazing when you call for help at the Heritage Council. The staff works hard and have numerous job descriptions. However, someone will direct you and help you if you and your organization help themselves. Then amazing things can happen.

With the Kentucky Lincoln Bicentennial and funding available for Kentucky Lincoln sites, it was a memorable era for Kentucky. Numerous locations across the state applied and received grants. It was tough competition.

I called Becky Shipp at the Kentucky Heritage Council and asked for assistance. Although she was very busy as the search continued for another executive director for the agency, Becky assisted with grant questions and writing and was available when I called for help. She and Dr. James C. Klotter both suggested using a wreath-laying ceremony as one of the main events to honor Judge Joseph Holt at the annual Holt Home Community Day. This was a wonderful idea, but I had to find a way to get a group to partner. This took work but it was worthwhile. Now the Friends of the Holt Home partner with the United States Army Cadet Commend and Fort Knox Office of the Staff Judge Advocate. This organization comes yearly to honor one of their own with a wreath-laying ceremony at Judge Holt's monument in the Holt family cemetery.

Becky along with former Breckinridge County Judge Executive Ray Powers, also attended meetings involving the purchase of the Holt Home. During Ms. Shipp's time as a consultant for the home, the Kentucky Heritage Council took its first field trip to the mansion with the entire staff. Mary Jean Atchison, a secretary stayed at the office to answer the phone and serve the people during this anticipated trip. Lindy Casebier, deputy secretary for Tourism, Arts and Heritage Council, made his first appearance and told me, "The stairs don't squeak when you walk on them." Members of the council were amazed. David Hall, historian from Bardstown, also was invited by the council to view the home that day. When asked how he compared the Holt Home to homes in Bardstown, he said, "We have nothing like this in Bardstown."

The grand lady as I call the Holt Home just needed love, grants, hard work, partnering and she would be grand once more.

This was a day to remember for the Holt Home! You can view the people in attendance that day on the www.jholt-houseky.org KET video on the home page.

At Becky Shipp's retirement party I wondered, "Now who will help?"

Not long afterward, Mark Dennen became the executive director and it was such a treat to work with Mark. I had become the go-between with county government and the council and worked behind the scenes as a volunteer, writing numerous grants for the Breckinridge County Fiscal Court.

The Friends began as a group working together as the Holt Home Steering Committee. A committee began its work with David Morgan. Then we worked as a committee of the local Breckinridge County Historical Society. We functioned in this manner until 2013 when the Friends needed to become a non-profit organization to work in a cooperative agreement with the Breckinridge County Fiscal Court.

A number of trips were made across Kentucky, especially for the Kentucky Lincoln site meetings in Frankfort and the Kentucky Lincoln Bicentennial Commission meetings from 2007-2010. The Kentucky Lincoln sites now have become a non-profit organization called the Kentucky Lincoln Heritage Trail Alliance (KLHTA), of which the Holt Home organization is also a member. This ties us to all the official Kentucky Lincolns sites in the Commonwealth. I serve on the board and have found this to be an enormous learning experience. It has also taken a lot of commitment and time to serve and bring back information to help support the KLHTA and the Holt Home.

Attending meetings helps place you in a network of many distinguished people and opportunities. What was learned has been used and friends made that have given enormous strength and growth to the Holt home project. This has taken an enormous number of hours, days and trips. However, work and learning makes your organization strong. When you surround yourself with wise people who have similar goals, this helps you increase knowledge about historical properties and you learn from the best. The Heritage Council staff also has attended KLHTA meetings from time to time.

Many times, people get excited, and work for a while and get tired and move on to something else, especially during times when there is not available funding. That is when you must stay stronger and unite your group to keep the focus on preservation and never give up! When funds are available and you receive grants people will get excited. When money sources are meager, you will find the true preservationists as they will work together to keep things moving. Remember, everyone is watching and you must stay strong as that is when the people will know you are for real, that you are serious about preservation.

Mark Dennen traveled to Breckinridge County numerous times for meetings along with Diane Comer, public relations specialist for the Kentucky Heritage Council/ State Preservation Office. Mark spoke at one of the Holt Home Community Days and was present often at the Kentucky Lincoln Bicentennial Commission meetings. With a massive project such as the Holt Home, we have had numerous obstacles to overcome, grants to find and grants to write.

One grant in particular comes to mind. We submitted a request three times before finally receiving it. And finally, writing the SAT the third time with the help of two experts to advise and assist, Diane Comer and Dana Beth Lyddan, the

SAT was won. Would you write a grant three times and spend several months pursuing it? You would if you are truly a preservationist. Sometimes, grants you do not receive make you work harder. However, I have been told that sometimes your grant application could not have been any better, but, in spite of your efforts, you did not win the grant. But you persevere and ALWAYS give your best!

After Mark Dennen's retirement Lindy Casebier became the acting executive director of the Kentucky Heritage Council. Lindy worked with the Friends in numerous ways. He attended meetings and spoke at several of the Holt Home Community Days. He answered questions and helped our rural community with many tasks. He gave encouragement when we had numerous hurdles to overcome without funding in the bank. Our community will always be grateful to Lindy. I have often called him seeking advice.

The power in a successful project is having wonderful Kentuckians working together as a team, searching for many ways how to be successful. Lindy always answered his calls and went once with me to speak to a very distinguished group. This materialized into good things.

Sometimes having someone put in a good word goes a long way. Your work can be measured, and will be. People learn who works and if you are working for your community, especially as a volunteer, the public will be willing to help.

The next Executive Director of the Kentucky Heritage Council was Craig Potts. His job was and is very demanding, as are all the preservation officer's positions. Numerous organizations and individuals across Kentucky call for help. It's rewarding to witness how local communities stand up for preservation, take leadership and work together with the Kentucky Heritage Council/ State Preservation Office to make it happen. During the years Craig Potts has spoken at numerous Holt Home Community Days. Craig attends preservation conferences, has numerous meetings, and carries a heavy load to give Kentucky the best possible plan to help communities like ours in rural Breckinridge County.

The Holt Home, and our community will forever be grateful for all those who have worked and continue to serve at the Kentucky Heritage Council.

For instance, Diane Comer has assisted us with answering questions and attending meetings. She also helped us get through the very first Holt Home Community Day, which was one of the most successful events of the Lincoln Bicentennial Celebration. Since 2006, Diane has assisted the Friends through many situations and events. She encouraged us to develop a website, get students involved and encouraged us to develop a non-profit organization. She has attended numerous Holt Home Community Days on her own time and continues to praise our rural community on the restoration efforts. We have been blessed with true preservationist who have guided us.

For all those at the Kentucky Heritage Council/ State Preservation Office who have assisted us, we are very grateful and have had remarkable success because of them and our other state partners. The Holt project definitely will be remembered as the community with little industry and big hearts and with people who were willing to join the team. Teamwork unites and gives strength that is sometimes unbelievable. All that has been involved in saving Judge Joseph Holt's home is unforgettable!

242nd JAG Birthday Celebration 101st Airborne Division of Fort Campbell, KY

The phone rang as we were planning a weekend getaway. Both my husband and I needed a break. The voice on the phone was Captain Todd Wayne, a specialist in the JA at Fort Campbell, Kentucky. Captain Wayne called to see if I would be the Special Guest speaker for the 242nd Birthday of the Army JAG Corp. He shared the JAGS would like for me to speak 30 minutes and then they would have a recognition of soldiers and end with a cake cutting ceremony.

Captain Wayne said, "We know you are the authority on Brigadier General Joseph Holt and would love for you to come here and speak." Captain Wayne said I would need to send speaking points before coming.

I explained being asked to be the Special Guest speaker was such an honor and with such a distinguished audience there, this was short notice, that normally I like at least one month in advance to prepare my thoughts. He continued to explain how busy every one of the JAGS had been. I told him I would love to accept however, I would think about it over the weekend and let him know for sure on Monday.

Captain Wayne shared that General Dana K. Chipman, the 38th TJAG spoke two weeks earlier and he had the same notice.

The weekend trip was amazing at French Lick Resort and West Baden as we also took my mother with us. Quiet time with freedom from labor of multi-tasking with the Holt project was relaxing and much needed, as the continued work is non-stop! Being a volunteer for a non-profit organization has many duties with new challenges along with opportunities presented.

During the weekend from time to time the thought persisted in my husband's and editor's opinion to go and speak. All speeches for Judge Holt's legacy, the Holt Home project, and *Lincoln's Advocate* present opportunities — of meeting new people, continuing the circle of connections for possibilities of partnering, grant opportunities, getting the word out beyond Kentucky of the restoration of the Holt Home, and networking with distinguished scholars who have exceptional expertise and connections.

Tour of the Air Assault School by Col. Marton

A project such as saving and restoring a national treasure has a strong empowering effect.

Monday soon came and decision time was at hand. Before leaving on Friday for the short retreat I called Ed Ford, my editor and he said, "Susan, you need to do this." Ed and I had planned to work together July 26-29 to complete details for the upcoming book and he had already rescheduled numerous appointments to come to Breckinridge Co.

Listening to a mentor like Ed Ford is very powerful especially from one who has had such a brilliant career. My heart felt I should accept the invitation and my mind thought different as

I understand the challenge of presenting a speech to such scholars as the 101 Airborne Division (Air Assault) JAG Office and the eminent audience.

Sitting in my study I drafted ten speaking points I thought the JAGS would enjoy and appreciate. Courage took hold of me again, and I phoned Captain Wayne explaining I would be glad to accept if the speaking points were acceptable. The e-mail with speaking points was sent and Captain Wayne's reply was "this will be great!"

Now the work began! Only ten days to prepare a distinguished speech for the Judge Advocate's Office! Monday flew fast while speech writing began. Writing by hand, typing, cutting, pasting, and composing a speech from the heart, which is the only way I deliver a talk. That evening I tried out the draft on my husband. He said, "This is really good!"

Ten days to polish the speech and deliver like telling a story. Eighteen hours of practice went into a twenty-minute speech with Q&A at the end. The first four days were exhausting with practice. However, with each practice the talk was coming together and the objective was to intrigue the audience, to share the story where everyone including children of officers would want to know more.

When giving a speech you must consider your audience, who they are, their educational interest, and include them in your talk sharing thoughts reaching them by being real. If you have their attention and their interest they will remember you and remember your cause!

My husband and I went the evening before the speech as it was a three-hour drive each way. Rest is important before giving a speech. We left around 2:00 p.m. and took our time driving the back roads to Fort Campbell; stayed at a nice hotel and enjoyed time together.

Shortly after accepting the invitation to speak for the 242nd JAG birthday party I phoned our former pastor Rev. Janet Carden and asked for her prayers for God to send me his thoughts. I would do the work, prepare and give my best! I also phoned my minster Rev. Rebecca Heid and asked for her prayers. My family prayed as well.

With prayers, you can feel God's presence and for this talk I could feel him beside me. I was not nervous, and spoke from my heart. Something many are not aware of is when I give a speech like this it takes a day or two to gain my energy back again. The reason is my heart and soul is in the talk!

Before speaking, a display of posters were placed around the Sportsman's Lodge at Fort Campbell. Using newspaper clippings, and magazines along with pictures and notes written by other, it told the story of how Holt's legacy and restoration of his home has occurred over the last two decades. The display also showed the courage, changing negatives into positives, never giving up, and with God leading you, anything is possible.

Invited guests enjoyed the buffet at The Smokehaus before the speech. Captain Todd Wayne and his wife Kendel ate with my husband and me along with COL Marton and his wife.

COL Marton gave the introduction slow and strong as I listened. I thought of the work it had taken to get here. The room was quiet, without a sound. I slowly walked with a smile to the lectern to deliver the speech for the 242nd Birthday of the Army JAG Corps.

The expressions on all the faces were sincere. Throughout the speech there were smiles and laughs. I could feel the audience was with me, they could feel my thoughts and words! After completing the talk COL Marton and his wife stood and everyone else followed. Receiving a standing ovation was heartwarming and with God answering the prayers I had delivered what the JAGS wanted.

After completing the speech, COL Marton addressed the question and answer portion. The audience asked numerous questions and answers were given.

Following this COL Marton asked me to come back to the lectern and presented a plaque thanking me for being the Guest speaker for the 242nd JAG Corps Birthday Celebration for the 101st Airborne Division (Air Assault) Fort Campbell,

Kentucky, for sharing my unique perspective on the history of the JAG Corp with them. He said my commitment to honoring the legacy of General Joseph Holt is an inspiration to their office and the entire U.S. Army JAG Corps. For a most wonderful surprise, COL Marton, Staff Judge Advocate, presented me a coin medal from the "Eagle Justice" from the Staff Judge Advocate 101st Airborne Division (Air Assault) Bring IT! This is usually only given to solders! Wow!

To be given compliments from the U.S. Army JAG Corps is a recognition that will always be remembered especially when others ask, "Do you ever get tired?"

Persistence, professionalism, passion, and changing negatives into positives when circumstances at many times have seemed overwhelming keeps you going! Numerous challenges made me work harder to carry the torch for the dream God placed on my heart. This has been the most difficult task in my lifetime to teach preservation to our community and what grants are, how they work and how to save Judge Holt's home with the help of many wonderful Kentuckians including the Kentucky Heritage Council/ State Preservation Office, our lifetime partner.

Continued prayer is sent to God for he is the leader of the Holt project. Now, that reality is happening, the Holt Home will soon be completely restored and others can now visualize the dream of 20 years ago.

Col. Marton gave a plaque and metal to the guest speaker.

Private Analuisa Ramolete, paralegal specialist, 96th Aviation Support Battalion, 101st Combat Aviation Brigade, 101st Airborne Division, Col. Andras Marton, staff judge advocate, 101st Airborne Division and Fort Campbell, and Susan Dyer, guest speaker and author of Lincoln's Advocate: The Life of Judge Joseph Holt, *prepare to cut the United States Army Judge Advocates Corps 242nd anniversary cake during a July 27th ceremony.*

When COL Matron told his entire JAG team he had now met his match and had found someone who had as much passion for the U.S. Army JAGS as he did and would not take no for an answer, but she did not even wear a uniform — these were some of the kindest words ever spoken to me by anyone with the Holt Project. This day will forever be pressed in my heart as I felt the closest ever to the U.S. Army JAG Corps! The touch of the medal will keep the memory strong for future challenges!

Finally, after the Birthday celebration COL Marton voiced he was going to try his best to visit the Holt Home on September 23, 2017 at the 9th Annual Holt Home Community Day. Hopefully, soon the 101st Airborne Division (Air Assault) Judge Advocates' Office will visit the historic Holt Home and grounds.

Lastly, my husband and I were given a private tour of Fort Campbell by COL Andras M. Marton, Staff Judge Advocate and Todd A. Wayne, Client Services, Office of the Staff Judge Advocate. Another step toward making the Holt Home a National meeting place for all the Army JAGS across the nation!

Friends of Holt at a Glance

The **Holt Home** and surrounding 19.5 acres were acquired by the county in 2008 through a Kentucky Heritage Council Preservation Grant, funded by the Kentucky Abraham Lincoln Bicentennial Commission, which designated acquisition of the Holt home as a Legacy Project. The home dates to the 1850's, and the site includes a cemetery where Holt and family members are buried.

The Kentucky Abraham Lincoln Commission worked together in a wonderful nonpartisan alliance; former Senator Dan Kelly Co-chair worked diligently to get funding for this most honorable celebration of the 200th anniversary of President Lincoln's birth along with Co-Chair Judge Tommy Turner who also served on the national Abraham Lincoln Bicentennial Commission where everyone worked together. Wonderful accomplishments were made. Many communities across the Commonwealth received funding for Lincoln connections to the 16th President.

At the time of the purchase of the Holt home it had been vacant for over 40 years. Today, exterior preservation is well under way via grants secured by Friends of the Holt Home, Inc. and Breckinridge County Fiscal Court, including two $500,000 federal Transportation Enhancement (TE) grants, a $150,000 Save America's Treasures grant that was mostly matched with volunteer time, along with other grants.

The Kentucky Abraham Lincoln Bicentennial began on June 20, 2005 and ended on June 30, 2010. During this time the Kentucky Abraham Lincoln Bicentennial Commission had many duties to study and recommend activities that would be carried out by the Commonwealth of Kentucky to honor Abraham Lincoln on the bicentennial anniversary of his birth. The Commission educated Kentucky residents and the nation about the life of Abraham Lincoln during the years he resided in and visited the state where he was born. The members of the Commission assisted local governments and organizations with planning, preparation, and grant applications for bicentennial events and projects. The group coordinated federal, state, and local bicentennial activities occurring throughout Kentucky. The Commission also planned and implemented appropriate events including celebrations and educational initiatives to commemorate the bicentennial. The commission and advisory committee helped perform other duties as necessary to help highlight Kentucky's role in the life of Abraham Lincoln and seek federal grants and philanthropic support for bicentennial activities.

During the years of the Kentucky Lincoln Bicentennial Commission meetings I was advised by the Kentucky Heritage Council/ State Preservation Office to work with county government as a go-between with the Kentucky Heritage Council/ State Preservation Office. This volunteer role/ job consisted of forming the Holt House Steering Committee, holding meetings, organizing meetings, attending every Kentucky Lincoln Bicentennial Commission meeting in Frankfort every three months beginning in 2007-2010 and bringing back information to my community, paying my own way and expenses along with writing grants as a volunteer.

I tried to get others to go with me to learn during this time. However, one event was done solo. I was invited to the Kentucky Lincoln Bicentennial Commission meetings by Kentucky State Senator Carroll Gibson, Co-Chair Tommy Turner and David L. Morgan, Executive Director at the Kentucky Heritage Council/ State Preservation Office, and by Warren Greer, the Program Coordinator of the Abraham Lincoln Bicentennial Commission whom I had met earlier at the 2006 Kentucky State Preservation Conference in Covington where we had both spoken. Warren had spoken about the upcoming Kentucky Abraham Lincoln Bicentennial celebration. I had spoken about the grassroots effort of saving the Holt Home.

Much was learned from attending these meetings and I learned about the possible grant opportunities. Since the Abraham Lincoln Bicentennial Commission named the Holt Home a Legacy Project there was an opportunity to submit a grant through the Heritage Council / State Preservation Office, which was submitted and written for the Breckinridge County Fiscal Court. This grant was submitted with assistance from Becky Shipp who at that time was at the Kentucky Heritage Council. It was remarkable news that the grant was won for the county government. However, before that could happen I had to organize a community meeting, and get the Fiscal Court to agree to be the entity for the ownership of the historic Holt Home. This was successful with the help of Breckinridge County Judge Executive Ray Powers, Executive Director at the Kentucky Heritage Council State Preservation Office, David L. Morgan, and the Holt House Steering Committee, which helped guide the direction for the entity that would purchase the Holt Home.

The Breckinridge County Fiscal Court won a grant through the Kentucky Heritage Council/ State Preservation Office. They had the funding thought necessary for the acquisition and purchase of the historic home. However, they did not own the home on February 12, in 2007 when they received the first grant of $108,000 for purchase through the Kentucky Lincoln Bicentennial when the home became an official Lincoln site in the Commonwealth. During this time the Preservation Officer at the Heritage Council, David Morgan, suggested for the Holt House Steering Committee to continue to meet, which we did. Members from four state agencies met at my home and then in the Fiscal Court room. During this time the grant of $108,000 was about to expire while the county was negotiating to buy the home. Not wanting to lose the grant I called Becky Shipp and asked what do we need to do? Ms. Shipp suggested doing an extension on the grant, which I did.

The Holt House Steering Committee decided to have an appraisal of the home in late October of 2006 which is written about in this book, and two appraisals had to be done as the first was not high enough to make the guardian of the private owner an offer. The guardian of the private owner had an additional appraisal done in the Louisville area making a third appraisal. This appraisal was of an historic home already restored, (not the historic Holt Home.) Now with the third appraisal, the Breckinridge County Fiscal Court did not have enough grant money to make an offer to buy the home.

I called the Kentucky Heritage Council seeking help and they advised me to submit another grant for the Holt Home. I submitted the second grant and Breckinridge County Fiscal Court received $50,000. Putting the two grants together county government had enough money to make an offer to purchase the home. The offer was made, and the rest is history. The Breckinridge County Fiscal Court became the entity for the Holt Home.

Not long after the purchase on December 5, 2008 we endured a terrible ice storm and parts of 22 windows of the Holt Home were broken with rain coming in the home. The Kentucky Lincoln Bicentennial Commission meetings continued, and I was asked to speak often thanks to Co-Chair Judge Tommy Turner. In giving my updated reports, I told of the grave condition of the historic Holt Home crying for help. I remember so strong saying, "It is raining in the Holt Home. It is ruining the floors. I cannot sleep at night for when I awake with rain hitting my window pane I think of how it is also raining in the Holt Home, which is breaking my heart, and we need help! My concern was heard and not long after that day, pleading for help in front of Kentucky's finest citizens the Kentucky Historical Society, another state partner assisted. A grant was won through the Kentucky Abraham Lincoln Bicentennial Commission placed in the Kentucky Historical Society for stabilization of Judge Holt's home. The threatening elements were stopped. Rain and snow was not falling into the beautiful home any longer.

Friends of the Holt Home began as a grassroots effort in 1997 through my work as a volunteer as I sought to bring recognition to preserve the home of Judge Joseph Holt (1807-1894). Holt, as mentioned earlier, was a prominent Kentucky attorney who served as Commissioner of Patents, Postmaster General and Secretary of War under President James Buchanan, and as Judge Advocate General (TJAG) of the Union Army under President Abraham Lincoln, a role in which he served as chief prosecutor in the trial of conspirators accused of Lincoln's assassination.

When the Kentucky General Assembly announced plans to form a Kentucky Abraham Lincoln Bicentennial Commission, Joseph Holt's home was identified as a site to be included in the planning, because of Holt's strong connection to Lincoln. Representatives from Breckinridge County were invited to commission meetings from 2006 through 2009. During this time I, along with others, advocated preserving the home, having been vacant since 1969 but still structurally viable.

Numerous presentations were given before the commission and other groups across the state and by me, who was also an invited speaker at the 2006 Kentucky Historic Preservation Conference. I published a biography about Holt, wrote grants and worked closely with the county and others to help create momentum for rehabilitating the home and restoring it to service for the community.

The home and surrounding 19.5 acres were acquired by Breckinridge County Fiscal Court in December 2008 for $158,000 through a Kentucky Heritage Council Lincoln Preservation Grant, funded through the Lincoln Bicentennial Commission, which also designated restoration of the home as a Legacy Project of the bicentennial. After the time of purchase, the Holt House Steering Committee met normally every three months with state partners attending. The Kentucky Heritage Council State Preservation Office suggested that we form a Friends group as a committee under the local Breckinridge County Historical Society. We worked as an umbrella under the local historical Society until it became necessary to form our own organization and The Friends became an official 501 (C)3 on August 29, 2013. We continue to work in a cooperative agreement with Breckinridge County Fiscal Court on raising funds and rehabilitating the home seeking to bring attention to Holt's life and contributions to our Commonwealth and nation restoring his Kentucky home.

The Friends organization is made up of ALL volunteers and we have a wonderful team of individuals who bring talents to the organization as we work together as a great team! As of this writing the members of the Friends of the Holt Home are: Breckinridge County Judge Executive Maurice Lucas who assists with tours of special guests; students, the Army and dignitaries, who make sure the grounds are meticulously kept and groomed. We all work with our life-time partner, the Kentucky Heritage Council/ State Historic Preservation Office who guides all things for the Holt project.

Kathina Bell, the judge's assistant attends meetings. She, along with the judge, works with the Kentucky Heritage Council making sure all the project is done with state guidelines. She completes the final program for the Holt Home Community Day, keeps the record of volunteer hours for matching grants and final reports along with all the paper work required for Fiscal Court relating to the Holt Home. And Kathina takes the minutes when the secretary is absent as numerous other tasks.

Charlie Corbet is one of the directors who has helped with a county-wide fundraising effort. This became necessary as we were told by the Kentucky Transportation Cabinet we needed to raise money to assist with matching grants. Charlie also continues to be a mover and shaker in assisting with numerous activities. He has also helped make the Holt grounds a place we are all proud of, using fundraising money along with grants to improve the grounds with nice items for the service to the people, like new picnic tables and a new flagpole along with flags. Charlie continues to help with the task of fund raising as most all the donations received go for preservation and matching grants as none of the Friends receive a salary.

Paul Joseph O'Donoghue was encouraged to join this team and helps us select the correct period music. Being a retired music teacher, he continues to help bring local musicians such as the Breckinridge County Band and the Breckinridge County Chamber Singers to perform on the Holt Home Community Day.

Paul Joseph, a lifetime scholar of trees, has an essential role in watching over the Holt grounds as it has such a great variety of trees, some from Judge Holt's era. Paul Joseph has given tree tours and continues to grow trees yearly to sell at the Holt Home Community Day. Mr. O'Donoghue also is the watch dog for caring for the trees on the Holt grounds. No one makes a move about anything concerning trees before consulting Paul Joseph, and he also helped the Friends with the restoration of the Holt fence.

Veronica Ent, another director, performs numerous tasks. She always helps with the planning for Army events at the home and helps support through the Breckinridge County Tourism. When it is time to plan the Student Day in September, Veronica contacts the GT students at the Breckinridge County High School and makes sure they are trained to conduct tours for the 5th Grade Student Day and the yearly Holt Home Community Day. Veronica enables the Friends to hold their meetings in the Chamber of Commerce until the Holt Home is complete. Each year Veronica helps in numerous ways to make sure the Holt Home Community Day is classic and ready to go.

Judge Kelly Easton, another director, is also a district judge who helps provide possibilities of what the Friends could and can do legally correct. Judge Easton assisted in revising the Holt Gift of Deed when a person wants a document saying they have donated a gift to the Friends of the Holt Home, Inc. (We also deeply appreciate John Nyberg for letting the Friends use his idea for the document of a gift, insuring it fits the needs for the Friends.) Judge Easton helped the Friends secure Dr. Phillip Mink's contact with the University of Kentucky in helping us get the Holt Family Cemetery radar testing completed. In addition, Judge Easton portrays Judge Joseph Holt at the annual Holt Home Community Day each September.

Sherry Stith, has been the Secretary and Treasurer since the beginning of the Friends organization. Her job is important in keeping the history of the organization correct, along with balancing the Friends' check book and paying the bills. Sherry has assisted in cleaning the historic home numerous times for the Holt Home Community Day. She has had an active part in the participation of the Boys Scouts Troop in bringing in the Colors and presenting the flag at Holt Home Community Days. Sherry manages the donation table at the yearly event, which is so very important, since the organization appreciates all donations. Sherry delivers free lunch tokens to individuals who travel a long distance and volunteers at the Holt Home Community Day, and manages the e-mails from the Friend's website.

Cleo Lee, a newly added director, comes to the Friends with much experience with the public. Cleo supports the work of the Friends with her presence, personal donations when sudden expenses occur that need immediate attention but are not in the budget. Cleo assists in preparing for the Holt Home Community Day and recently received a donation for the Friends for a nice shop vacuum to prepare the Holt Home for the Community Day.

My job as volunteer, President of the Friends of the Holt Home, Inc., involves on average 20-25 hours a week. The job description covers grant writing, writing and answering e-mails, planning the Holt Home Community Day (with help from the Friends), reconnecting with individuals who have been essential in the restoration of the Holt home, delivering lectures and speeches (regionally, state, and nationally) about Holt's career and the restoration of his home, keeping in touch with the JAG School and the TJAGS at the Pentagon and the United States Army, writing articles for the events of the Holt Home and continuing to take pictures and write captions for the webmaster page, calling about, writing and submitting articles promoting all events and the Holt Home Community Day, appearing on television and radio promoting Holt's legacy and home, representing the Holt Home on the board of the Kentucky Lincoln Heritage Trail Alliance, taking care of furniture and items donated for the home, giving private tours, and completing the follow-up book on how the historic Holt Home has been saved. Basically, this job has been doing anything lady like and professional that has contributed to the success of saving the Holt Home and bringing back Judge Holt's legacy along with continuing to carry the torch, and turn all negatives into positives. And all this can be done with God as your leader and having a magnificent team! For team work and faith are the keys to success!

The first (TE) grant funded exterior restoration including a new roof and masonry repairs, restoring the chimneys, putting back lightening rod protection because appraiser Claude Galloway indicated that homes of this type were prone to lightning strikes. Front and back windows were restored inside and out excluding the built-on kitchen, not original to the home, but old enough to be considered historical. A decision was made by the Friends of the Holt Home to have the original, wavy glass placed on the first floor of the home.

The second (TE) grant received in 2015 will be used for restoration on the front twin entrances, the front porch including cast iron works. The home received a $199,000 tax credits (same as cash) from life-time partners with the Kentucky Heritage Council/ State Preservation Office in 2015 to continue restoration. The tax credits will be used for service of rest rooms and restoration of the kitchen not original to the home but old enough to be historical. In 2015 the Friends received a grant from the National Trust for Historic Preservation for a site-use plan of what the home will become.

The Friends group is working in partnership with the home's owner, Breckinridge County Fiscal Court, to raise funds, secure the home's status as a viable and treasured historic landmark, and bring together all interested people, and organizations. Friends of the Holt Home, Inc. is a non-profit organization formed in 2013 dedicated to preserving and rehabilitating, along with state and federal agencies to work toward opening the home to the public and ensuring its long-term operation. Visit www.jholt-houseky.org

The Friends of the Holt Home have pursued state and federal grants and grant matches, and created special events including a local fundraising campaign. Since 2009, volunteers have sponsored an annual Holt Home Community Day at the site, which draws hundreds of people for tours, period music and project updates. The organization continues to work with Kimberly Nyberg, Consultant to assist with the community and Friends to complete a planning process to articulate a final vision for how the home and site will be used. We know it will have numerous uses for the region, state and nation.

Friends of Holt continue to grow for with passion and vision people want to be a part of preserving an important story of our American history. We now need many torch carriers, continued partnering with state agencies, foundations and private investment along with the continued support of the locals whom have given ALL THEY HAVE TO SAVE AND RESTORE Holt's legacy!

Judge Holt's Legacy Lives Again

Judge Holt's legacy lives again! How does a legacy return that was suppressed for over a century and a half? How is a national treasure on the Register of Historic Places saved, and restored to its former glory when it was the show place of Breckinridge County?

"Over two hundred years ago Joseph Holt was born, and over two hundred years have passed. Great occurrences have progressed in history. Leaders and successors have brought both pain and strength, allowing our country to proceed into today's destiny."

To progress with great dignity, people must first understand, appreciate, protect, and carry the past in their hearts! It is only fair to speak of every man's story to get the truth, sometimes lost in the heart and soul of those who fought as well as lived to preserve a wholesome way of life and strive for goodness over evil and power.

Searching the records, scouring the archives and unveilng the past, show Judge Holt's work still encourages the nation to stand for its beliefs, to work together instead of dividing our power, to unite the nation to work for a solution, to heal a nation by joining our talents, continuing the good works the world needs.

The centuries have past. And the inscriptions on Judge Holt's monument display his significance in America's national history. It is unique to have Judge Joseph Holt buried on the grounds of the Holt Home property, the only place he ever really loved and the only place he ever called HOME!"

Vision is the key for a legacy to be reborn. Believing in something that could not be seen in 1997 when things appeared in grave condition, without funding, without support of a gracious team, without the deed to the property, without resources, and the circle of wonderful Kentuckians, state agencies, the U.S. Army and partnering of local community, state and nation.

Having faith, "keeping the faith" as Lindy Casebier has always told me, praying for direction, guidance and following God's will, knowing it is all possible, is how a legacy is reborn! First, you must believe yourself, and then carry the touch. When God puts something on your heart and you have the passion to follow his will,

Historic Holt home, 1890's. Lady believed to be Vanna Holt, wife of Washington D. Holt, Judge Holt's nephew. Courtesy of Margaret Rose Badger, great-great niece of Judge Joseph Holt.

Front view of the Holt home with deer grazing, 1890's. Courtesy of Margaret Rose Badger, great-great niece of Judge Joseph Holt.

The Holt Grounds, 1890's. Courtesy of Margaret Rose Badger, great-great niece of Judge Joseph Holt.

he will guide you. In the case of saving the Holt Home it has taken more work than most would do! Your spirit must stay strong, not tiring, and you will work until there is a team, until others believe in your cause. For it takes a commuity of like-minded champions, a nation, and a calling higher than the enormous obstacles you must overcome to climb that mountain.

The yellow-covered moss that embraced the red brick Holt Family Cemetery encasing the grave yard of seven family members, for so long sealed with a black gate and rusty chain surrounded by walls with huge crevasses has been restored by the Holt Family Trust. Unaware of the grave condition of the family cemetery, they were contacted and became impressed with the work to preserve Joseph Holt's home. The Holt Family Trust has graciously transferred the ownership to the Friends of the Holt Home, Inc. for lifetime care!

The Holt Home is about 200 yards from the Holt Family Cemetery. In the beginning of the restoration it was difficult to see the beauty of the Holt Home as two non-historical buildings, a decaying Jim Walters home from the 60's and a garage, blocked the beautiful view to what the Holt grounds originally looked like. But it is now back to its original state. The Kentucky Heritage Council/ State Preservation Office, a silent but essential partner continues guiding the correct way to bring back the Holt home to the prominent years when Judge Holt served three presidents with national positions by his service in Washington City.

Holt's own words, "It is encouraging to know that behind every cloud the sun still shineth, that if we are patient every cloud will see it light again" perfectly tells the story of how Holt's legacy has been brought back. Holt's own words speak to us today in the 21 Century saying, with vision, hope and thinking it is possible to restore a national treasure and bring back Holt's distinguished works. The possibility is always there. When we work diligently with patience and guidance our dreams are possible! However, if we had let the negative rule our hearts, and quit when told there is not a thing we can do to help, there would be a sign at the site in the future saying, "This is where Judge Joseph Holt's home once stood." However, 20 years later all the hard work is paying off and visitors can now walk the grounds, tracing footsteps of our most famous son, who became Brigadier General during the Civil War serving President Abraham Lincoln as his TJAG of the U.S. Army.

Visiting the Library of Congress today in person or online researchers will continue learning how President Lincoln chose Joseph Holt for his TJAG because Joseph Holt was a nationally famous lawyer. Dr. James C. Klotter, The State Historian of Kentucky and Professor of History has stated numerous times, "everyone across America knew the name Joseph Holt during the Civil War." Lincoln needed the most qualified and intelligent lawyer to advise him and the United States Army during one of the most critical times our nation has ever experienced, one that threatened the very existence of our nation.

The Holt project did not happen overnight. We did not make partners quickly. Everything has been done by the book, with patience, and professionalism, overcoming obstacles, turning all negatives into positives as former Kentucky State Representative Dwight D. Butler has stated numerous times, "If you want this project to be successful then you will turn ALL negatives into positive work." My response in the beginning, "I don't know if I can do that," has changed into, "What an exciting time for the Judge Joseph Holt Home."

Even for those who did not believe this project could happen, together with those who have given their hearts and a huge part of their lives for something greater than themselves, Judge Holt would be proud of his community for finally giving him the recognition he deserves. We have paved the path for historians of the future to make Judge Holt's last wish come true for his family to celebrate the centennial celebration of the Holt Plantation in 1911 and for the land to always stay in the family, with perhaps even better outcomes than Judge Holt might have imagined. For not only his family, and Holt's relatives still living in America today, but for the country to understand the military history and national significance of the Life of Lincoln's Advocate, Judge Joseph Holt will be recognized and celebrated at his beloved Kentucky home. Holt's legacy is alive once more! And it is not too late to get involved.

The people and the United States Army are now Judge Holt's family and we are celebrating the rebirth of Judge Holt's legacy and his home as it will have local, regional, state and national uses for the people because Holt Home is "The Peoples' home" as Judge Holt himself would have wanted. It belongs to America and our national history!

Now that the Holt Home has been saved, and restoration is in full swing after almost two decades of gaining partners, winning grants and bringing Joseph Holt's importance back to Kentucky and America, visitors who come will be able to study and carefully examine history, learning about Joseph Holt, how he worked, and helped keep our nation strong and united. Citizens will learn how the people of the past and people of present day work to learn the mistakes of history, and hopefully, will not make them again.

The strength of knowledge, the truth tested over time makes us stronger. Visitors will continue to be amazed at the wonderful legacy of Joseph Holt and how he is admired by the U.S. Army still today and how he is compared with today's Army as Holt led the way for the Judge Advocates. President Lincoln's family deeply appreciated what Joseph Holt did after President Lincoln's assassination. For there is a letter that hangs today in the Executive Suite of the TJAG office at the Pentagon that I had the privilege of viewing on my invited visit to meet General Darpino on May 5, 2017. Lincoln's family wrote the letter to Joseph Holt and thanked him for all he did during the Lincoln Conspiracy Trial where Holt presided as the prosecuting judge.

It is long overdue that Joseph Holt be remembered and honored as a brave patriot of our nation. He stood up for what he believed as his family was torn apart, along with our nation. Holt believed in something more than his personal wealth, he believed in the future of his country. He did all that was possible to stand up and keep Kentucky in the union. After the Civil War Holt worked for the rest of his life for the rights of all citizens including former slaves. Judge Holt did not want the state he loved to not have protection by the federal government. Without Joseph Holt, President Abraham Lincoln would not have been as successful. Lincoln believed in Joseph Holt and his gifted mind. I have been told numerous times by the United States Army JAGS of today Joseph Holt's spirit is surely smiling down on the work of bringing back Holt's legacy and restoring his beloved home.

Because of God we have witnessed a miracle in rural Breckinridge County, KY as a national treasure has been saved. The restoration of Judge Holt's home is more than restoring an OLD HOUSE. It is not only the restoration of a structure, a home with national significance but the restoration of the last official Kentucky Lincoln site in the Commonwealth, of the "only home in America today that tells the complete story of the Lincoln Conspiracy Trial", said David L. Morgan. It also preserves Joseph Holt's legacy in the story of "My Heart of Hearts!" as Judge Holt signed his letters to both wives — Mary Harrison Holt and Margaret Wickliffe Holt.

Believe in your dreams! But much work goes into them! Many of us believed in the dream to save and restore the Holt Home — and now, it is, and always will be, an American National Treasure in our own back yard! The Friends of Holt Home invite you to come to Holt, KY and view for yourself, "My Heart of Hearts!"

Appendix

Holt House Commission Accomplishments 2006-2010

1. On February 15, 2006 a public meeting was held in Breckinridge Co. to inform the community possibilities available with the connection of Judge Joseph Holt and his home in Breckinridge County identified by the Kentucky Lincoln Bicentennial Commission.
2. The Kentucky Heritage Council/ State Preservation Officer, David Morgan presented information about possible grants through the Kentucky Lincoln Bicentennial, and Susan Dyer, volunteer, briefed the audience about Joseph Holt, his career, national, state, and local connection, and his contributions to the nation.
3. The Holt House Commission was formed to work with guidelines from the Kentucky Heritage Council/ State Preservation Office in regards of negotiating with the private owner of the Holt House, Louise Doda/ guardian Kevin Ford.
4. Preservation Kentucky selected the Judge Joseph Holt House as one of the 2006 Most Endangered Historic Places in Kentucky.
5. Heritage Council's David Morgan contacted the guardian, and the guardian was open to a proposal to sell the Holt House.
6. The Holt House Commission met on June 29, 2006 deciding who would buy the Holt House? What the price would be? The logical way to purchase? How to reach agreement for the offer? How would the project be put together?
7. A proposal letter was sent to the guardian on August 21, 2006 from Breckinridge County Judge George Monarch III with a partnership with the Kentucky Heritage Council/ State's Preservation Officer and Executive Director David Morgan.
8. The Holt House Commission received a response from guardian Kevin Ford on September 25, 2006 saying he would welcome a proposal for the amount of property that is to be purchased and the specific price.
9. Susan Dyer shared information from E-mails and phone calls from Judge Tommy Turner, co-chair of the Kentucky Lincoln Bicentennial Commission, with the Holt House Commission about the May 11, 2006 meeting of the Commission in Frankfort. This concerned approval of their budget for the next two years. The Commission placed $670,000 in the Heritage Council for preservation of such properties as the Holt House.
10. Susan Dyer, community volunteer for Breckinridge County, was an invited speaker at the 2006 Kentucky Historic Preservation Conference on September 30, 2006 in Covington. The speech gave a perspective of work and interest with Judge Joseph Holt, his home in Breckinridge County, Lincoln ties and grass root efforts to preserve the Holt House.
11. With continued communication with Judge Tommy Turner, Susan Dyer asked for help to find a way to pay for the appraisal of the Holt House. She contacted Chris Goodlett of the Kentucky Historical Society seeking information about mini-grants to pay for the appraisal.
12. Susan Dyer submitted an application for a grant through the statewide funds through the Kentucky Historical Society's Abraham Lincoln Bicentennial with letters of support mailed on November 9, 2006 to the Kentucky Historical Society. The effort sought a matching grant of $2,5000 to pay the historical appraiser.
13. Local appraiser Beck Ruskowski located an historical appraiser. Claude Galloway from Mayfield was contacted to see if he would do the appraisal for the Holt House Commission and wait several months to receive money for his work.
14. Permission was granted by Kevin Ford for Claude Galloway, historical appraiser, to conduct an appraisal of the Holt House and desired twenty-five acres on October 23, 2006.
15. Susan Dyer attended The Lincoln Bicentennial Commission Meeting on November 13, 2006 in Frankfort, and was asked to report efforts on trying to save the Holt House.
16. The Holt House Commission met on November 20, 2006 to evaluate the appraisal.
17. The low appraisal of $60,000 for twenty-five acres and the Holt House was too low to make the family an offer. A re-evaluation of the 25 acres and house was done with the value increased to $108,000.
18. January 4, 2007 Susan Dyer made a visit to meet Larry Cox, State Director for Senator Mitch McConnell. She asked for assistance from the office

for connections to contribute to this massive project. A booklet of the Holt House Commission's accomplishments of 2006, information about Judge Holt, his home, and his contributions to the nation were discussed.

19. On January 6, 2007 a beautiful red wreath was placed on the gate to the graveyard of the Holt Family Cemetery to honor Judge Holt on his 200th birthday.
20. A short speech was given honoring Judge Holt for the dedication he gave our nation without any fanfares or parades.
21. Breckinridge County Judge Executive Ray Powers met in person with Kevin Ford, guardian of Mrs. Doda, on January 15, 2007. Judge Powers made the offer to purchase the twenty-five acres and the Holt House. The judge in Louisville will decide if the offer is fair and will make her final decision after the guardian, Judge Ray Powers, and children have given their perspectives about the home and property.
22. Becky Shipp from the Kentucky Heritage Council/ State Preservation Office is guiding the Holt House Steering Committee since the retirement of David Morgan.
23. A letter was written to Erin Hower in Washington D.C. requesting Senator Mitch McConnell to accompany Judge Powers - Breckinridge County Judge Executive, Kentucky State Rep. Dwight D. Butler, and retired teacher/writer Susan B. Dyer to meet with Mrs. Laura Bush in regards to saving Judge Joseph Holt's home in Breckinridge County.
24. Susan Dyer worked on the application to nominate the Holt House for 11 of America's Most Endangered Historic Places after speaking to State Representative Dwight D. Butler
25. After speaking to Preservation Kentucky's Executive Director Joanna Hinton, we decided for Preservation Kentucky to take the application and for them to become the nominator. On January 12, 2007 Preservation Kentucky mailed the application for 11 of America's Most Endangered Historic Places. Joanna Hinton asked for support letters to be written by the Kentucky Historical Society, The Heritage Council, and The Holt House Steering Commission.
26. The Kentucky Heritage Council met on January 17, 2007 and did endorse the Holt House project of $108,000 for statewide grants available through the Kentucky Lincoln Bicentennial.
27. Chris Goodlett sent an E-mail with congratulations on the request for funding through the Kentucky Historical Society's Abraham Lincoln Bicentennial grant program for the mini-grant for $2,500 to pay for the appraisal of the Holt House.
28. An E-mail was received from Judge Tommy Turner, co-chairman of the Lincoln Bicentennial Commission with congratulations. Judge Turner gave approval to the Holt House application to receive the $108,000 to purchase the home and twenty-five acres if the judge agrees to sell.
29. Brittany Fausey, field representative from Ron Lewis's office, attended the last core meeting of the Holt House Steering Commission and is helping locate a speech from the Library of Congress given by Joseph Holt at the Baltimore Convention in 1835. In that speech, Holt tied the Democratic Party together and helped Richard Johnson of Kentucky receive nomination for Vice-President for 1836.
30. Representative Dwight D. Butler, Senator Carroll Gibson, Breckinridge County Judge Executive Ray Powers and Susan Dyer attended a ceremony at the capitol Rotunda February 12, 2007 (Lincoln's 198th birthday) receiving two grants for the Holt House. One for $2,500 from the Kentucky Historical Society would pay for Claude Galloway's appraisal of the Holt House and 25 acres, and $108,000 from The Kentucky Heritage Council was provided through the state wide Kentucky Lincoln Bicentennial Celebration.
31. An Ear Mark Request was completed through Ron Lewis' Office requesting funding consideration for the fiscal year 2008. Sarah Davasher helped with this request and follow up.
32. A letter was received from Congressman Ron Lewis stating he was going to request consideration for Breckinridge County's Fiscal Court to receive an Ear Mark to help with renovation of the Holt House.
33. After speaking to Bryant Brooks in Washington D.C., director for Senator Mitch McConnell, Susan Dyer was asked to summit a letter to Senator McConnell and fax it to Larry Cox requesting an Ear Mark for Breckinridge County on February 27, 2007. She said Mr. Cox would contact us if he needed anything additional. We have not had a response about the letter. Ms. Brooks also stated Larry Cox took care of Ear Marks for Kentucky.
34. Senator Carroll Gibson sent a letter of endorsement to Ron Lewis' office in regards to the Ear Mark request.
35. Susan Dyer submitted an application for a grant from the Heritage Council through the Lincoln Bicentennial Preservation Grant for $240,800 with a match of $51,200. The application was mailed on

March 9, 2007 with 24 letters of support from the community of Breckinridge County.

36. The Holt House Commission met to discuss the grant of "Save America's Treasures" through the National Parks.

37. Susan Dyer wrote a grant for "Save America's Treasures" through the National Parks requesting $300,000 dollars on April 26, 2007 for the Breckinridge County Fiscal Court.

38. On March 17 a letter was received from Allison P. Barrett, director of scheduling for First Lady Barbara Bush. Ms. Barrett appreciated the opportunity and said the request to meet the First Lady will be given every consideration, and that she would contact us when a final decision had been made.

39. On April 3 Susan Dyer received a card thanking her for her letter requesting a meeting with the First Lady from Allison P. Barrett. But unfortunately she said the volume of similar requests and complexities of her schedule prevented her from being able to meet with Breckinridge County Judge Executive Ray Powers, Representative Dwight D. Butler and Susan Dyer.

40. Susan Dyer attended the Summit of Kentucky Lincoln Sites and the Lincoln Bicentennial Commission meeting on May 21, 2007. Judge Joseph Holt's home was listed in the Activities By Type of Program as a Legacy Project-Purchase.

41. On June 21, 2007 Susan Dyer received a message from Becky Shipp of the Heritage Council that the Council and the Lincoln Bicentennial Commission both approved an additional $50,000 for stabilization of the Holt House pending transfers of the property.

42. Becky Shipp will issue the letter of agreement to the county once the initial grant is completed for acquisition.

43. On July 2, 2007 Representative Dwight D. Butler phoned to announce the presence of a new Historical marker of Judge Holt on Highway 60.

44. The Historical marker of Judge Holt was funded through grants of the Lincoln Bicentennial through efforts of the Kentucky Historical Society and Stuart Sanders.

45. The Heritage Council/ State Preservation Officer Donna Nearly, Becky Shipp, council members, and Director of Preservation Kentucky Joann Hinton were invited to view the inside of the Holt house on August 24, 2007.

46. Judge Powers was granted permission from the guardian, Kevin Ford, to enable the Heritage Council to view the Holt house on August 24, 2007. The Council will be a lifetime partner with the Breckinridge Fiscal Court.

47. On August 6, 2007 Susan Dyer received an E-mail from Joanna Hinton, director of Preservation Kentucky, requesting her to bring her chair and Judge Kelly Easton to Frankfort.

48. On August 7 Susan Dyer spoke with David Banks of the National Parks in Washington D.C. about the grant submitted by the Fiscal Court. He said the panel has not met yet and the grants would not be awarded until early October. Banks stated that Save America's Treasures Grants were one of the biggest bureaucracy in the nation. (Ms. Dyer asked how the recipients of the grants will be notified.) Banks said the winners of the grants would be notified by E-mail or by phone by the first of October Judge Powers' office will give special attention to any phone calls or E-mails from "Save America's Treasures".

49. On August 9, 2007 The Holt House Commission met with Jim Askins, field representative for Senator Jim Bunning. The meeting was to inform Jim Askins about the work, grants, community support, and state support from the Lincoln Bicentennial Commission, Kentucky State Historian James C. Klotter, the Heritage Council, Preservation Kentucky, Kentucky Historical Society, and the opportunities for Breckinridge County. Previously, on August 8, 2007 Joanna Hinton sent an E-mail stating that it is very exciting that the Heritage Council has decided to make its first real field trip to view Judge Holt's home.

50. On August 24, 2007 Breckinridge County was honored by hosting the Heritage Council. All were amazed by the beauty of the Judge Holt's home. Patrick Kennedy, restoration project manager, stated that the house was sound but had three areas of concern with leaks.

51. Lindy Casebier from the Commerce Cabinet fell in love with the Holt House. He said the stairs were better than the ones in his own house and he would do everything he could to help with this project.

52. Becky Shipp, from the Heritage Council and Preservation Officer Donna Neary are working to combine the grants of $108,000 and $50,000 for the purchase of the Holt House.

53. The Heritage Council is working to complete reports with suggestions on what the next steps will be for the Holt House project.

54. Susan Dyer contacted Becky Shipp from the Heritage Council requesting an extension of the grant of $108,000 that expires the first of September. A

letter was written and the extension has been taken care of to preserve the awarded grant that was in jeopardy because of the six month wait for the final appraisal requested by the family of Ms. Doda.

55. Judge Executive Ray Powers received the completed appraisal from the guardian on August 17 for $255,000. Judge Powers is negotiating with the guardian for a lower price
56. The Heritage Council is working to locate funds for the needed purchase.
57. Susan Dyer attended the Lincoln Bicentennial Commission meeting on August 27, 2007 at Springfield. Afterwards KET representatives Carolyn Gwinn and Joy Flynn discussed interest in doing a documentary on the Holt House and Judge Holt.
58. An application was mailed on October 4, 2007 for the Abraham Lincoln Bicentennial Grants Program through the Kentucky Historical Society. The request is for a matching grant of $5,000 through the Fiscal Court to pay for the cost associated with producing a Lincoln-themed book. The funds will be used to help complete research for the project, pay design, layout, and printing costs of publication on the biography of Judge Joseph Holt.
59. A letter was received on October 5, 2007 from the Governor's Office from Regina Crawford, executive director of Boards and Commissions, thanking Susan Dyer for her recommendation for Steve Collins for continued service as an appointee of Governor Fletcher on the Kentucky Heritage Council.
60. On October 5, 2007 Breckinridge County Judge Executive Ray Powers, discussed with Kevin Ford, court appointed guardian of Mrs. Louise Doda, the offer for the purchase of the Joseph Holt home in Breckinridge County.
61. Breckinridge County Judge Executive Ray Powers mailed a letter on October 10, 2007 for the proposed $158,000 for the purchase of Joseph Holt's home and twenty-five acres.
62. Susan Dyer has conferred with Becky Shipp from the Heritage Council about the differences in the two appraisals of $108,000 and $255,000. The judge in the Disability Court in Louisville will probably not accept the offer of $158,000 and another grant from the Lincoln Bicentennial must be written hoping to award the Breckinridge County Fiscal Court more funds to get closer to the $97,000 difference with the last appraisal to secure the property.
63. Sarah Davasher, from Congressman Lewis' Office spoke with Hampton Tucker, Historic Preservation Grants Division of the National Parks, who said that the 2007 Save America Treasures Grants would be awarded mid November.
64. On October 25, 2007 Governor Fletcher came to Hardinsburg. Susan Dyer spoke to Governor Fletcher personally about the Holt house and shared with him how the Holt House has become a Legacy Project of the Lincoln Bicentennial. She explained that Preservation Kentucky named the home One of the Most Endangered Historic Places in Kentucky in 2006. She also explained that the Heritage Council and Preservation officer Donna Neary has made a field trip to view the home, and that the Heritage Council is working with us. Ms. Dyer asked for the governor's support and asked Governor Fletcher how his administration could make this project happen.
65. On October 25, 2007 retired County Court Clerk Charles Allen Wilson brought Larry Cox, state director for Senator Mitch McConnell, to speak to Susan Dyer. Ms. Dyer updated Cox on all accomplishments since their meeting on January 4, 2007, and Cox said he could help when the Holt house became a national project and that Senator McConnell cared about saving such homes as the Holt house. He also stated he was going to call Bryant Brooks in Washington to see if it was not too late to make a call to Save America's Treasures to put in a good word for the efforts of the work being done to save the Holt house.
66. Governor Fletcher's office called on October 30 wanting to be informed about a packet of information about Judge Holt's home. Ms. Dyer explained that the information was given to Governor Fletcher while in Hardinsburg. Ms. Dyer told the Governor's office that she had asked for the Governor's support after sharing with him the work that has already been done before asking for his help. She was told that all of the state offices had been contacted about the accomplishments and are working to assist.
67. On November 2, 2007 Governor Fletcher's office called to tell Susan Dyer that Governor Fletcher wanted her to know that he had looked over the packet of information given to him about the Holt house while traveling the Commonwealth on his campaign bus. Ms. Dyer expressed appreciation for the phone call and that Governor Fletcher's support could make the project happen
68. On November 6, 2007 Judge Ray Powers made a personal visit to see Mrs. Doda's guardian, Kevin Ford. The guardian explained he had gotten another lawyer Stanley Chavan to assist with the project. Kevin Ford told Judge Powers that Stanley Chavan and he would take the offer of $158,000 to the

that a court date would be set in December for the court judge to decide if the property would be sold and for what price.

69. Susan Dyer wrote an application for the Breckinridge County Fiscal Court and mailed on November 14, 2007 for the Lincoln Heritage Preservation Grants of 2007-2008. The grants are for $50,000 with a $10,000 match in cash and in-kind for stabilization of Judge Holt's home.
70. Susan Dyer attended the Lincoln Bicentennial Commission meeting on November 19, 2007 at Hodgenville. Judge Tommy Turner, co-chairman of the Lincoln Bicentennial Commission, asked Mrs. Dyer to give an update to the Commission about progress of the legacy project of Judge Joseph Holt's home.
71. Mrs. Dyer was the guest speaker at the Breckinridge County Retired Teachers Association on November 26, 2007. She was asked to brief the organization about the work and project of Judge Holt's home and the book she is completing on Joseph Holt.
72. Sarah Davasher, from Congressman Ron Lewis's office e-mailed information from her Washington contact about Save America's Treasures Grants. Breckinridge County has applied for $300,000 for renovation of the Holt house. The grants are expected to be awarded next week. The awards were pushed back again.
73. On December 6, 2007 Breckinridge County Judge Executive Ray Powers and Becky Shipp met in Louisville for a hearing about the Holt House. Some of the family of Mrs. Doda was unable to attend the hearing and it was rescheduled for January 17, 2008.
74. On January 11, 2008 a grant alert was received from Congressman Ron Lewis' office based on the interest in funding for the Judge Joseph Holt house from the federal and state agencies. Congressman Lewis wanted to share the information about a few grant opportunities. And if we choose to apply for any of these grants, Congressman Lewis would be pleased to write a letter of support for the application.
75. On January 17, 2008 a hearing was held in Louisville concerning the negotiation between the Breckinridge County Fiscal Court and Guardian Kevin Ford representing the owner of the Holt House. The judge of the court approved a contract to be written and signed on the 17th of January for purchase of the Holt house. Becky Shipp represented the Heritage Council and Mark Dennen, staff architect for the Kentucky Heritage Council, attended. Finalizations will be made on February 7, for the Breckinridge County Fiscal Court to purchase the Holt House and transfer the deed. The Holt House will be purchased by using awarded grants received by the Breckinridge County Fiscal Court through the Lincoln Bicentennial Celebration and the Heritage Council.
76. January 17, 2008 Susan Dyer spoke to David Morgan, planner of the Lincoln Bicentennial National Kick off on February 11-12. She discussed a conversation she had had with Larry Cox in November of 2007. Cox stated that when the Holt house became a federal project Senator McConnell would come aboard. Morgan stated that when a historic home is listed on the Register of Historic Places it is marked with the significance of being local, state, or federal. Morgan stated that Judge Holt's home was listed in 1976 as nationally significant, which makes the house federal.
77. On January 29th 2008, the Breckinridge County Fiscal Court members voted in favor of a resolution to enter into a contract to purchase the Holt house and twenty-five acres for $158,000.
78. On February 7, 2008 Judge Martin in the Louisville Court ordered the sale of the Holt house to the Breckinridge County Fiscal Court. Kevin Ford, guardian of owner, Louise Doda, signed the contract to sell. The Fiscal Court will purchase the Holt house for $158,000 through grants from the Heritage Council. The Council will partner with the Breckinridge County Fiscal Court. Breckinridge County Judge Executive Ray Powers represented Breckinridge County and Becky Shipp represented the Heritage Council.
79. On February 11, 2008 Susan and Eddie Dyer attended the symposium at the Henry Clay Hotel in Louisville with Pulitzer-Prize-Winner Doris Kearns Goodwin as the speaker about Lincoln. During the beginning of the program it was announced that 10 per cent of the proceeds from the National Lincoln Bicentennial Kickoff will go to the Holt house.
80. On February 12, 2008 Susan Dyer was invited by the Kentucky Historical Society to attend a celebration at the Capitol Rotunda in Frankfort for the work she has done on the Holt project. Mrs. Dyer was asked to invite Senator Carroll Gibson, Representative Dwight Butler, and Judge Executive Ray Powers. The Kentucky Lincoln Heritage Trail and Lincoln Sites were recognized. The Holt House was officially recognized as a Lincoln Site and on the Kentucky Heritage Trail location on February 12, 2008.

81. On February 14, 2008 Susan Dyer hand delivered a federal request to Sarah Davasher with Congressman Lewis' Office.
82. On March 17, 2008 Susan Dyer presented at Kentucky Days at Hardinsburg Elementary School information about Joseph Holt, the Holt house, the Lincoln Bicentennial and Holt's connection to Lincoln. A station was set up for 90 fourth graders who interacted with Mrs. Dyer.
83. On April 14, 2008 (Warren Greer, with the Kentucky Historical Society and program Coordinator for the Lincoln Bicentennial Commission) did a joint power point presentation about the life of Joseph Holt. Susan Dyer made a presentation about saving the Holt house, local efforts, and community leaders. The Heritage Council's Becky Shipp provided information about restoration of the Holt house and the Council's field trip to the Holt house.
84. On April 19, 2008 the Breckinridge County Fiscal Court received notification of a $852.67 grant from the ALBC state grant funds directed to Lincoln Sites and its government organization through the Abraham Lincoln Bicentennial/Kentucky Historical Society. The Holt House, Lincoln Site will receive a marker showing the connection of Joseph Holt to President Lincoln.
85. April 22, 2008 Susan Dyer was the guest speaker at the Breckinridge County Historical Society. Ms. Dyer gave a talk about the Holt House Team/Lincoln Bicentennial/ Lincoln connections, how the project began, discussed the accomplishments, and the state organizations involved.
86. May 19, 2008, Susan Dyer submitted an application for Save America's Treasures Grant for $600,000.
87. May 30, 2008 Eddie and Susan Dyer attended the retirement party of Becky Shipp from the Heritage Council, who has guided the Holt House Steering Committee with grant writing, court appearances, advice, support, and partnering with the organization since the retirement of David Morgan in December 2006. Patrick Kennedy, project restoration manger for the Heritage Council, explained he would be assisting with the Holt project upon Ms. Shipp's retirement.
88. June 17, 2008 Warren Greer, program coordinator for the Kentucky Abraham Lincoln Bicentennial Commission and Kentucky Historical Society, was the guest speaker at the annual Breckinridge Chamber of Commerce Dinner. He delivered a talk about the Lincoln Bicentennial, what is happening with the celebration across the state and how Kentucky is leading the way, making the United States aware about Kentucky's significance with Lincoln. Greer spoke about Breckinridge County's connection with Joseph Holt and his home.
89. June 18, 2008 David Banks with the National Parks System was contacted to make sure the organization had received the Save America's Treasures Grant. He explained there was more money to be awarded this year.
90. June 24, 2008 Kevin Ford, guardian of Mrs. Doda, (owner of the Holt house), had his lawyer, Stan Chavan, expedite a hearing at the District Court in Louisville to speed up a decision that has been pending since March 8, 2008. This was done because of a grant pending at the Heritage Council for $50,000 to stabilize the Holt House. Breckinridge County Judge Executive Ray Powers, Peggy Guier, Heritage Council attorney, and Becky Shipp, retired, attended for the Heritage Council. The appeals judge stated he would make his decision in writing.
91. On July 14, 2008, Susan Dyer attended the Lincoln Sites/ Lincoln Bicentennial Commission meeting, and was asked to report on the Holt house.
92. On July 15, 2008, Judge Powers called with good news that the appeals judge in Louisville ruled in favor of the Holt House, and agreed with Judge Martin's first ruling to approve the sale of the Holt house to the Breckinridge County Fiscal Court.
93. On July 20-26 a packet was made with a copy of the Save America's Treasures Grant application, the complete list of accomplishments for the Holt house, a recent picture of the Holt house, and a personal letter thanking each individual for their support in assisting with the Holt Project. A phone call was made to each person informing them of the packet they would be receiving and also to remind them of the three federal requests that were made from their offices.
94. August 20, 2008 at the Kentucky Fair and Expo Center in Louisville, the Lincoln Heritage Trail and the Joseph Holt house were promoted, encouraging folks to travel the trail.
95. On September 5, 2008 Susan and Eddie Dyer attended the 2008 Preservation Conference at Bardstown. Judge Tommy Turner, Co-chair of the Lincoln Bicentennial Commission and member of the National Lincoln Bicentennial Commission, gave a talk about the Lincoln Bicentennial and discussed the Holt project, giving complements for the job well done. Lindy Casebier, executive

director of Arts, Cultural Heritage and Tourisms, and acting preservation officer from the Heritage Council Mark Dennen, stated the Holt house was becoming a reality because of the dedicated work.

96. Friday October 10, 2008 a meeting was held in Breckinridge County for the Holt house. Many ideas were discussed and the issue of transferring money from the F & A cabinet was discussed with ideas to help speed up the process. Those attending were Diane Comer from the Heritage Council, Warren Greer from the Historical Society and program coordinator for the Lincoln Bicentennial Commission, Representative Dwight D. Butler, Breckinridge County Judge Executive Ray Powers, Susan Dyer and Eddie Dyer.
97. Saturday, October 11, 2008 Susan Dyer volunteered for the Breckinridge County government hosting the Kentucky Lincoln Heritage Trail Exhibit at Hoedowns Days in Hardinsburg. The public enjoyed learning about their Lincoln connections. Stamping the passport map with the Holt House, (now an official Lincoln site and on the Lincoln Heritage Trail) was enjoyed by citizens. Maps, bookmarks and information on Lincoln were distributed.
98. Friday, October 17, 2008 Judge Powers phoned to say that the MOA's were in order; the F and A Cabinet was looking over things. Mrs. Bradley was going to contact Judge Powers with the issue of the environmental assessment for the Holt House.
99. Lindy Casebier, deputy secretary of Tourisms, Arts and Heritage Cabinet, Representative Dwight D. Butler, and Warren Greer, program coordinator for the Lincoln Bicentennial Commission, assisted in speeding up the process of the environmental assessment.
100. On October 21, 2008 Eddie Cooke performed the Environmental Assessment on the Holt House.
101. Representative Dwight D. Butler phoned on October 23 to say that the environmental survey was passed and the F and A Cabinet sent its own person not costing the county government anything.
102. On November 13, 2008 Judge Powers E-mailed to say he had completed all that Natalie Holloman had asked with issues for the RFT (legal services) for a title search of the Holt house and the title search had been completed. Everything for the Holt house has been signed on Breckinridge County's end and the Finance & Administration has signed a MOA from Judge Powers.
103. On November 18, 2008 Susan Dyer was the guest speaker at the Breckinridge County Chamber Breakfast at Rough River State Park Mrs. Dyer spoke about the Holt house project, Judge Holt, Breckinridge County's connections to President Lincoln, and discussed the top three honors the House has received: Preservation Kentucky listed the Holt House as One of the Most Endangered Historic Places in Kentucky in 2006, The Lincoln Bicentennial Commission named Judge Holt's home as a Legacy Project of the Lincoln Bicentennial in 2000, The Preservation Office and the Kentucky Historical Society honored the Holt House as officially being on the Kentucky Lincoln Heritage Trail and an official Lincoln Site in Kentucky on February 14, 2008. Ms. Dyer shared that acquisition is almost complete, that two grants are pending for the Holt House, and discussed that the dream of writing a book to help save the Holt House is becoming a reality.
104. On November 18, 2008 Susan and Eddie Dyer attended the Lincoln Bicentennial Commission Meeting at Hodgenville. Toward the end of the meeting, Mark Dennen, acting preservation officer from the Heritage Council, updated the commission with the Holt house, discussing the environmental assessment, the title search and addressed that the closing for the acquisition of the Holt house should be soon.
105. December 5, 2008, Susan Dyer received a phone call from Breckinridge Judge Executive Ray Powers informing her that the historic Holt House and surrounding property of 19.5 acres now was in the procession of the citizens of Breckinridge County.
106. Susan Dyer submitted a cemetery grant for the Breckinridge County Fiscal Court to Office of State Grants Department of Local Government on December 31, 2008 for the Holt Family Cemetery. This is where Judge Joseph Holt is buried and property of the Holt Family Trust.
107. Susan Dyer gave a presentation and update on the Joseph Holt House at the Lincoln Bicentennial Commission meeting in Frankfort on January 5, 2009. Breckinridge County Judge Executive Ray Powers and Eddie Dyer attended. Kent Whitworth, executive director of the Kentucky Historical Society, told the audience that the Lincoln Bicentennial helped make it possible to save the Holt House.
108. On February 2, 2009 the first private donation to the Holt House was given by Dan Lee of Cecilia, Kentucky.
109. A phone call was received from Brian Smith, director for Brett Guthrie. He discussed the material that was sent to him concerning the work and

accomplishments of the Holt House project. He said he was going to research the Save America's Treasures Grants and was looking forward to viewing the Holt House, and coming to Breckinridge County.

110. On February 20,2009 The Heritage/ State Preservation Office and the Historical Society met in Frankfort to discuss long-term planning for Judge Joseph Holt's House in Breckinridge County.

111. Federal Requests for FY 2110 were made to Senator Mitch McConnell, Senator Jim Bunning and Congressman Brett Guthrie on February 24, 2009 from the Breckinridge County Fiscal Court.

112. WULF radio called and did an interview with Susan Dyer on February 28, 2009 about updates of the Holt House Project, grants, state, local and federal support and about the book to be published in 2009 by Douglas Sikes with Acclaim Press.

113. On March 18, 2009 the first local steering committee was formed to represent the follow up and action plan for the Holt House. Those representing Breckinridge County were Judge Executive Ray Powers, Advocate Susan Dyer, Representative Dwight D. Butler, Lee Stinnett, and Suzanne Miles from Congressman Brett Guthrie's office. Also, Mark Dennen, Heritage Council acting executive director and State Historic Preservation Officer; Diane Comer, Heritage Commission Public Information Officer; Warren Greer, program coordinator for the Kentucky Abraham Lincoln Bicentennial Commission/Kentucky Historical Society; Dana Beth Lyddan, Elizabethtown Heritage Council executive director and chair of Preservation Kentucky, Inc.; and Hardin Circuit Judge Kelly Easton. The Save America's Treasures Grant was discussed. Dana Beth and Diane will work with Susan to provide support before the May 22 deadline. Susan Dyer emphasized that restoration of the Holt House is a community based project that will employ 50 people – mirror language of stimulus funding/ identified needs –focus on local jobs and local business contacts. A Kentucky Colonel Grant application will be submitted and contacts will be made to have individuals support the Holt House. Mark Dennen suggested for Susan to talk to Shane Tucker regarding TEA21 Funding for next year, * Susan noted that Holt's father was a commissioner of roads in Breckinridge County. Dana Beth will contact transportation Cabinet Secretary Joe Prather for support. Dana Beth and Diane will assist Susan in grant writing and along with Mark get her contact information and suggestions for the next steps. Preserve America Susan/ Diane/Dana Beth: Explore opportunities to apply for PA status follow up with a grant application in the next available grant cycle. Organization needs, Local Advisory Committee, State, National Steering Committee, 501(c)3 partner, begin to establish relationships with key partners. Promotional Opportunities/ Media opportunities, media tour, develop long-term media and marketing plan, Abraham Lincoln Bicentennial Commission involvement, also Civil War Sesquicentennial, open house. Funding: SAT application-deadline May22, Congressional Earmark Holt House Restoration and Interpretation: Status of Easement, Next steps—stabilization and Rehabilitation/ Convene Resource Team.

114. March 27, 2009 Brian Smith for Congressman Brett Guthrie's office called saying another detailed budget must be submitted to the Washington D. C. Office with a 50-50 match. Susan Dyer wrote another detailed budget and it was faxed on March 30, 2009 with Breckinridge County's Judge Executive Ray Powers' approval.

115. March 31st 2009 Susan Dyer submitted another grant application to the Kentucky Colonels for a $20,000 grant to help with stabilization for the Joseph Holt House. Since the partnering of state agencies and the forming of a steering committee Susan Dyer now has help with grants. Dana Beth Lyddan, Elizabethtown Heritage Council executive director, and Diane Comer, Heritage Council /State Preservation Office.

116. Wednesday April 15, 2009 Susan Dyer met with Dana Beth Lyddan in Elizabethtown and worked on the SAT application for the Holt House.

117. On April 17, 2009 the second steering committee for the Holt House met in Hardinsburg. Those attending were Breckinridge County Judge Executive Ray Powers, Kentucky State Representative Dwight D. Butler, Mark Dennen, preservation officer of the Heritage Preservation Office, Diane Comer, the Heritage Office, Brian Smith, executive director for Congressman Guthrie's Office, Chris Goodlett, Historical Society, Warren Greer, coordinator for the Abraham Lincoln Bicentennial Commission and the Historical Society, David Hayes, editor of the Breckinridge County Herald News and tourisms director for Breckinridge County, Susan Dyer, grant writer and advocate for the Holt House, and Douglas W. Sikes, publisher of Acclaim Press. Grants and funding update from Susan Dyer. Susan shared about submitting the Kentucky Colonels grant application and the work on the current SAT with assistance of Dana Beth and Diane. The Heritage Council Holt

House Site Visit Report was given by Jen Williamson. Media and public relation were discussed with Open House/ media tour date, Lincoln Bicentennial Commission update from Warren Greer. Begin draft of short and long-range goals. Updates of 501(c)3 organization/ Susan Dyer shared that Dana Beth thought it would be a good idea if the county attorney would write a letter stating he was working on the 501(c)3 to be attached with the grant application for SAT. Judge Powers stated he would ask Bradley Butler to write the letter. Judge Powers will follow the suggestion of Heritage Council Site's visit in regard to cleaning debris from around the house. Susan expressed Lee Stinnett's suggestion of having a community clean up date soon before the grasses got higher, and Diane Comer stated that an announcement sometime in May will be made on the clean up date.

118. Judge Powers called saying Save America's Treasures called the Heritage Council asking about a budget submitted to Congressman Brett Guthrie's office for funding for a federal request. Mark Dennen shared with Susan Dyer that the National Parks asked many detailed questions about the Holt House Project.

119. On April 20, 2009 Susan Dyer was the guest speaker at the Hancock County History Dinner. She presented information about Judge Joseph Holt, the Holt House Project and the book on Judge Joseph Holt and the Holt House to be published in September 2009.

120. April 22, Susan Dyer attended the Lincoln Bicentennial Commission meeting in Springfield. Mark Dennen, the new preservation officer at the Heritage Preservation Office, presented plans and updates for the Holt House. He talked about the Heritage Council's site visit on April 3, 2009 and the Holt House Steering Committee meetings, the work involved with Susan Dyer submitting the grant to the Kentucky Colonels and the Save America's Treasures Grant application with which Diane Comer from the Heritage Council and Dana Beth Lyddan are assisting.

121. Susan Dyer was the guest speaker at the Irvington Woman's meeting May 18, 2009. She gave an update of the progress of the Holt House Project and discussed the upcoming book on Judge Holt. The club members offered to help in any way.

122. On May 22, 2009 the Save America's Treasures Grant was submitted to the National Parks. The Heritage Preservation Office and the Elizabethtown Heritage Council assisted. Federal request were made in February with Senator Mitch McConnell, Senator Jim Bunning, and Congressman Brett Guthrie's offices. This is the third year to apply for this worthy project.

123. June 5, 2009 the Holt House Steering Committee met. The Save America's Treasures Grant was discussed; the Kentucky Colonels Grant with Cabinet support was discussed. Stabilization was a great concern. The Lincoln Bicentennial funds will help with covering windows until new windows can be purchased. Volunteer contractor Charlie Corbett volunteered to help install Plexiglas and help repair the five major leaks in the roof. The Holt House will be spotlighted on the Lincoln Heritage Trail on August 15, 2009. The committee decided to open the house for the public to tour before renovation begins.

124. On July 1, 2009, the Holt House Steering Committee met discussing the planning and crucial work that must be completed for the Spotlight on the Holt House Community Day. Susan Dyer shared with the committee that Michael Gish, the person in charge of the Holt Family Cemetery, had given permission for Breckinridge County government to have a ceremony at Judge Holt's grave on August 15 to honor him and also to share that the county had received in grant of $1, 900 for the Holt Cemetery. Much work was done getting Fort Knox's Public Affairs Office assistance to help with a wreath laying ceremony. A phone call was received from Sec. Sparrow's Director, Sue Helmberg. She said the packet of information had been passed to Sec. Sparrow's Office and that Lindy Casebier, director of Tourisms, Arts, and Heritage Cabinet, would be attending. Ms. Helmberg suggested contacting magazines in Kentucky who have always been kind to Kentuckians and suggested sending information about the Spotlight on the Holt House. Ms. Helmberg said she would pass the information about the Holt House to their Executive Director of Communication Gil Lawson, and that they would also send the press release to travel writers that the Department of Travel has on hand. The event would also be put on Sec. Sparrow's schedule. We were advised to contact our senator and representative. Both Senator Carroll Gibson and Representative Dwight Butler were called as they serve on the Steering Committee for the Holt House.

Massive work was done preparing a packet of information to Governor Beshear and speaking to the Director of Scheduling Courtney French concerning efforts to get Governor Beshear to attend the August 15 event. An article for the *Kentucky*

Monthly Magazine was written by Susan Dyer and edited by Dr. James C. Klotter and Diane Comer about the event, which came out in the August issue. David Hayes, local newspaper editor, prepared invitations for guests of the Lincoln Bicentennial and groups that have diligently assisted with the Holt project. Hayes also worked with the county home makers on preparing food for the event and helped assist with tours for the Holt House, helped to write scripts for the guides, and assisted with numerous other tasks. Local musicians were contacted to perform music from the period. All were asked to volunteer. Violinist Scott Moore, Allison O'Donoghue and Kathy Tabor performed as Paul Joseph O'Donoghue accompanied the singers and performed selections from the period. Jackie Miller performed with a flute ensemble. Heather Mercer, sponsor for the National Honor Society, was contacted to encourage local students to be guides for the event. Students from Breckinridge County High School volunteered.

125. July 8, 2009 the local steering committee members met to continue organizing for the August 15 event at the Holt House. Carol Hinton was called to schedule two weeks before the event. The Honor Guard from Fort Knox was called and speakers were contacted. Local musician also were contacted, the local steering committee members recorded commercials to promote the event, and invitations were mailed to guests. Preservation Kentucky paid $160 for the 16 Lincoln holiday ornaments for the Holt House prizes, a project board and a massive notebook were prepared for guests. The Holt House Steering Committee met on July 14, 2009. Judge Powers gave a report on the cleanup and status, the installation of windows was discussed. Judge Powers worked diligently getting the grounds clean for the event, and the Holt House ready. He also helped by providing a tent for the event. The Breckinridge County Chamber of Commerce helped with a stage and sound system and numerous other tasks for the event. The Breckinridge County Historical Society helped with parking, and tours. Updates were given on grants and the 501© 3 status, Judge Powers and Susan Dyer went over the agenda of the day and discussed the special guests that would attend the event.

126. LaRue County Judge-Executive Tommy Turner, State Senator Carroll Gibson, Marcheta Sparrow, secretary, and Lindy Casebier, deputy secretary Kentucky Tourism, Arts and Heritage Cabinet, Mark Dennen, Kentucky Heritage Council executive director and State Historic Preservation Officer, U.S. Representative Brett Guthrie, were contacted. Warren Greer gave a Lincoln Bicentennial Commission update. Cabinet/Tourisms, open house/ and media tour date were discussed. Upcoming events were discussed for a Resource Team, planning and funding. An archaeological survey was also discussed. Diane Comer worked diligently on programs, organization, contacting people, and gathering items needed for the August 15 event.

127. The premiere release of "Lincoln's Advocate," the life of Judge Joseph Holt, was held on August 14, 2009 at the Community Building behind the Breckinridge County Extension Office, with more than 200 people attending. A reception was held with violinist Scott Moore performing with guest speakers, local and statewide speaking on behalf of author Susan B. Dyer. Ms. Dyer also spoke about her new biography of Judge Joseph Holt. Publisher Douglas W. Sikes from Acclaim Press was on hand to help with the special community event.

128. The Spotlight on the Holt House/Community Day was held on August15, 2009, as Judge Holt's home was spotlighted on the Lincoln Heritage Trail and welcomed as an official Lincoln Site in Kentucky. Numerous guests were available, homemakers served food, provided guided tours of the house, the local historical society helped with parking and numerous other activities.

129. Union soldiers camped out the evening before and Susan Dyer was on had to autograph her new biography on Lincoln's Advocate. The public waited for more than an hour and a half to tour the house and get a signed copy of the new release.

130. September 25, 2009. Numerous people have contacted the Holt House committee with congratulations for a very successful event on August 15. Eileen Mackevich, executive director of the National Abraham Lincoln Bicentennial, said she was going to write a blog about the project on the national web site. All the comments from the guests were typed and sent to Diane Comer, Heritage Preservation Office. A list was formed of future volunteers for the Holt House. Cathy Cowan brought Judge Holt's Congressional Records on site and shared with Susan Dyer on August 15. A picture was made to document the books. We discussed how to keep the excitement going for the Holt House. How to involve Todd Cassidy and Kentucky Films with Judge Holt's home. The meeting discussed getting Cloverport High School involved with writing a grant through the History Channel to establish a web site for the Holt House. Our new Washington contact for Senator Mitch McConnell will be Ally

Bird. Paul Joseph O'Donoghue had a report conducted by Steven Gray, district forester, to check about the trees on the grounds of the Holt House. Holt and Henry Clay's paths did cross and more research needs to be done to see if the Emperor of China gave Henry Clay seedlings to Clay that Clay could have given to Holt

131. The tree report is essential for the Holt House because there is a Basswood or American Linden. In the back yard there is a stump about three feet tall, which is the remnant of a base wood. There is a sprout coming off the stump at the ground level. Gray suggested we do what we can to cultivate that sprout. If you carefully cut the stump, you may be able to count the growth rings.

132. David Morgan, Washington D.C. resource, suggested contacting Melton Porter Hay–Historical Society–concerning the connection of Clay and Holt.

133. October 17, 2009 Fred Bennett (his mother grew up in the Holt House) spoke to Susan Dyer about the house and about coming to visit and sharing pictures of his mother's to be possibly scanned to help with renovation.

134. October 24, 2009 Hugh H. Bland from Glendale, Kentucky came to True Kentucky and spoke to Susan Dyer about giving an antique 1840's Astral Lamp to the Holt House.

135. November 7, 2009 Peggy Evans, formally of Breckinridge County, visited Susan Dyer at the Kentucky Book Fair. She wants to leave in her will a beautiful bed from the period. The bed is in fine condition, with all the parts in place. It is walnut, has heavy hexagonal posts with detachable finials, a blanket roll, and paneled headboard. It is in the same time period as the prime era of the Holt House and could be used in a bedroom decorated for the period. This is an old Breckinridge County artifact and will be given to our group when needed.

136. Dave Shuffett visited with Susan Dyer on November 7th and she shared that KET was interested in doing a documentary. Doug Krawezy from the Louisville Civil War Roundtable invited Susan Dyer to speak at the roundtable. He said they would donated up to $2,000 for renovation of the Holt House.

137. November 16, 2009 Susan Dyer attended the Lincoln Sites meeting in Frankfort which is forming the Lincoln Sites Alliance. This alliance is very important for the Holt House and its future. The alliance was formed with the primary objective of strengthening and maintaining a vibrant Lincoln heritage alliance in Kentucky. The Alliance is a partnership of Lincoln Sites and affiliates to ensure continued growth and development of Lincoln Heritage. The number of directors constituting the initial Board of Directors is seven. These same seven persons are also the incorporations. They are Iris Larue, the Lincoln Museum; Gwen Thompson, Mary Todd Lincoln House; Mary Kozak, Camp Nelson Heritage Park; Christy Pritchard, Hardin County History Museum; Eric Brooks, the Henry Clay Estate; Andrea Saylor, Farmington; and Susan Dyer, Judge Joseph Holt House. There will be $10-20 million dollars distributed in grants in the next five to ten years for Lincoln Sites.

This was the final meeting of the KY Lincoln Bicentennial Commission.

138. On January 6, 2010, Don Wojcik from the Denver Planning Division of the National Parks, visited the Holt House. (Judge Holt's birthday) The meetings continued today at Farmington. Wojcik called this morning to say that the turn out was large. Wojcik toured the Holt House, grounds and Judge Holt's grave. He was amazed at the beauty of the house and compared it to White Hall. He said there was an 80 percent chance that the Kentucky National Heritage Area would become a reality. He also stated there was more of a chance to become a national heritage area because of the Holt House. He was very impressed with the community for its support, letters and huge interest in the restoration of the Holt House.

139. On January 26, 2010 the Kentucky Heritage Council presented a special screening of *Historic Archaeology: Beneath Kentucky's Fields and Streets.* This one-hour documentary explores new archaeological investigations into the life of farmers, slaves, soldiers, immigrants and labors during the historic era in Kentucky. Eddie and Susan Dyer attended to learn more as the Holt House will have an archaeological dig in the near future to help understand the history of the house.

140. February 12, 2010. The Kentucky Historical Society honored the conclusion of the Abraham Lincoln Bicentennial and initiated the commemoration of the Civil War Sesquicentennial. Eddie and Susan Dyer represented Breckinridge County as the Lincoln Bicentennial has been essential in partnering with the Joseph Holt House.

141. Eileen Mackevich e-mailed that the transition stage from the commission to the foundation will maintain its web site.

142. At the Ancestral Trails Historical Society Genealogy & History Book Fair on April 12, 2010, Susan

Dyer was approached by local Breckinridge Countian Mickey Storms of Storms Electrical Construction Company. Mickey is a master electrician who has volunteered to do any electrical work for free for the Holt House.

143. May 26 event recognizes 2010 Ida Lee Willis Memorial Foundation Preservation Award winners.

2010 Ida Lee Willis Memorial Foundation Historic Preservation Awards were presented during a special ceremony May 26 at the Kentucky Governor's Executive Mansion in Frankfort. The ceremony is presented each year in partnership with the Kentucky Heritage Council. Also during the ceremony, student winners in the 12th Annual Statewide Photo-Essay Competition were honored, a competition co-sponsored by Preservation Kentucky, Inc., and the Heritage Council.

Ida Lee Willis Memorial Preservation Awards are presented each May, in observance of National Historic Preservation Month, and recognize those who have demonstrated an understanding of and an appreciation for the value of preserving and reusing Kentucky's historic and prehistoric resources, whether through the restoration of an important structure or community resource or through a lifetime commitment to encouraging and promoting historic preservation. The awards are named for the late Ida Lee Willis, who was appointed first executive director of the Kentucky Heritage Commission (now the Kentucky Heritage Council) in 1966. The Ida Lee Willis Memorial Award is presented to the individual who has demonstrated outstanding dedication to the cause of historic preservation in the Commonwealth. The 2010 recipient is Clyde Reynolds Carpenter of Lexington, chair of the University of Kentucky Department of Historic Preservation, who is being honored for his lifelong commitment to preservation and design, his leadership in the UK College of Architecture and his dedication to educating students and others of the value of Kentucky's built environment. Preservation Project Awards recognize outstanding examples of restoration or rehabilitation of historic buildings, or other types of projects that have had a positive impact on Kentucky's built environment. 2010 winners are:

Bishop Flaget Log House, Nelson County, for the historically accurate restoration of the earliest structure representing the Catholic faith to be built west of the Allegheny Mountains.

The Grand Theatre, Frankfort, in recognition of the restoration of the historic theater in downtown Frankfort and its return to the community as a multi-use performing and visual arts center.

Pearce-Wheeler Farm, Hart County, in recognition of owner Bruce Cohen's commitment to preserving the historic house, barns and outbuildings of the farm, helping to preserve the heritage of Kentucky's rapidly changing rural landscape.

Service to Preservation Awards honor those who have furthered historic preservation activities or had a positive impact in their communities, including individuals, organizations, public officials, financial institutions, news media, and/or volunteers. 2010 winners are:

Charles Cash, Louisville, in recognition of his long service as an architect and administrator for Louisville Metro Government, his work helping to preserve historic buildings and neighborhoods, and a career championing good community planning and design.

Donald Clare, Rabbit Hash, for his commitment to preserving the buildings and heritage of Rabbit Hash and all the time and effort he has committed as an advocate for historic preservation causes throughout Boone County and Northern Kentucky.

Susan Dyer, Breckinridge County, for her persistence advocating for the preservation of the Judge Joseph Holt House in rural Breckinridge County, and for all she has done to educate others about his legacy and role in President Abraham Lincoln's administration.

144. The Kentucky Lincoln Sites Alliance Meeting was held at Camp Nelson Civil War Park on April 26, 2010. The Preservation of Lincoln Bicentennial and Lincoln Trail Materials were discussed. Warren Greer gave an update about the KALBC Grant Update, and the development of Kentucky Lincoln Trial Products. The National Heritage Area Update was given by Warren Greer.

145. Gwen McCall Smallenburg E-mailed on June 22, 2010 confirming receipt of her letter to include the Breckinridge County Fiscal Court for potential grant applications when the grant applications are mailed in mid-January. This will be through the Kentucky Bar Association Foundation.

Accomplishments and updates of the Joseph Holt Home

2013 was a most distinguished year with numerous accomplishments for the Joseph Holt Home!

1. The 6th Annual Holt Home Community Day was a huge success with a 500 plus crowd!
2. General Dana K. Chipman, the 38th Judge Advocate General of the United States Army was one of the key speakers and told the crowd there was much patriotic pride in Judge Holt's communi-

ty. He spoke about the man and the crowd was spell-bound.

3. Retired Colonel Frederic Borch, the keynote speaker told me the event could not have been better. (Col. Borch gave a very dramatic delivery about the Father of the Judge Advocates, Joseph Holt.) Recently, Fred wrote an article in the Annual Bulletin a magazine he edits for the Judge Advocate General's Legal Center and School about Judge Holt and included a photograph he personally took on his private tour of the home.
4. Rick Brown, Production Manager of Wave 3TV kept his promise and came and filmed for half the day and aired a segment on the Saturday night news and then again on the Sunday morning news.
5. Was invited to view the segment at Wave 3TV edited for the local web site and a copy was made for the JAG School.
6. KET/ Kentucky Life did a segment on the efforts of saving the Holt Home
7. Both videos can be viewed on www.jholt-houseky.org and the Friends now have a webmaster, Greg Hicks who will maintain updates of renovation, events of the Judge Joseph Holt Home, honors it receives and continued improvements as they occur.
8. The Friends of the Holt Home, Inc. officially became a non-profit organization on August 29, 2013.
9. A Cooperative-Agreement has been voted on and approved by the Breckinridge County Fiscal Court (owner of the home) to work with the Friends of the Holt Home, Inc. (a non-profit organization that does fundraising), holds events, writes grants and works with county government in a partnership with the home.
10. As President of the Friends of the Holt Home wrote and submitted a grant to Brown-Forman of Louisville in June and the Friends of the Holt Home have received a $20,000.00 grant for the interior renovation for the Holt Home.
11. Phase 2 Transportation Enhancement grant for interior renovation was submitted in fall of 2013. We will use tax credits, fundraising money we raised in 2012, and the money remaining in the Holt Family Trust, volunteer labor and logs of work on the grounds to help match the grant. The Friends organization has made a commitment to raise the remaining amount it will take to match the federal grant. This will be in the form of seeking other grants, more fundraising, seeking partners, and finding sources for the 20% required match.
12. The heavy metal roof was delivered in February to the roofing subcontractor along with the metal roof panels, half-round gutters and downspouts.
13. The Holt Family Trust transferred the ownership of the Holt Family Cemetery to the Friends of the Holt Home, Inc. in February of 2014.)
14. Lanham Brothers Contractors of Owensboro were awarded the bid to begin exterior renovation with the phase 1 $500,000.00 TE Grant. (We went through two biding processes in the summer of 2013 and renovation began in April 2014.
15. Wrote a grant application for the Friends used by the Breckinridge County Fiscal Court to Bluegrass Pipeline. And county government was awarded $10,000 hopefully this can apply to the $150,000.00 SAT grant for the Holt Home.
16. Delivered a lecture on Judge Holt for the Owensboro/ Davis Co. Public Library, February 6, Remembering: The Civil War/ including updates with the Judge Joseph Holt Home
17. The Judge Joseph Holt Home is included on the Kentucky Lincoln Heritage Trail 2014 Summer Promotion tear off sheets.
18. Frederic Borch, the Historian and Archivists at the Judge Advocate Legal Center and School in Charlottesville recently wrote an article in the "Annual Bulletin about Judge Joseph Holt and included a picture of his beloved home. This magazine is based nationwide.

Accomplishments for the Friends of the Holt Home, Inc. 2014-2015!

1. January 3, 2014 SAT/ Kathina Bell/ SAT correspondence with Joshua Wilks has answered questions regarding volunteer time used as match. Joshua Wilks has answered yes to Susan's retired teacher volunteer time for letter writing, and researching for the home. Activities have to be directly used to the home's preservation related to the project. Time developing website to educate people about the home's preservation, research for the 5th George S. Prugh Lecture on the Career and Military Life of Judge Joseph Holt and other lectures educating people about the preservation of home. Updates with the Holt website, writing press releases, and planning the annual Holt Home Community Day. All members are turning in volunteer time.
2. January 16, 2014 The Friends of the Holt Home received the original deed conveying the cemetery real estate from BB& T as Trustee of the Holt Cemetery Trust to the Friends of the Holt Home, Inc./ Charlie Corbett
3. February 6, 2014 delivered a lecture on Judge Holt for the Owensboro/ Davis Co. Library: The Civil

War/including updates with the Judge Joseph Holt Home.

4. February 7, 2014, Ted Guillaum/ Organ Grinder from Tennessee/ has been scheduled and will be present at the 6th annual Holt Home Community Day (NEW EVENT) March 7, 2014 Rick Brown/ Wave 3TV completed the Holt Home Community Day video for the 5th annual Holt Home Community Day in 2013. (Partnering with Wave 3TV.) Included on the www.jholt-houseky.org website. This will assist in grant efforts!
5. April 4, 2014 The Friends of the Holt Home, Inc. received a grant for the amount of $500.00 for our organization.
6. Donors Robert W. Whayne and Suzanne Wallace Whayne were issued a tax receipt for a $500 gift/ grant through the Community Foundation of Louisville.
7. April 18, 2014 Lincoln-Holt Presentation to Breckinridge County Elementary Schools. Susan Dyer accompanied Larry Elliott as he gave performances and mentioned Holt's importance as Lincoln's JAG/spoke briefly to students about Holt, Community Day and renovation.
8. April, 2014 renovation began on the Judge Joseph Holt Home/ Lanham Brothers Contractors of Owensboro.
9. Spring, 2014 Frederic Borch, Historian and Archivist at the Judge Advocate Legal Center and School in Charlottesville wrote an article in the " Annual Bulletin" about Judge Joseph Holt and included a picture of his home. (Nationwide distribution)
10. Summer 2014, Lincoln Memorial University in Harrogate, TN will be doing an educational series on Joseph Holt (General Orders No. 100)
11. May 2, 2014, The Friends of the Holt Home Inc. received a check representing the final net proceeds from the distribution of the Holt Family Trust. These funds will be used for the upkeep and maintenance of the cemetery. And has been deposited in a local bank.
12. May 2014 The Judge Joseph Holt Home is included on the Kentucky Lincoln Heritage Trail 2014 Summer Promotion tear off sheets. Permission was given from Mrs. Parks to use her colored picture of the Holt Home for the icon.
13. June 12, 2014, Phillip Mink, Archaeologist, Kentucky Archaeological Survey /final report and invoice ($1,000.) for the GPR survey conducted in June of 2013 at the Judge Joseph Holt Home Cemetery. The report states it is likely that Holt was buried in a vault and there are two unmarked graves in the cemetery. The Friends paid for this survey that was the beginning of understanding more about the site and grounds.
14. Wrote a grant application for the Friends used by the Breckinridge County Fiscal Court/ submitted by Kathina Bell/ to Bluegrass Pipeline. Breckinridge County Fiscal Court was awarded $10,000.
15. June 16, 2014 Judge Joseph Holt Home wayside panel. Mudpuppy & Water dog developed the text and proposed images for an interpretation panel of Joseph Holt at the Holt Family Cemetery. The Holt Family Cemetery Grant written in 2008 by Susan Dyer for the Breckinridge County Fiscal Court was used to make the match. Total cost was $1,763.00
16. June 18, 2014 A License Agreement was entered into with James L. Wimsatt "Artist" allowing Mrs. Dyer and The Friends of the Holt Home, Inc. to use Mr. Wimsatt's beautiful artwork depicting the Joseph Holt Home/Charlie Corbett
17. July11, 2014, Finalized all scheduled performers/ exhibits for Holt Home Community Day.
18. July11, 2014 Submitted all articles for the media's coverage for the 6th annual Holt Home Community Day.
19. August 1, 2014, Holt website can take donations online on www.jholt-houseky.org New sign with renovation picture designed for the Holt Home Community Day (can take donations with credit cards Sherry Stith) Donated $250.00 for the sign.
20. August 21, 2014 Jessica Burdette, Personal Trust Specialist with BB&T asked for the Friends to pay the cost for closing the Holt Trust in the amount of $ 443.85. The Holt Family Cemetery is now owned by the Friends of the Holt Home, Inc.
21. September, 2014 Invited by Wave3TV for interview about the Holt Home Community Day. Can view under Events on www.jholt-houseky.org
22. September 3, 2014 Friends of the Holt Home received a gift The Works of Robert Burns; with His Life as Allan Cunningham two volumes Vol. II 1834 belonging to Joseph Holt signed by Holt from historian, John P. Behen of Elizabethtown.
23. September 27, 2014 The 6th Annual Holt Home Community Day was very successful with a 600 plus crowd! Over $2,500 worth of donations were received. The most on record!!!
24. Friends of the Holt Home, Inc. received a patriotic historic hat rack donated by Wayne and Mary Hill. Ms. Hill said she had owned the hat rack for over 40 years and was told it was over 100 years old.
25. Susan Dyer attended the Kentucky Heritage Council Fall Conference in Paducah, KY. (highlights/

panel discussion "Be the Future of the Past in Kentucky." Thoughts about parking areas and how they should not distract from natural or historic aspects of the property were shared with the committee.

26. Susan Dyer, Vice-Chair Attended the Kentucky Lincoln Heritage Trail Alliance meeting September 10, 2014 Lincoln Memorial University in Harrogate, TN.
27. Because of continued communication with Centre's President, Dr. John Roush and his wife Susie, a private tour of the Judge Joseph Holt Home was given a couple years ago. Centre College learned Holt attended there and now there is a new Holt/ Lincoln sign at Centre College.
28. January 8 received $200.00 donation from Southern States and $100.00 donation from Cleo Lee for drain pipes for the Holt Home.
29. January 8, 2015 Relatives of Susan Dyer, Fannie Mae Berry, niece of her grandfather (has period pieces from Breckinridge County) is giving a fainting couch, table, bed and two period lamps to the Holt Home.
30. Gave Carl Thomas, President of the Gheens Foundation and Kathy Knotts grant administrator a private tour of the Holt Home on February 11, 2015.
31. Friends of the Holt Home, Inc. submitted a grant to the National Trust on February 1, 2015 for a site use plane.
32. Susan Dyer attended KLHTA Board Officers meeting April 30, 2015, in Hodgenville.
33. Received word from David J. Brown, Executive Vice President & Chief Preservation Officer on March 31, 2015 that the Friends of the Holt Home received a grant for the use site use plan of the Judge Joseph Holt Home.
34. Indiana National Guard Office E-mailed the Friends' website, Roger Wilson, the legal Administrator. Wanted information about a print of President Lincoln along with Joseph Holt, signing General Orders 100. Contact information was given for the JAG School who released the print.
35. New this year for the 7th annual Holt Home Community Day is a Civil War Baseball game, and Jonathan Bennett is the coach. The Holt Home will be the first official KY Lincoln site in the state to host a game such as this.
36. Updates for the Holt website at www.jholt-houseky.org can be viewed by clicking on Events and Renovation. Susan Dyer took new pictures of renovation, wrote captions, and composed new Holt promo along with preservation updates and an article for the www.jholt-houseky.org sent to Greg Hicks webmaster, and has been placed!
37. The Judge Joseph Holt Home will be hosting one of the Kentucky Lincoln Heritage Trail Alliance's meetings in 2016 where the Holt Home is the last official Kentucky Lincoln Site in the state to be restored.
38. All events have been planned for the 7th annual Holt Home Holt Community Day on September 26, 2015, which has taken the past year.
39. Received another grant from Robert & Suzanne Whayne on May 8, 2015 for $500.00 through the Community Foundation of Louisville! As always thank-you notes were sent to both the giver and Community Foundation.
40. Much effort and time was spent informing the Gheens Foundation with state partners Diane Comer, PR at the KY Heritage Council/ State Preservation Office and Susan Dyer, President of the Friends of the Holt Home Inc. had a personal meeting on December 15, 2014 upon invitation by President, Carl Thomas. A private tour of the Holt Home was given on February 11, 2015, and the grant submitted February 12, 2015. Recently, Carl Thomas has contacted Susan Dyer with news that he is retiring on June 25, 2015. And that he has made sure his replacement Barry Allen, knows about the spear header's mission and team to fully restore/preserve the Holt Home. Susan has been invited to meet with the new President Barry Allen.
41. Received a personal call from President John Roush of Centre College in May, 2015 saying he and his wife Susie were keeping a watch over the Holt project from a distance and to keep updating him with events, renovation, grants and the continued hard work.
42. The Friends received a Hamilton Victorian Parlor organ to be placed in the Judge Joseph Holt Home once restored from Georgia (Davis) Whelan in May, 2015.
43. A new interpretative marker was placed at the Holt Home Family Cemetery on May 19, 2015 by Paul Joseph O' Donoghue and Michael county worker. The Holt Family Cemetery has been transferred to the Friends of the Holt Home Inc. from the Holt Trust. The interpretative marker was made possible by a grant.
44. Positive works with a cooperative agreement with Breckinridge County Fiscal Court continues/ Judge Maurice Lucas/ Charlie Corbett/ Susan Dyer

Renovation with the TE grant from Phase1/ $500,000 that Governor Beshear has assisted

Recently, the new beautiful roof has been added and completed in fall of 2014, 80% of the old tile on the kitchen was used and the kitchen tiled roof restored, soffit/ trim/crown/ fascia replacement restored, dormers have been removed, repaired, repainted and reinstalled, the guttering has been added, chimneys have been restored, and lightening rod protection was added in February 2015.

Work is continuing now on restoration of the historic windows and pediments.

The 7th annual Holt Home Community Day is September 26, 2015. (This is the last opportunity to thank Governor Beshear publically while still serving the Commonwealth!

Accomplishments for the Friends of the Holt Home, Inc. 2016

1. Gheens Foundation/ Past President Carl Thomas encouraged a meeting with the new President Barry Allen and grant administrator. It was a memorable meeting on December 3, 2015. The magnitude of the Holt Project is impressive to the new president. The Friends received compliments, and that this was the most passion, humble, worthy, and genuine work the Foundation has met with yet. That this project is real and for the people! President Barry Allen said the Gheen's Foundation may be able to change their vision to fund beyond Louisville.
2. Roger Wilson, Legal Administrator for the Indiana National Guard JAGS 38th Division contacted Susan Dyer to say the JAGS have confirmed March 5, 2016 for the Onsite Training date at the Joseph Holt Home.
3. January 4, 2016 a request was granted from Roger Wilson, Legal Administrator of the Indiana National Guard JAGS for the media to be present on March 5, 2016.
4. Kimberley Nyberg/ Consultant for the site use plan from the National Trust for Historic Preservation grant met with the Friend's organization on January 7, 2016.
5. Planning for the Indiana National Guard Onsite Training was discussed with a handout from Susan Dyer at the January 7, 2016 Friend's meeting.
6. The funds from the Historic Preservation (Electronic funds) were transferred to the Friends' bank account to pay Kim Nyberg as the Consultant. / Sherry Stith
7. Diane Comer was called after speaking with Judge Lucas about the pending SAT grant with concerns that Kimberly Tompkins who now leads with the Transportation Phase 2 grant was familiarized with the knowledge that the SAT 150,000 grant must be used by September 16, 2016. Ms. Tompkins knows the grant exist and has said the grants could be done separately, that the SAT money could be used on the back of the home and Jon Rollins could write them separately for the stairwell, back porch and back windows. This was officially approved in March of 2016!
8. Gaye Clark 14th Kentucky Light Artillery Cannon has been scheduled for 2016!!!! Gaye rescued us for the 7th Annual Holt Home Community Day when the 113th cancelled two days before our event.
9. Larry Elliott and H.E.S. have called and have requested Abraham Lincoln to be present at the Holt Home on April 12 for a presentation, and tour of the home. Much effort has been put into introducing Larry Elliott to Breckinridge County Elementary Schools. For the past, several years Susan Dyer and Larry Elliott have gone together to all the schools and Elliott has presented and portrayed Lincoln. He has shared about Lincoln's Advocate, Joseph Holt, Lincoln's JAG, how Holt was famous nationwide and how his home has been saved and under restoration for new uses.
10. On January 6, 2016, the Kentucky Historical Society requested information be sent out about the Kentucky Local History Trust Fund to our friends, and supporters. This helps KHS, local history and ourselves. Information was distributed to the Breckinridge Co. Library along with follow-up.
11. Susan Dyer contacted Diane Comer to get Charlie Corbett's request to get started as a prequalified contractor. The website address was sent on 1/8/16 to Charlie Corbett to complete the application.
12. Request was filled for the KY Home Guard Band to perform at the 8th Annual Holt Home Community Day on September 24, 2016.
13. January 21, 2016 continued planning for the Indiana National Guard JAGS Onsite Training/ Veronica Ent ordered food, and heaters, details were planned on menu, eating table wear, hand washing, necessary items for classic luncheon for Army JAGS with Veronica Ent, Sherry Stith and Susan Dyer.
14. January 25, Names were completed with contact /email& phone numbers for work in progress to schedule meetings with community for Kim Nyberg/ Consultant for Site Use Plan for National Trust Grant/ Veronica Ent/ Susan Dyer/ Maurice Lucas
15. January 25, Private Property Utilization Agreement allowing Army's Blackhawk helicopters to land at Holt Home for Onsite Training/Delivered/ Signed/ Sent/ to Roger Wilson, Indiana National

Guard JAGS/Judge Lucas/ Kathina Bell/ Susan Dyer

16. Request for Hosting JAGS completed January 26, 2016 (All details for event, preparing home, media contacts, and press releases written)/ Judge Lucas/ Kathina Bell/ Veronica Ent/ Susan Dyer
17. Kim Nyberg/ Consultant requested a one-page overview of the Holt project with general information and project goals to be handed out at the community meetings for the Site Use Plan. Susan Dyer wrote the overview sent on January 26, 2016
18. February 2, 2016 new lighting has been installed around the Holt Home and three security cameras on motion detect with a local DVR lockbox have been ordered. Charlie Corbett/ Judge Maurice Lucas/ Made possible by the Kentucky Bluegrass Grant/ Kathina Bell & Susan Dyer
19. Video Surveillance signage put up at Holt Home on February 6, 2016. Charlie Corbett/ Made possible by KY Bluegrass grant.
20. Removal of most decorative iron, historic Holt fence and delivered to TGH Machining/ February 6, 2016/Charlie Corbett/ Made Possible by Friends of the Holt Home, Inc. and the Brown-Forman Grant/ Susan Dyer
21. February 10, 2016 Media Advisory was sent informing local, regional and state media about the Indiana National Guard JAGS Onsite training (closed to the public. / Susan Dyer
22. February 10, 2016 Updates of Onsite Training sent to President Roush, President, Centre College.
23. Trees trimmed, removal, fence removal and delivered to TGA machining February 11, 2016 Charlie Corbett/ Paul Joseph O'Donoghue
24. February 11, 2016 Jefferson County Civil War Round Table, President Gerry Reilly rescheduled talk by Susan Dyer on Judge Joseph Holt, Holt project and upcoming book "The New Jewel in Kentucky's Civil War Crown" for May 13, 2016 in Madison, Indiana.
25. Updates for Onsite Training sent to Roger Wilson, Indiana National Guard JAGS February15, 2016
26. Continued communication with COL Fred Borch, Top Historian and Archivist at the JAG School. Fred stated in an E-mail on February 16, 2016 "Holt would be proud to see what has been done for his legacy!" An update with the Indiana JAGS was given as the Friends continue striving to make the Holt Home become a National meeting place for the Army Judge Advocate across the nation.
27. On February 22, 2016, a letter was E-mailed to COL Frank King, XO OTJAG requesting LTG Flora D. Darpino to be the 2017 Key-note Speaker for the 9th Annual Holt Home Community Day. Answer received from COL King, February 22 stating with certainty the Army cannot say LTG Flora D. Darpino can attend, please know that we will evaluate this request along with her other travel and professional engagements. That said, the Holt Home holds a special place in the JAG Corps' history so please be assured that we are working very hard to support this request. / Susan Dyer
28. February 16, 2016 Completed application for proposed change to property/ KY Heritage Council/ Preservation Easement/ KHC Form 9PE-1)/ Charlie Corbett
29. February 23, 2016 Picnic tables installed, anchored and locked. Charlie Corbett/ Funding made possible by the Friends of the Holt Home, Inc.
30. Andrew M. Condia, Field Representative for Senator Mitch McConnell was given the private tour requested on February 29, 2016. Judge Lucas/ Susan Dyer
31. March 4, 2016 Roger Wilson, WO1, JA Legal Administrator Indiana National Guard sent updates stating 22. JAGS would be arriving by Blackhawk (as long as the weather cooperates) and four by vehicle. Supreme Court Justice David is wanting to give a power point presentation. And all JAGS are excited about coming to the Holt Home.
32. History was made!!!! The Indiana National Guard JAGS (Judge Advocates) held its Onsite Training in the Judge Joseph Holt Home March 5, the first new reuse for the historical home. The Guards Onsite Training program consisted of a training session partly in Bloomington, Ind., because of heavy fog and then later at the Holt Home, arriving in three Blackhawk helicopters. Following an official welcome, a luncheon was given in honor for the 26 JAGS, including the Indiana Supreme Court Justice Stephen David. There was a short meeting in the classroom set up in the historic home for the JAGS, a tour given by Susan Dyer - President of the Friends of the Holt Home, and Interviews by area media. Media covered the landing of the three Blackhawk helicopters flying from the Guards 2002 South Holt Road location. And Wave 3TV, Rick Brown, Production Manager was on site all day for the event which aired on Wave 3TV on Sunday March 6, 2106! The Friends of the Holt Home, Inc. worked diligently to make this happen!!!!!
33. March 7, 2016 The Ambrose Meador DAR organization's guest speaker spoke about restoration of

the historic Holt Home, updates for the project, and Judge Joseph Holt was delivered in a talk by President of the Friends of the Holt Home, Inc. and author of "Lincoln's Advocate." Susan Dyer.

34. Regina Stivers, Deputy Secretary E-mailed on March 8, 2016 to say she would be visiting the Holt Home once the General Assembly session has been completed.
35. Charlie Corbett sowed grass on the Holt grounds and it looks beautiful.
36. March 10 and 11 The National Trust for Preservation Grant for the site use plan of the Historic Holt Home meetings were held at the Breckinridge County Public Library. The summary of the meetings was discussed at the Friends of the Holt Home, Inc. special called meeting on March 11, 2016 at 1:30 led by Kim Nyberg, consultant. The meetings were all positive, and ideas of what the public want for the Holt Home to become were all recorded and will be included in the final report composed from these meetings by Kim Nyberg. Comments were shared by Kim about the Friends of the Holt Home's work as.... The Non-Profit organization is very professional, do what they say. And everyone was very excited on all that has happened and they are very proud of the hard work that has been done to get where the home is today! And the community is taking ownership of the recent success of the Indiana National Guard JAG Event Onsite Training. And many thanks were received at the meetings for the tremendous progress that has been made to save and restore the Holt Home.
37. The planning of these meetings took much effort from the Friends of the Holt Home, Inc.'s board. The meetings were over the course of two days.
38. Doug Sikes, Publisher from Acclaim Press visited on March 15, 2016 to discuss Susan Dyer's upcoming book "The New Jewel in Kentucky's Civil War Crown" (working title) on how the Holt Home has been saved.
39. The Press Release and pictures along with captions of the Holt Home Hosting Indiana National Guard JAGS were sent to Greg Hicks, webmaster for the Friends of the Holt Home, Inc. to place on the www.jholt-houseky.org

Website under Events. Veronica Ent purchased the Indiana JAGS banner (given by the Breckinridge County Chamber) displayed in the picture and used at the JAG event. The Chamber also supported the luncheon, and numerous things making the event classic!!! Many thanks go to Veronica Ent!!!

The successfully JAG Event was shared On March 30, 2016 at the KLHTA meeting in Springfield. "The Board of Directors stated, "How clever to come up with an idea on making the Holt Home have such a prestigious title and goal to become the National meeting place for all the Army JAGS across America."

40. Roger Wilson Legal Administrator, Indiana National Guard Office of Staff Judge Advocate confirmed on March 18, 2016 COL Daniel Kozlowski will be speaking at the 8th Annual Holt Home Community Day on September 24, 2016.
41. Brittany M. Fausey, attorney from Ohio presently who was the former Field Representative for Ron Lewis E-mailed to Congratulate the progress on how much has been done for the Holt Home. She stated it feels her heart with so much happiness with ALL the success! Ms. Fausey was from the first Office of a Congressman to come to assist in 2006 and helped Susan Dyer address concerns with the Department of the Interior in Washington D.C.
42. Paul Joseph O'Donoghue contacted TGH on 4/8/2016 regarding restoration of the historical Holt Home fence. The Hardesty's have devised a plan on how to reset old cast iron post and method to reinstall fence rails.
43. The Friends of the Holt Home, Inc. received a check on April 11, 2016 by mail from Father Richard of Brunswick, MO for $50.00, Sherry Stith secretary.
44. Hardinsburg Elementary and Irvington Elementary came to the Holt Home on April 12, 2016 for a presentation from Larry Elliott portraying President Abraham Lincoln, and blending in history of Lincoln's lawyer, Joseph Holt along with a tour of the historic home. Those assisting were the two schools, Judge Maurice Lucas, Veronica Ent, and Susan Dyer. This was a first tour for Breckinridge County Schools.
45. Hardinsburg Elementary School requested a follow-up article on April 15, 2016 for their school website. The article also appeared in the Breckinridge County-Herald News and the Meade County Messenger. The Friends received numerous compliments from both schools and their students.
46. On April 18, 2016 Diane Comer, PR for the KY Heritage Council/ State Preservation Office (lifetime partners) posted pictures for the Kentucky Heritage Council on the Kentucky Heritage's Facebook page and on the Save the Judge Joseph Holt Home, Facebook page, "What a difference time makes!)
47. May 5, 2016 the Friends of the Holt Home, Inc. approved a 16x20 plaque to be designed, purchased

and hung in the historic Holt Home for remembrance of the First New Use of the Holt Home/ Indiana National Guard Onsite Training. Veronica Ent/ Susan Dyer

48. The Friends of the Holt Home, Inc. received word from the KY Heritage Council on May 9, 2016 to proceed on the historical Holt Home fence, Kathina Bell.
49. Tear Away Maps for Kentucky Lincoln Heritage Trail sites were shipped by Warren Greer, Director of the KLHTA on May 10, 2016. The Holt Home received 600. These maps are used at the KY State Fair, Holt Home Community Day, and are kept in the Breckinridge County Chamber's Office for visitors.
50. May 12, 2016 the Friends were told advertisements will be placed ASAP for the Save America's Treasures Grant/ work will be completed by September 30, 2016. Salutes go to Jon Rollins with GRW architects for his persistence and professionalism to get things moving as this is the last SAT grant to be distributed and used in America.
51. Congratulations to the Friends of the Holt Home, Inc., who volunteer hundreds of hours for the Holt Home along with county workers grooming the grounds and Kathina Bell who did paper work making the $150,000 match for the SAT grant mostly with volunteers. Thus, meeting the deadline and requirements to receive full funding to remove the dilapidated back porch of the Holt Home and reconstruct as original.
52. Ken Knouf, President of the Jefferson County Civil War Round Table in Madison, IN invited Susan Dyer as Key-note speaker for the Round Table Gordon Whitney Memorial Dinner on May 13, 2016 on Judge Joseph Holt, the Holt project, restoration and the upcoming book "The New Jewel in Kentucky's Civil War Crown."
53. Graham Shelby, writer for " Kentucky Living" magazine who composed the featured story about the Holt Home and the effort behind the project E-mailed May 17, 2017 for updates about school field trips and the March 5th Indiana National Guard JAGS on-site training, along with continued restoration of Holt home (SAT grant) and work on historical Holt fence (a part of the historical home) made possible by the Brown-Forman grant, and work on the grounds by the Friends of the Holt Home, Inc.
54. Phil Huddleston, Chief of Staff for former Lt. Governor Luallen with 30 years in state government, who has worked behind the scenes for the Holt Home E-mailed May 18, 2016 to say he and his wife Pat would attend the 8th Annual Holt Home Community Day on September 24, 2016.
55. Kate Sowada, Coordinator for the KY History Mobile E-mailed May 18, 2016 to confirm the History Mobile is scheduled at the Holt Home for Saturday, September 24, 2016. Made possible by KY Historical Society, State Partner.
56. On May 26, 2016 Jon Rollins, with GRW architect of Lexington E-mailed stating Lanham Brothers will begin work on May 30, 2016 for the Save America's Treasures grant.
57. On May 30, 2016, the Breckinridge County Historical Society requested Susan Dyer to write an article on updates for the Holt project for the historical society's newsletter. The article was also sent to Greg Hicks, webmaster for the Friends to place on the www.jholt-houseky.org under restoration.
58. May 2016 Touritz is launching new Kentucky Lincoln Heritage Trail "apps" and web site and tourism page for the Judge Joseph Holt home. Warren Greer.
59. Friends of the Holt Home, Inc, received a gift from Ellen Austin (a period rocking chair) belonging to former lawyer, Henry Gibson's mother. Judge Lucas picked up the gift for the Friends.
60. June 2, 2016 A Progress Report for the Holt Home restoration was submitted to Breckinridge County Historical Society for their newsletter upon request and sent and placed on the Holt website. / Greg Hicks & Susan Dyer
61. June 4, 2016, Deed of Gift document for gifts received for Holt Home requested by Susan Dyer/ written by John Nyberg/ Edited by Judge Kelly Easton.
62. June 7, 2016 Permit for Holt Fence KY Highway Dept./ R/W Encroachment Permit completed by Charlie Corbett and signed by Judge Maurice Lucas. The permit will allow Friends to move historic fence closer to the road.
63. Right of Way permit approved on June 8, 2016. / Charlie Corbett The Friends of the Holt Home can proceed with fence installation.
64. On June 14, 2016 Gaye Clarke responded with request that the 14th Kentucky Light Artillery will be present for the Holt Home Community Day on September 24, 2016.
65. Jon Rollins, Architect with GRW has informed Friends permission was granted for the go-ahead from SHPO (KY Heritage Council/ State Preservation Office to proceed with historic Holt fence restoration made possible by the Brown-Forman grant.
66. Charlie Corbett spoke with Richard Butler, Assistant Superintendent of Breck. Co. Schools on July

1, 2016 regarding a Student Day for all students in Breckinridge County Schools previously approved by the Friends organization. Details were requested with an outline of purposes, objectives and importance of the Holt Home and Holt's legacy by Susan Dyer, lunch at Holt, and date was set for September 21, 2016.

67. July 1, 2016, Susan Dyer, President of the Friends composed an outline with objectives for Breckinridge County Schools. Veronica Ent did much planning with the scheduling and contacting all the schools including a follow-up, and the training of Gifted and Talented students from Breckinridge County Schools. Several meeting times, numerous E-mails and follow -ups organized the very worthy Student Day with a practice tour for tour guides at the historic Holt Home. Those assisting were Judge Lucas, Veronica Ent, Charlie Corbett, Richard Butler, Janet Meeks, Paul Joseph O'Donoghue and Susan Dyer
68. Received a note from Steve Oldfield designer of www.abelincoln.tours. Steve is designing the website and will be working with the Friends when the time is right.
69. The Kentucky Civil War Bugle wrote an article in the July-September issue, 2016 about Holt cakes sent by Susan Dyer for over a decade to organization and individuals whom have assisted with helping bring attention to the Holt Home with kind deeds of contacts, assisting with grants, putting in kind words and numerous other things.
70. Shannon Brook, managing editor at Kentucky Living sent a thank-you for assisting with fact-check in making the featured article on the Holt Home and efforts of saving it appearing in the September, 2016 issue as great as it can be.
71. July 18, 2016 Carmon Imagining did the enlargement print of the JAG picture of the On-Site training for the Indiana National Guard JAGS, taken by Eddie Dyer for the First new-reuse of the Holt Home.
72. July 21, 2016 the assigned contract for the Friends and parking information was sent to Julie Kemper, KY Historical Society for the KY History Mobile. / Susan Dyer (One of the Holt Home's state partners grants this wonderful asset for the Holt Home Community Day. / Kent Whitworth, Director, KY Historical Society.
73. August 4, 2016, Charlotte Taul is donating a baby crib to the Holt Home.
74. August 16, 2016 The completed list of former KY Lincoln Bicentennial Commission members and Advisory Committee names and contacts as requested by the KY Heritage Council were researched and compiled and sent to Kathina Bell to send invitations to these individuals for their efforts in believing in the Holt project, making the Holt Home an official KY Lincoln site in the Commonwealth with help from the KY Heritage Council, Legacy Project of the Lincoln Bicentennial in 2007 which purchased the Holt Home for the Breckinridge County Fiscal Court with acquisition through grants!/ Susan Dyer/ Kathina Bell/ Diane Comer/ Warren Greer, and Iris Larue.
75. August 23, 2016 Jerome D. Klein, MSG, USA Chief Paralegal sent a note saying the Staff Judge Advocate LT. COL Bagwell will support the 8th Annual Holt Home Community Day with the Wreath-Laying Ceremony at Holt's monument.
76. A wonderful note was received from Byron Crawford on August 23, 2016 sending kind words with great praise for the success of the Holt Home project! Mr. Crawford helped raise $25,000 for a fun-raiser for the Friends of the Holt Home in 2012 when he came to speak about saving a National Treasure.
77. August 25, 2016 SHPO approved the alternative flagpole location on the Holt cemetery side of the gravel drive. Jon Rollins/ Charlie Corbett/ Jen Williamson
78. Craig Potts, Executive Director, and Preservation Officer at the KY Heritage Council Preservation/ State Office responded on August 29, 2016 and has accepted to speak at the 8th Annual Holt Home Community Day.
79. Fred Borch, Historian and Archivist at the JAG School replied September 2, 2016 on updates of the Holt Project. "This is really great news about all the progress, for Holt Home." The importance continues with updates to the JAG School where the Friends continue to partner with the Army to make the Holt Home a National meeting place for the Army JAGS across America. / Susan Dyer
80. The Greens Foundation sent a note of congratulations on the work for the SAT grant! Updates on the Holt website are very important in keeping the public informed!
81. September 9, 2016 the Owensboro-Messenger called and they are going to write a story about the 8th Annual Holt Home Community Day. The Owensboro-Messenger is a great media partner with the Holt Home.
82. Andrew Effron former Supreme Court Judge for the U.S. Army e-mailed to say "it is gratifying to see interest in Holt remains strong!"
83. September 15, 2016 a radio interview with WXBC promoted the 8th Annual Holt Home Community

Day/ Judge Kelly Easton, Jonathan Bennett, Civil War Baseball coach, and Susan Dyer.

84. Information was sent after a phone call with Janet Meeks, Breckinridge County Superintendent of Public Schools to help promote the 8th Annual Holt Home Community Day. On September 21, 2016, the article was sent to all staff in the district. / Susan Dyer

85. On September 22, 2016, A Face Book Ad was purchased and run by KLHTA Warren Greer, Director to promote the 8th Annual Holt Home Community Day. The ad was seen by 12, 267 people with 310 likes and 13 comments. Many people were familiar with the Holt Home and expressed interest in visiting. The Holt Home is a member of the KLHTA.

86. Community Day Brochure complied with a rough draft and final draft prepared for the 8th Annual Holt Home Community Day/ Kathina Bell/ Susan Dyer

87. September 24, 2016 *A Holt Home blog . . .Highlights of the day, A year's work!*

They came and saw how historic mansion becomes an educational, tourism anchor

It was a grand day at the Holt Home.

More than 3,000 visitors came Sept. 24 to explore the history of Joseph Holt's legacy when he served President Abraham Lincoln as the top lawyer for the United States Army.

They toured the antebellum mansion during the 8th Annual Holt Home Community Day, walked the beautiful grounds graced with trees and marveled at the renovation progress of the Hardinsburg structure. Smiles were a highlight of the day as visitors viewed the numerous improvements, such as the restored front and back windows. The beautiful replica of the back-stair tower gave insight to master workmanship.

The crowd began arriving early pointing out and admiring the restored Holt fence. Throughout the day, the grounds were filled with compliments and people, locally and from across the state and beyond. Those who attended enjoyed eating on the new picnic tables, seeing the recently placed flagpole with "Old Glory" waving among the treetops, and watching the Civil War baseball game, the first official Kentucky Lincoln site to host one.

Bands played, stirring the atmosphere with patriotic, traditional, and period music. Breckinridge County students took great pride in performing songs from the period and sharing Holt's history and national significance.

The echo of "Taps" at Holt's monument was very moving at the wreath-laying ceremony performed by the U.S. Army Cadet Command and Fort Knox soldiers with Lieutenant Colonel Jimmy Bagwell, the staff judge advocate. The Indiana National Guard Judge Advocates (JAG) – COL Daniel Kozlowski – discussed the Onsite Training at the historic home in March and the importance of Joseph Holt's legacy. Col. Kozlowski came to lend a hand supporting the Friends of the Holt Home to make Judge Holt's dwelling become a national meeting place for Army JAGS across the nation. Judge Holt's home holds a special place in the history of the JAG Corps.

Numerous speakers spoke briefly explaining the roles their stations contributed to the Community Day. Ninety-eight-year-old James Wimsatt was recognized and honored for his gift – the famous Holt print used for all events, promotions and programs. Tamara Langman, Louisville Actor's Theatre Costume Shop coordinator spoke about the significance of history and costume connections. One of four state partners, the Kentucky Historical Society, provided the Kentucky History Mobile with the Civil War exhibit. Judge Tommy Turner, former Co-chair of the Kentucky Lincoln Bicentennial Commission, spoke about "The Legacy Project" of the Kentucky Lincoln Bicentennial, the acquisition grant that made possible the purchase of the home for the Breckinridge County Fiscal Court.

Craig Potts, executive director of the Kentucky Heritage Council, shared how partnership with the Holt Home, local partners and community support is shaping tourism, economic development and community pride across the state. Former State Representative Dwight D. Butler relayed the vision of saving the home, and how taking actions to protect and preserve our local community's important history saves Kentucky's rich heritage.

Keynote speaker, David L. Morgan, who was executive director at the Kentucky Heritage Council from 1984-2006, delivered heartwarming comments about preservation, the importance of protecting history and the numerous benefits it brings to local communities, the state and nation.

Field Representative Isaac Myers attended and spoke briefly telling the people that Governor Bevin would do whatever he could.

The cannon firings, Civil War campsite, fragrance of food and the community pride event will long be remembered as the Friends of the Holt Home continue to take actions to protect, preserve and promote Breckinridge County's historical jewel.

Friends President Susan Dyer emphasized in the morning welcome, "the Holt Home is our compass, a link to our past and our gift to the future." She asked visitors to keep updated at www.jholthouseky.org as the Holt Home is being developed to become an educational and tourism anchor for South Central Kentucky.

88. Received a request from LTC Bagwell, Staff Judge Advocate USACC& Fort Knox about bringing his entire JAG team for a professional development session at the Holt Home in Spring of 2017! Susan Dyer
89. Numerous Thank-you letters from the Friends were sent from October through November for the 8th Annual Holt Home Community Day along with eight Holt cakes to organizations who partnered and individuals who did special things for the event! Susan Dyer
90. A request was submitted to Jean Williams, Assistant for Gov. Matt Bevin on September 30, 2016 by Isaac Myers, Field Representative for Gov. Matt Bevin from the Friends of the Holt Home, Inc. to invite Gov. Matt Bevin to be a Key-note speaker for the 9th Annual Holt Home Community Day on September 23, 2017. Charlie Corbett/ Isaac Myers, Susan Dyer
91. October 7, 2016 Jon Rollins sent a note about the Friends of the Holt Home, Inc., meeting concerning tax credits that have been approved and how to proceed to the Cecilian Bank, Don Wise, Amanda Kincard, Maurice Lucas, Charlie Corbett, Kathina Bell, Judge Kelly Easton, and Susan Dyer
92. Preservation Trail Blazers (Our Future, Our Legacy) in Frankfort had very many interesting sessions exploring Kentucky's Historic Preservation legacy, October 14, 2016. Susan Dyer attended sharing the summary of the Conference with the Friends.
93. November 4, 2016 Julie Kemper, Senior Curator at KHS E-mailed to see if the Friends wanted two large Mid-Century carpets, 212 inches x 210. Julie thought of the Holt Home because of the wonderful examples of floor coverings still in the home she saw on Sept. 24, 2016. Ms. Kemper said please consider the carpet as a special piece to use now during restoration. / Julie Kemper/
94. Carol Campbell, Program & Tourism Director at Lincoln Memorial University/ E-Mailed on November 11, 2016 to say she is researching and designing an educational packet on Joseph Holt/ and the Lieber Code.
95. Received a letter from Colonel Sean McGarry, Judge Advocate for Flora D. Darpino/ The Judge Advocate General of the United States Army on November 11, 2016 explaining appreciation for the work of the Friends of the Holt Home, and will plan to provide a more definite response about General Darpino being the key-note speaker for the 9th Annual Home Community Day requested in 2015.
96. December 7, 2016 David Morgan organized a meeting with state partners Judge Lucas, Kathina Bell, Jon Rollins, Diane Comer, Craig Potts, David Morgan and Susan Dyer in Frankfort to discuss unanswered questions concerning Tax Credits at the KY Heritage Council in Frankfort. The meeting was very productive as many questions were answered and numerous items clarified for tax credits.
97. Judge Exec Maurice Lucas E-mailed December 28, 2016 announcing a ceremony with Don Wise and the Cecilian Bank to give them publicity they deserve for purchasing tax credits for the Holt Home granted from the KY Heritage Council/ State Preservation Office in the next few weeks.
98. Received a letter from John A. Roush, President of Centre College on December 28, 2016 mailed on November 29, 2016. The letter discussed the great story about an important man in our nation's history, (our beloved Joseph Holt.) Both President Roush and Susie send their best wishes!

Accomplishments for the Friends of the Holt Home, Inc. 2017

1. Susan Dyer received information from COL James Bagwell, Staff Judge Advocate at the United States Army Cadet Command and Fort Knox on steps to be admitted to Fort McNair in Washington D.C. 12/28/2016.
2. On 12/30/2016 Judge Maurice Lucas closed on the tax credits received from the KY Heritage Council/ State Preservation Office for the Friends of the Holt Home, Inc.
3. Congratulations was received from Craig Potts, Exec. Director at the KY Heritage Council on 1/3/2017 on receiving tax credits for the historic Holt Home.
4. Andrew M. Condia, Field Representative for U.S. Senator Mitch McConnell responded to a request regarding attending a Friends' meeting 1/3/2017.
5. Received an E-mail from John A. Roush of Center College 1/4/2017. President Roush is working on a chance to revisit the Holt Home.
6. 1/5/2017 Received word from Isaac Myers, Field Representative for Governor Bevin saying the Friends' accomplishments for 2016 are quite impressive!
7. Received an E-mail from Brittany Fausey on 1/6/2017, now an attorney, formally with Con-

gressman Ron Lewis' Office stating she is blown away by how far the Holt project has come along.

8. Dr. Timothy Spaulding of Louisville contacted Susan Dyer saying he has 2 sets of girandoles, one period acquired in Fredericksburg, VA and one obtained by a local antique dealer in Louisville he wants to donate to the Holt Home.
9. Susan Dyer, President of the Friends of the Holt Home, Inc. participated on 1/12/2017 with the Kentucky Lincoln Heritage Trail Alliance representing the Holt Home in a conference call to discuss progress, momentum and planning for KLHTA in 2017.
10. Received an E-mail from Former Supreme Court Justice for the U.S. Army, Andrew Condia on help to set up planning for visiting the newly restored Lincoln Conspiracy Court Room in Washington, D.C. where Joseph Holt prosecuted the Lincoln Conspirators.
11. Paul Joseph O'Donoghue discussed completion of the historic Holt fence with TGH and Wayne Hardesty for the Friends of the Holt Home, Inc. on 1/13/2017.
12. Received an E-mail from COL Sean McGarry, Exec. Officer for General Darpino, The Judge Advocate General of the United States Army at the Pentagon thanking Susan Dyer for recent E-mails and updates, efforts on behalf of the Holt Home. And Col McGarry shared the Pentagon recently featured photographs of COL James Bagwell, Staff Judge Advocate at Fort Knox with the wreath-laying ceremony at the Holt Home in their Regimental Quill and Sword publication and the Office of the Judge Advocate General continue to look forward to future updates from the Holt Home.
13. Received word from COL Sean McGarry, Exec. Officer for General Darpino assisting with information on how to schedule the Pentagon tour. Col McGarry stated he would plan for a separate escort after the official tour of the Pentagon and would bring Susan Dyer to meet everyone in the front office and take a picture in front of the Holt portrait on 2/2/2017.
14. Received an E-mail on 2/2/2017 from COL McGarry after sending the 2016 accomplishments of the Friends of the Holt Home, COL McGarry replied, "This is fantastic!"
15. Sherry Stith forwarded an E-mail sent to the Friends website about submitting an advertisement for the Breckinridge County Guide for 2017.
16. Veronica Ent and Susan Dyer gave Dr. Timothy Spaulding and his mother a tour of the Holt Home, and accepted the girandoles gift for the Holt Home.
17. 2/4/2017 Received information for the Pentagon Tour/ Security information.
18. Received phone call from Charlotte Jenkins inviting Susan Dyer for book discussion on Joseph Holt in Louisville 2/6/2017.
19. Susan Dyer wrote and submitted an ad included in the 2017 Breckinridge County Guide.
20. Warren Greer, Director of the KLHTA requested Susan Dyer to contact the Hardin Co. History Museum, Jefferson Davis State site and Farmington all KY Lincoln sites along with Holt Home for their yearly visitation numbers.
21. Susan Dyer assisted with information on 2/9/2017 for KY Lincoln membership letters for the KLHTA.
22. Received an E-mail on 2/9/2017 from Robert Love SSG US Army as POC from the Fort Knox legal Community. The Judge Advocate's Office are gathering numbers for the visit to the Holt Home and asked what the expectations are as the date gets closer for the Fort Knox JAGS' visit.
23. Received an E-mail from Brown-Forman inviting the Friends to submit a grant in 2017.
24. Holt water line service planning consulting/ Jon Rollins/ Charlie Corbett and Judge Lucas on 2/18/2017.
25. Water meter and service plan approved from Jen Williamson in October 2016. Beginning after reviewing approved plans from Jen Williamson at the KY Heritage Council/State Preservation Office/ Charlie Corbett, Jon Rollins, and Judge Maurice Lucas.
26. E-mail from Diane Comer, PR for the KY Heritage Council/ State Preservation Office saying great news from Brown-Forman that 2nd grant is an option! Offered to assist and congratulated Friends with the great updates and things to come!
27. After KY Heritage Council/ State Preservation Office approved in late 2016 for residential water service at Holt Home Charlie Corbett recommended going ahead following the guidelines from Jon Rollins with GRW architects and SHPO and getting Fiscal Court to apply for residential water service at the Holt Home.
28. Susan Dyer compiled information from the point of view of restoration of the Holt Home on 2/21/2017 and along with importance of unity and benefits from being a member of the KLHTA to Warren Greer, Director as Holt Home is an official member of KLHTA.
29. Received E-mail on 2/21/2017 from SSG Robert Love from Fort Knox JAGS community upon request for site visit, professional development for

JAGS to be given a guided tour of the Holt Home, and Holt Family Cemetery. Soldiers will present from JAG office different aspects of Judge Jolt's life. Combination of field trip, training, session, and professional development. JAGS are looking forward to learning as much as they can in addition to building camaraderie and getting out of the office.

30. 2/22/2017 Communications with COL Sean McGarry and Susan Dyer on upcoming Washington D.C. trip/ confirmed/ Pentagon tour.
31. March 2, 2017 Tax credits of $129,000 were granted from the KY Heritage Council/ State Preservation Office/ with a check celebration from the Cecilian Bank who purchased the tax credits/ Don Wise, and members of the Cecilian Bank / Judge Lucas/ Charlie Corbett and the Friends of the Holt Home, Inc.
32. 2/27/2017 received E-mail from SSG Robert Love about private tour of the historic Holt Home.
33. On March 3, 2017 Judge Lucas made an appeal to the Mayor of Hardinsburg and the Mayor has agreed to set the water meter for the Friends of the Holt Home, at no charge. Friends will put down $50.00 deposit.
34. March 3, 2017 Veronica Ent and Susan Dyer gave SSG Love, his wife and little daughter a tour of the historic Holt Home. SSG Love is impressed with what the Friends are doing for the JAGS. SSG Love stated, "He was interested in coming to the Holt Home but now is inspired to bring the JAGS!"
35. Review of SSG Love's visit was sent to the Friends of the Holt Home 3/4/2017. Highlights were half-day combination, professional development/ luncheon/ field trip, two soldiers making presentation on Joseph Holt's life, sending soldier's talk to Susan Dyer to examine and asked Mrs. Dyer to speak with additional information about Holt Home and Holt to the JAGS. 26 JAGS are attending, and they will donate for part of the luncheon. The event is closed to the public.
36. 3/7/2017 Gay Clarke with the KY Light Artillery has confirmed for September's 9th Annual Holt Home Community Day.
37. March 15, 2017 Susan Dyer signed a contract with Doug Sikes, Publisher for Acclaim Press to publish the upcoming book with working title, "The New Jewel in Kentucky's Civil War Crown." A 20-year collection on how the Holt Home has been saved.
38. The Committee from members of the Friends of the Holt Home met on 3/7/2017 for planning the Fort Knox JAGS event on April 20, 2017.
39. Susan Dyer received and E-mail from retired COL Fred Borch, Historian and archivist at the Judge Advocate General's Legal Center and School in Charlottesville, VA. Fred has agreed to write the preface for the upcoming book on how the Holt Home has been saved.
40. Received an E-mail from Leah Rubalcaba, Community Relations Officer Joint-Base Myer-Henderson Hall assisting with forms for upcoming visit to restored Lincoln Conspiracy Court Room where Judge Holt prosecuted conspirators.
41. Received itinerary from SSG Love for Holt Home visit from Fort Knox JAGS on April 20, 2017.
42. The media background and news release for the JAG event on April 20, 2017 was written and submitted to local, regional, and state.
43. Jon Rollins, with GRW architect E-mailed on 3/30/2017 saying he has begun creating drawings for the proposed work that needs to be done for TE Phase 11.
44. Received word from President John Roush of Centre College on 4/9/2017 stating he wished both Susie and he could be present for the JAG event. President Roush sent kind words to say the Holt Home has gathered strength and he and Susie are proud and happy for the Friends of the Holt Home.
45. Heard from Leah Rubalcaba, Community Relations Officer at Fort McNair regarding the May 6, 2017 Grant Hall open house. Susan Dyer has requested to sit in Judge Holt's chair.
46. COL James Bagwell E-mailed to say the JAGS are looking forward to a good time on 4/1/2017.
47. On behalf of the Friends of the Holt Home, Inc, Susan Dyer accepted some wonderful gifts for the Holt Home from Joyce and Thomas Wheatley's family after speaking to Judge Lucas. The period correct furniture includes a marble top dresser, marble top washstand, Lincoln bed, marble top coffee table, and chest of drawers. Eddie and Susan Dyer volunteered to drive their pick-up truck to Dawsonville, GA 373.5 miles each way, 6 hours and 39 minutes to load and bring back to Kentucky an entire period Lincoln bed room suit.
48. The final itinerary and update for the Fort Knox JAGS event at the Holt Home was sent to the Friends on 4/18/2017.
49. Special Report from April 20, 2017/ Fort Knox, Pentagon Honor Holt Friends, Susan Dyer for Development of Home. /(TJAG) at the Pentagon have honored the Friends of the Holt Home and its president.

The Friends received a plaque of appreciation and its president, Susan Dyer, received a medal for outstanding selfless service. The awards took place

April 20 at the Breckinridge County historic mansion of Joseph Holt, Lincoln's judge advocate general.

The award to Dyer was presented on behalf of Brig. Gen. Flora D. Darpino, Judge Advocate General for the U.S. Army. The Friends president was cited for 20 years of dedicated service and duty to Holt's legacy and restoration of his home. She also was given a certificate of appreciation.

COL James Bagwell, Fort Knox Staff Judge Advocate, brought his entire JAG team to the event along with the legal community from the Army Cadet Command and Fort Knox for a historical professional development/field trip exercise.

The colonel, in his remarks, praised Holt for his tireless energy and work "during a crucial time in our nation's history" as the top legal advisor and lawyer for the U.S. Army during the Civil War. PFC Christian Arbec and Specialist Caroline Bedoy reviewed Holt's career under President Abraham Lincoln.

Breckinridge County Judge Executive Maurice Lucas welcomed the team of JAGS and briefly shared how Holt is remembered as the Prosecuting Judge of the Lincoln Conspiracy Trial.

Efforts continue to develop the Holt Home into a national meeting place for the JAG corps.

50. On 4/22/2017 an E-mail was sent to the Friends of the Holt Home as they were honored at the JAG event at the historic Holt Home. A grand day, glorious weather, and the JAGS hold high regards to the "Father of the Judge Advocates". All Army officers present gave numerous compliments to all efforts with continued work for Judge Holt's legacy and beloved home. The Friends were complimented with progress and service of Judge Holt's home as an historical landmark! Special thanks were sent to Breckinridge County Judge Executive Maurice Lucas for having the grounds meticulously groomed for the distinguished guests and special thanks to Veronica Ent, Exec. Director of the Breckinridge County Chamber of Commerce/ Tourism/ for dedication for numerous tasks completed to make the event classic and memorable for the Fort Knox JAGS.
51. Local and regional media coverage for the Fort Knox JAG Corps visit to the historic Holt Home was covered widely in newspapers and radio the week of April 24, 2017.
52. After meeting with the KY Heritage Council/ State Preservation Office in Frankfort in December 2016, David L. Morgan, former Preservation Officer and Executive Director asked if the Holt Home could apply again for tax credits. Craig Potts, Executive Director at the KY Heritage Council answered, yes, the approved part 2 tax credit application can be submitted. And on April 29, 2017 Kathina Bell, Judge Lucas's assistant submitted the application for part two tax credit for the Holt home.
53. April 26, 2017 received a phone call from David Taylor of Owensboro, KY. Mr. Taylor wanted to donate a mahogany wardrobe measuring 81 inches T, 48 inches W and 19 inches D. Mr. Taylor is also donating sections of an iron fence.
54. Received a note from MSG Konkadu Nikolao U.S. Army Cadet Commend and Fort Knox. Thanking the Friends for the pictures from the April 20th event and expressing the JAGS deep appreciation of how our team continues to preserve the legacy of a remarkable leader who has paved the way for their Judge Advocates and Paralegals.
55. Susan Dyer took photos and wrote captions and an article for the JAG event and sent to the Holt webmaster, Greg Hicks to place on the www.jholthouseky.org website.
56. Paul Joseph O'Donoghue forwarded information regarding requesting the Breckinridge County Band and the Breckinridge County Chamber Singers to perform for the 9th Annual Holt Home Community Day on September 23, 2017.
57. COL Jeffery Miller, Executive Officer for TJAG General Flora D. Darpino the 39 Judge Advocate General of the U.S. Army invited Susan Dyer to meet personally with General Darpino on May 5, 2017 at the Pentagon. COL Miller greeted Mrs. Dyer and her husband at the Pentagon and took Mrs. Dyer and her husband through security giving them a private tour of the Pentagon and meeting General Darpino for over one hour in the executive suite. Mrs. Dyer received a medal from General Flora Darpino for 20 years of selfless service for the Holt Home and bringing back Judge Holt's legacy. COL Bagwell assisted with the medal. Col Bagwell's Officer told the JAGS and the Friends of the Holt Home at the Holt event where Dyer received the medal that General Darpino does not give medals to civilians, only to soldiers.
58. On May 5, 2017 at the end of visiting General Darpino in the Pentagon Dyer was promised by General Darpino, "The TJAGS will work on making it a tradition to send the Judge Advocate General to the Holt Home during their 4-year term because of Holt and his leadership and what his legacy means to today's JAGS!"
59. COL Fred Borch, Historian and Archivist at the JAG School coached Danny Huston who por-

trayed Joseph Holt in Robert Redford's movie "The Conspirator" shared with Susan Dyer about the restoration of the Lincoln Conspiracy Court Room restored in 2013. And on May 6, 2017 the long-anticipated visit happened. Permission was granted for Susan Dyer to sit in Judge Joseph Holt's chair. The happenings of that day are composed in a chapter titled "The Lincoln Conspiracy Trial Court Room Revisited" in the upcoming book released on September 21, 2018, published by Acclaim Press.

60. On 5/12/2017 COL Jeffery Miller, Executive Officer for General Darpino E-mailed to say the picture of Susan Dyer next to Judge Holt's portrait in the Pentagon is being sent.
61. Andrel Ross II SPC Administrative Paralegal, for the Fort Knox JAG office wrote saying the office would be mailing a gift to BG Holt's home.
62. 5/18/2017 David Taylor dropped a note saying he had personally delivered the mahogany wardrobe to the 3rd floor of the old court house and the iron fence is in the Breckinridge Co. maintenance garage.
63. Charlie Corbett wrote a fundraising letter and shared with the Friends to be mailed in June for raising funds for the Friends of the Holt Home, Inc. to assist with educational programs at the historic Holt home for students and to assist with the Annual Holt Home Community Day and numerous other functions and events.
64. 5/31/2017 Sherry Stith forwarded the 990-form completed by Drane & Company PLLC CPA's.
65. May 31, 2017 Charlie Corbett E-mailed to announce the Holt Home's exterior brick had been cleaned by approved method of the KY Heritage Council and guidance from Jon Rollins, GRW architect. The Friends payed the bill for cleaning the brick and the equipment rental along with labor.
66. On June 23, 2017 Dr. Janet Meek, Superintendent of Breckinridge County Schools and Susan Dyer discussed the 2nd Annual Student Day at the Holt Home to make sure the new Superintendent, Nick Carter was up to date with the event for all Breckinridge County students and their partnering.
67. On June 26, 2017 Sherry Stith, Secretary of the Friends and Susan Dyer, President of the Friends went to the bank and got a cashiers check for the Friends of the Holt Home, Inc. for the fee payment for the tax credit application and mailed the payment fee.
68. June 26, 2017 Susan Dyer wrote and submitted an article and updated picture of the Holt Home to appear in the September 2017 issue of Kentucky Living magazine to promote the 9th Annual Holt Home Community Day on September 23, 2017.
69. Received the 2nd check of $500.00 from Bob Owsley of the Cecilian Bank to pay on exterior lights to the main entry doors that will be purchased later after approved by KY Heritage Council and Jon Rollins.
70. June 1, 2017 Susan Dyer submitted grant to Brown-Forman for the Friends of the Holt Home, Inc.
71. July 13, 2017 received a message from COL Jeffery Miller as his replacement will be LTC Jeri Hanes the new POC going forward with the TJAGS at the Pentagon.
72. July 17, 2017 Received a call from CPT Todd Wayne, Chief Client Service Officer of the Staff Judge Advocate, 101st Airborne Division (Air Assault) Fort Campbell, KY inviting Susan Dyer to be the Special Guest speaker for the 242d Birthday of the United States Army JAG Corps with the 101st Airborne Division and Fort Campbell, Office of the Staff Judge Advocate, speaking about the life of Judge Joseph Holt and his home.
73. July 27, 2017 Susan Dyer, Special Guest speaker for the 242nd Birthday of the U.S. Army JAG Corps with the 101st Airborne Division and Fort Campbell for the Office of the Staff Judge Advocate delivered the speech on Joseph Holt and his home and received a standing ovation from the JAGS. COL Andras Marton, Staff Judge Advocate presented Dyer with a medal and plaque for her commitment to honoring the legacy of General Joseph Holt that is an inspiration to their office and the entire U.S. Army JAG Corps. COL Marton told the audience, "I have now met a match from someone who does not wear the uniform, but shares the passion of our great history and preserving it. Afterwards COL Marton requested Susan to help cut the cake with the sword." Dyer and her husband were given a private tour of Fort Campbell following the JAG Corps Birthday event.
74. John and Kim Nyberg of Madison, Indiana preformed work of photography, measuring, collecting samples from each room of the Holt Home with wall paper remnants, wall paper location, and map documentation. Judge Lucas closed the home after the work was completed. The wallpaper is stored in acid free tissue boxes left with Susan Dyer upon departure. The fee of $500.00 with travel pay of $109.00 will be paid by the Friends.
75. Received an E-mail from COL Bagwell confirming he would be the keynote speaker on 9-23-2017 at the 9th Annual Holt Home Community Day.

76. 8-3-2017 Charlie Corbett talked with Phillip Jennings, Breckinridge County Music Director and Mr. Jennings wants to bring the Chamber Singers to the Holt Home to perform on Holt Home Community Day 9-23-2017.
77. Received an E-mail from Judge Easton with the list of KBF grants.
78. Sherry Stith forwarded information on checks received from the fund-raising letter of the Friends written by Charlie Corbett.
79. Judge Lucas E-mailed saying he has keys to the water on the Holt grounds now.
80. 8/24/2017 Troops were needed, and requests for help was sent to Ed Ford from Richmond and Connie Morris from West Point helped get out the word for re-enactors needed for September 23, 2017 at the September event at the Holt Home.
81. Jennifer Rose Escobar, Director for the Berea Festival Dancers and Susan Dyer discussed the schedule and final details for the 9th Annual Holt Home Community Day on August 27, 2017.
82. An article was written for the Student Day and current picture of the Holt Home sent to Superintend, Nick Carter on 8/28/2017 to be made into a brochure by Dale Butler and distributed to all Breckinridge County Students for the 9th Annual Holt Home Community Day.
83. On August 28, 2017 Charlie Corbett sent information on receiving two more very nice money donations for the Friends of the Holt Home, Inc.
84. 8-28.2017 received email from Bob Jones and he will present a cavalry living history on September 23, 2017 at the Holt Home.
85. September 7, 2017 Friends finalized planning for the 9th Annual Holt Home Community Day on September 23 and Student Day on September 20, 2017. And the Friends recently received 10 very nice money donations with the fund-raising letter written by Charlie Corbett.
86. Received the proof of article and photo for the Breckinridge County student brochure about the 9th Annual Holt Home Community Day to be sent home by students. A wonderful classic brochure and great partnering by Breckinridge County Schools!
87. Press releases were written and sent to local, regional and state media to promote 9th Annual Holt Home Community Day on September 23, 2017.
88. Judge Kelly Easton E-mailed for image of Holt Home as he is working on a nice gift for the key -note speaker for September 23, 2017.
89. Veronica Ent contacted and sent the schedule for Student Day to all Breckinridge County principals.
90. The 2nd Annual Student Day at the historic Holt Home was very successful. Students, teachers and principals gave continuous complements for the tours of the home, Holt Family Cemetery, and the enjoyable day! Special thanks go to Veronica Ent for training tour guides and assisting with the day. Larry Elliott for portraying President Abraham Lincoln and tying the connection with Holt and his legacy. All Breckinridge County Schools who partnered with the Friends and for the Friends paying Mr. Elliott and all the hard work preparing the home and cleaning by the Friends! This event can be viewed by visiting www.jholt-houseky.org/Events.
91. 9/13/2017 Paul Joseph O'Donoghue E-mailed with the major trees for sale on Holt Home Community Day from the Holt property; pecan, shagbark hickory, a few Chinese chestnuts and a grafted Holt gingko. Proceeds go for restoration of the Holt Home.
92. On 9/21 2017 Veronica Ent and Susan Dyer met with the B.C.H.C. gifted students at the historic Holt Home who are tour guides who requested Mrs. Dyer to meet with them to, give them a tour, and share additional history of the home from their research. Special thanks go to Veronica Ent for doing an outstanding job with tour guides and providing t-shirts for guides to have a uniform appearance for the distinguished guests.
93. Received an E-mail from Breckinridge County Sheriff, Todd Pate saying he would be present at the 9th Annual Holt Home Community Day.
94. Received a note from Ben Sheron, editor of the New-Enterprise of Elizabethtown, KY stating they would schedule a story about the 9th Annual Holt Home Community Day on September 18, 2017.
95. On 9/18/2017 Veronica Ent and Susan Dyer composed information and ordered a distinguished plaque for the Keynote speaker for the 9th Annual Holt Home Community Day. Breckinridge County Tourism purchased the plaque! Many thanks to Veronica!
96. Charlie Corbett found graves of the Holt brothers James & Robert and shared with Friends on 9/19/2017! Thanks to Charlie Corbett!
97. 9/21/2017 Kathina Bell completed the final program for the 9th Annual Holt Home Community Day.
98. 9/23/2017 The 9th Annual Holt Home Community Day was very successful! Highlights of the day: Record crowd, the Berea Festival Dancers were a crowd favorite, the wreath-laying cer-

emony with the Fort Knox JAGS continues to grow with partnering, the Breckinridge County High School band made its debut, the Breckinridge County Chamber Singers with new director performed, the Civil War Baseball game continues to be a big hit for the visitors, tour guides did a tremulous job along with period groups of bands, and two encampments of re-enactors with COL James Bagwell as key note speaker. Thanks goes to all the Friends who work the entire year to make the Holt Home Community Day a continued classic event for the local community, region and state. Special thanks to Judge Kelly Easton for being the Master of Ceremonies, portraying Holt and keeping schedules flowing with numerous activities for the guests!

99. 9/25/2017 Susan Dyer sent an E-mail to the Friends saying, "Congratulations on a classic, period, correct event for the 9th Annual Holt Home Community Day. Thank you for working diligently!!! Complements continue to come in from state partners, the media, people from across the Commonwealth and locals such as: You all did a great job, had a record crowd, with many wonderful events moving smoothly during the entire day. The Holt Home looks fantastic! Dyer sent words to the group stating, "Working hard for something we love is called passion." The Holt Home is our compass, a link to our past, and our gift to the future!"
100. Personal hand-written notes were sent on 11/1 2017 to the many volunteers for the 9th Annual Holt Home Community Day and a Holt Home cake was made and sent to COL James Bagwell and the Fort Knox Office of the Staff Judge Advocate for their continued partnering.
101. Neil Tindle CTSD Dean of Cloverport Independent Schools called to say he had found Joseph Holt's Bible in the Cloverport United Methodist Church Library. The Bible was in French signed by Holt. The church will vote on whether to give the Bible to the Holt Home and if yes, Bobby Stinnett, the Pastor will say a prayer over the Bible at the 10th Annual Holt Home Community Day on September 22, 2018.
102. Received an E-mail on November 2, 2018 from LTC Jeri Hanes, Office of the Judge Advocate General/ Pentagon. Receiving compliments on work for Holt for the past 20 years and the TJAG office is working to determine if LTG Pede's schedule will enable him to speak and attend the 10th Annual Holt Home Community Day on September 22, 2018. Efforts continue to make the Holt Home become a National meeting place for the Army JAGS across the nation!
103. On November 2, 2017 Preservation Kentucky one of the state partners of the historic Holt Home asked for help from advocates across Kentucky to call their Senators and Representatives with voices of concern for the eliminating of the historic federal tax credit. After conversation with David Morgan and learning of the severe nature of this Susan Dyer called Senator McConnell's office and Congress Brett Guthrie's offices. Representatives from both offices were not aware of what had happened. Both offices spoke personally with Senator McConnell and Congress Brett Guthrie. At the Friends meeting on December 7, 2017 the information was shared with the Friends, and Craig Potts, Exec. Director at the KY Heritage Council discussed the importance of getting the tax credits put back in the tax reform. Charlie Corbett called the Congressman and Senator's office, and all were encouraged to contact their Senator and Congressman. "A significant victory was won for the preservation community especially considering the House eliminated federal tax credits in their version. The inclusion of the FGTC is attribute to relentless grassroots advocacy and the preservation community's ability to champion historic preservation as sound federal policy that is good for the nation. A modified version of the 20% Federal Historic Tax Credit was saved on December 20, 2017 when the Senate and the House voted on Tax Reform!
104. Sherry Stith forward an E-mail from Randy Kunath of Elizabethtown, KY and his request to donate a period Victorian couch to the Holt Home he paid $1,600 for 20 years ago. Susan Dyer made a trip to view the couch and after the Friends viewed pictures Mr. Kunath sent the Friends voted to accept the wonderful gift.
105. On December 7, 2017 the KY Heritage Council/ State Preservation Office provided 106 training for the Friends of the Holt Home, Inc. as Nicole Konkal did a power point on the 106 training. Phase 1 Archaeological survey was discussed with funding available 80/20 match required. Nicole Konkal, Craig Potts and Diane Comer from the KY Heritage Council attended, and the site visit was made to the Holt Home.
106. December 8, 2017 John Campbell, Public Relations from Fort Knox sent an E-mail thanking The Judge Advocate's Office for their continuing partnering with the Friends for the wreath-laying ceremony and other partnering after Col Bagwell personally replied saying the JAG office would be

there on September 22, 2018 and they have assisted for several years.

107. Received an E-mail from Jon Rollins saying he had been in contact with Mike Jones, Kim Tompkins and Nicole Konkal as the Friends wish to go with the 80 KY TC/20/ Friends funding option for Phase 1 Archaeological Survey at the Holt Home.

108. J Rollins with GRW architects did an advertisement for the Phase 1 Archaeological Survey and it is has been placed for a 21-day clock on the www.jholt-houseky.org home page.

109. David Williams of Bloomfield, KY called with a beautiful donation of a square grand piano 1850 gift for the historic Holt Home. On December 7, 2017 Susan Dyer called Mr. Williams to say the Friends would accept the square grand piano for the Holt Home. And Judge Maurice Lucas will bring it to Breckinridge County.

110. On December 16, the Breckinridge County Historical Society recognized Susan Dyer as Historian of the Year 2017 for her continued work with Judge Joseph Holt and his home.

Index

A

Adamove, Robert 11
Allen, Barry 207, 208
Arbec, Christian 15, 159, 217
Arinage, Kathryn 19
Armstrong, Henry J. 153, 154
Arnold, Glenn 97
Askins, Jim 16, 195
Atchison, Mary Jean 6, 36, 50, 55, 109, 116, 119, 120, 121, 179
Austin, Ellen 211

B

Badger, Margaret Rose 15, 155, 156, 190, 191
Bagwell, James 10, 15, 158, 159, 160, 164, 168, 212, 213, 214, 215, 216, 217, 218, 220
Banks, David 195, 198
Barrett, Allison P. 195
Bartholomy, Suzi 16
Beach, Stephanie Prugh 61
Bedoy, Caroline 15, 159, 217
Behen, John P. 28, 61, 206
Behen, Mrs. John P. 5, 28, 61
Bell, Bob 18, 96
Bell, Kathina 14, 20, 85, 127, 187, 205, 206, 209, 211, 212, 213, 214, 217, 219
Bennett, Fred 16, 203
Bennett, Jonathan 12, 207, 213
Bennett, Marguerite 149
Bernson, Barry 16
Berry, Fannie Mae 207
Beshear, Steven 12, 15, 20, 97, 201, 207, 208
Bevin, Matt 148, 213, 214
Biagi, Michael 14
Bland, Hugh H. 203
Booth, John Wilkes 88
Borch, Fred L. 8, 10, 13, 24, 52, 60, 61, 62, 63, 64, 84, 99, 100, 114, 115, 116, 118, 119, 120, 164, 169, 173, 176, 205, 206, 212, 216, 217
Bostic, Michael 16
Bowen, Edmond 10, 100
Bowen, Mrs. Edmond, Jr. 10
Bowne, Ann 16
Boyd, Jonathan 12
Boyd, Steven 12
Bradley, Barbara 17, 199
Bramlett, Lee 8, 18
Breckinridge County Historical Society 6, 12, 16, 41, 55, 95, 180, 187, 202, 211, 221
Brooks, Bryant 194
Brooks, Eric 203
Brook, Shannon 212
Brown, David J. 207
Brown, Elizabeth 147
Brown, Rick 13, 101, 102, 120, 205, 206
Buchanan, James 16, 22, 23, 39, 56, 86, 98, 160, 187
Buckles, Mark 18, 107, 109
Bunning, Jim 195, 200, 201
Burdette, Jessica 19, 206
Burns, Robert 206
Bush, Barbara 195
Bush, Laura 164, 194
Butler, Aggie Harpe 2, 13, 28, 121, 122, 130, 133
Butler, Bruce T. 16, 108, 109
Butler, Dale 219
Butler, Dwight D. 5, 34, 35, 42, 43, 47, 48, 60, 91, 92, 105, 108, 109, 111, 137, 175, 177, 178, 191, 194, 195, 197, 199, 200, 201, 213
Butler, Jackie 13
Butler, Mitchell 13
Butler, Morton Levi 2
Butler, Richard 211, 212
Butler, Yale Lori 13

C

Campbell, Carol 214
Campbell, John 21, 220
Carden, Janet 8, 61, 121, 122, 123, 183
Carden, Tim 121
Carpenter, Clyde Reynolds 204
Carter, Nick 219
Carter, Virginia 20
Casebier, Lindy 7, 49, 55, 122, 123, 181, 190, 195, 198, 199, 201, 202
Cash, Charles 204
Cashman, Tiffany 17, 101, 158
Cassidy, Todd 202
Chandler, Ben 21
Chavan, Stanley 196
Chiarelli, Pete 16
Chipman, Dana K. 4, 9, 13, 52, 63, 64, 84, 92, 114, 115, 116, 118, 119, 120, 164, 166, 167, 169, 175, 182, 204
Civil War 4, 15, 22, 23, 26, 39, 61, 86, 88, 92, 100, 104, 133, 147, 159, 160, 169, 170, 191, 192, 205, 206, 213, 217
Civil War Baseball game 5, 12, 15, 96, 98, 101, 207, 213, 220
Clare, Donald 204
Clarke, Gaye 208, 211, 216
Clay, Henry 34, 203
Cohen, Bruce 204
Collins, Stephen L. 13, 122, 196
Coll, Ray, Jr. 153
Comer, Diane 17, 84, 104, 105, 106, 122, 126, 177, 180, 181, 199, 200, 201, 202, 207, 208, 210, 212, 214, 215, 220
Condia, Andrew M. 14, 209, 214, 215
Cooke, Eddie 199
Corbett, Charlie 17, 78, 79, 140, 187, 188, 201, 205, 206, 207, 208, 209, 210, 211, 212, 214, 215, 216, 218, 219, 220
Cotell, Robert 11, 55, 84, 175
Cowan, Cathy 202
Cox, Larry 8, 193, 194, 196, 197
Crawford, Byron 17, 81, 82, 84, 111, 121, 122, 123, 128, 212
Crawford, Regina 196
Cunningham, Allan 206

D

Darpino, Flora D. 9, 10, 138, 160, 164, 165, 166, 167, 168, 192, 209, 214, 215, 217
Davasher, Sarah 6, 34, 194, 196, 197, 198
David, Stephen 100, 102, 209
Davis, Michael 55
Dennen, Mark 7, 122, 123, 147, 148, 177, 180, 181, 197, 199, 200, 201, 202
Diehl, Karen 18
Distler, Ken 17
Doda, Louise 40, 41, 43, 46, 47, 193, 194, 196, 197, 198
Dowel, Clifford 16
Dutschke, Fred 40
Dutschke, Herman 40
Dyer, Brook Family 18
Dyer, Eddie 5, 8, 28, 29, 30, 31, 32, 35, 46, 52, 59, 61, 64, 81, 89, 91, 92, 102, 104, 110, 112, 116, 119, 120, 121, 122, 161, 162, 165, 166, 168, 170, 182, 183, 184, 197, 198, 199, 203, 212, 216
Dyer, Jaydyn 8, 13, 117, 132
Dyer, Justin 12
Dyer, Quince 12

E

Eakin, Jordan 16
Easton, Kelly 20, 56, 117, 188, 200, 211, 213, 214, 219, 220
Effron, Andrew S. 20, 60, 64
Egerton, John 5, 6, 27, 29, 105
Elliott, Larry 16, 118, 133, 135, 206, 208, 210, 219
Elliott, Mary 118, 133
Ent, Veronica 18, 100, 188, 208, 209, 210, 211, 212, 215, 216, 219
Escobar, Jennifer Rose 219
Evans, Peggy 203

F

Fausey, Brittany 6, 34, 35, 41, 43, 177, 194, 210, 214
Fletcher, Governor Ernie 34, 137, 196
Flood, Sarah 14
Flynn, Joy 196
Ford, Ed 5, 25, 182, 219
Ford, Edward 25
Ford, Kevin 43, 46, 193, 194, 195, 196, 197, 198
Ford, Mark 15
Frank, Monica 20
Frasier Museum of Louisville 15
Fredrikson, Christopher 11, 138
Friendlier, John 17
Friends of the Holt Home, Inc. 5, 6, 7, 9, 10, 11, 12, 13, 14, 15, 16, 17, 18, 19, 20, 21, 53, 56, 75, 77, 78, 79, 82, 83, 84, 85, 94, 95, 97, 98, 99, 100, 101, 106, 112, 115, 120, 127, 128, 139, 143, 148, 150, 155, 156, 157, 158, 160, 161, 162, 163, 164, 168, 178, 179, 180, 181, 185, 187, 188, 189, 191, 192, 205, 206, 207, 208, 209, 210, 211, 212, 213, 214, 215, 216, 218, 220, 221
Fugue, Angie 19

G

Galloway, Claude 6, 43, 44, 46, 47, 125, 148, 179, 189, 193, 194
Gheens Foundation 83, 84, 85, 207, 208
Gheens, Mrs. 85
Gibson, Carroll 7, 48, 49, 91, 92, 108, 137, 177, 185, 194, 197, 201, 202
Gibson, Henry 211
Gish, Michael 19, 201
Gleason, Howard 21
Glover, Alice 20

Godwin, John 147
Goodlett, Chris 7, 46, 48, 193, 194, 200
Goodwin, Doris Kearns 197
Grant, Ulysses S. 23, 56, 169, 172
Gray, Steven 203
Greer, Warren 11, 21, 46, 49, 91, 105, 106, 161, 185, 198, 199, 200, 201, 202, 204, 211, 212, 213, 215
Guier, Peggy 198
Guilderoy Byrne Band 19, 132
Guillaum, Ted 15, 206
Guthrie, Brett 14, 84, 127, 199, 200, 201, 202, 220
Gwinn, Carolyn 196

H

Hall, David 180
Hanes, Jeri 9, 220
Hardesty, Wayne 215
Harrison, Burr 39
Harrison, Elizabeth 39
Harrison, J.O. 39
Harrison, Smith 33
Hawkins, Pam 41
Hayes, David 8, 111, 200, 202
Hay, Melton Porter 203
Haynes, Doris 13
Heavrin, Kyle 21
Heid, Rebecca 8, 183
Heithpath, Keith 6, 34
Helmberg, Sue 201
Henderson, Pat 20
Hendry, Ida Dutschke 40
Henning, Cindy 21
Henning, Terry 8
Henry, Patrick 152
Herford, Kevin 15, 160
Herford, Marla 15
Hicks, Greg 19, 207, 210, 211, 217
Hill, Mary 206
Hill, Wayne 206
Hinton, Carol 8, 107, 110, 202
Hinton, Joanna 19, 194, 195
Hisgen, Jennifer A. 15
Hobb, Joe 90
Holloman, Natalie 199
Holt, Eleanor Stephens 38, 140
Holt Family Cemetery 19, 20, 75, 84, 88, 99, 103, 139, 140, 141, 142, 144, 155, 158, 179, 188, 191, 194, 199, 201, 205, 206, 207, 216, 219
Holt Family Trust 19, 75, 139, 155, 158, 191, 199, 205, 206
Holt Home Community Day 5, 6, 7, 8, 9, 10, 11, 12, 13, 14, 15, 16, 17, 18, 19, 20, 21, 50, 52, 55, 56, 61, 75, 84, 92, 95, 96, 101, 115, 116, 118, 119, 120, 127, 132, 133, 147, 150, 158, 162, 164, 167, 169, 175, 179, 180, 181, 184, 187, 188, 189, 204, 205, 206, 207, 208, 209, 210, 211, 212, 213, 214, 216, 217, 218, 219, 220
Holt, James 219
Holt, J.B. 149
Holt, John 38, 92, 140
Holt, Joseph 4, 5, 7, 8, 9, 10, 11, 12, 13, 14, 15, 16, 17, 18, 19, 20, 21, 22, 23, 24, 25, 26, 27, 28, 29, 31, 32, 33, 34, 35, 36, 37, 38, 39, 40, 41, 43, 46, 47, 48, 49, 50, 51, 52, 53, 54, 56, 57, 58, 60, 61, 62, 64, 66, 82, 83, 84, 85, 86, 87, 88, 89, 91, 92, 94, 96, 98, 99, 100, 101, 105, 106, 107, 108, 110, 111, 112, 115, 116, 119, 120, 121, 122, 123, 124, 127, 128, 134, 138, 140, 144, 150, 154, 155, 158, 160, 162, 164, 166, 167, 168, 169, 173, 176, 177, 178, 179, 181, 182, 184, 187, 188, 190, 191, 192, 193, 194, 195, 196, 197, 198, 199, 200, 201, 202, 203, 204, 205, 206, 207, 208, 209, 210, 211, 213, 214, 215, 216, 217, 218, 220, 221
Holt, Margaret Wickliffe 31, 32, 33, 36, 37, 39, 58, 59, 192
Holt, Mary Harrison 33, 39, 57, 58, 59, 61, 62, 192
Holt, Robert 23, 219
Holt, Rose 155, 156, 157
Holt, Rosina Board 140
Holt, Thomas 140, 155
Holt, Vanna 148, 155, 190
Holt, Washington D. 155, 190
Hopkins, Paris 12
Hopkins, Stephens 20
Hower, Erin 194
Huddleston, Pat 211
Huddleston, Phil 12, 211
Hultgren, Bill 19, 150, 151
Huston, Danny 17, 61, 64, 123, 169, 173, 217
Huston, John 61

J

Jasper, Charles Foster 11, 86, 88
Jenkins, Charlotte 215
Jennings, Phillip 219
Jesse, Ken 19
Johnson, Andrew 23, 169, 173
Johnson, Richard M. 39, 194
Jones, Bob 219
Jones, Mike 221

K

Kelly, Dan 7, 185
Kemper, Julie 212, 214
Kennedy, Patrick 21, 125, 195, 198
Kentucky Heritage Council 5, 6, 7, 12, 13, 14, 17, 18, 21, 36, 38, 41, 78, 84, 91, 92, 94, 95, 104, 105, 106, 107, 110, 111, 114, 118, 121, 122, 124, 125, 145, 147, 148, 155, 177, 178, 179, 180, 181, 185, 186, 187, 194, 195, 196, 197, 198, 199, 200, 201, 202, 203, 204, 206, 209, 210, 211, 212, 213, 214, 217, 218, 220
Kentucky Heritage Council/State Preservation Office 5, 6, 7, 11, 43, 46, 54, 83, 85, 92, 93, 98, 104, 113, 121, 122, 124, 147, 177, 178, 181, 184, 185, 186, 187, 189, 191, 193, 194, 195, 207, 210, 211, 214, 215, 216, 217, 220
Kentucky Historical Society 7, 11, 15, 29, 46, 48, 91, 112, 179, 186, 193, 194, 195, 196, 197, 198, 199, 200, 203, 208, 211, 212, 213
Kentucky Humanities Council 20, 21
Kentucky Lincoln Bicentennial Commission 5, 6, 7, 11, 14, 19, 37, 43, 46, 48, 49, 55, 65, 66, 91, 92, 94, 95, 104, 111, 114, 125, 179, 180, 185, 186, 187, 193, 194, 195, 196, 197, 198, 199, 200, 201, 202, 203, 212, 213
Kentucky Lincoln Heritage Trail 7, 11, 54, 106, 107, 110, 118, 137, 178, 189, 197, 198, 199, 201, 202, 205, 206, 207, 211, 215
Kincard, Amanda 214
Kincheloe, Dr. 87, 88
King, Francis P. 9, 164, 167, 168
King, Frank 209
King, Horace 147, 148
King, Preston 173
Kirby, Bruce 6, 26, 27
Klein, Jerome D. 11
Klotter, James C. 5, 6, 29, 30, 35, 37, 50, 61, 63, 81, 85, 89, 105, 107, 111, 123, 127, 145, 179, 191, 195, 202
Knotts, Kathy 84, 85, 207
Knouf, Ken 211
Konkal, Nicole 220, 221
Kozak, Mary 203
Kozlowski, Daniel 10, 99, 148, 210, 213
Krawezy, Doug 203
Kunath, Randy 220

L

Lane, James 173
Langman, Tamara 8, 213
Larue, Iris 11, 203, 212
Lawson, Gil 201
Lee, Cleo 20, 188, 207
Lee, Dan 199
Leonard, Elizabeth D. 6, 15, 40, 125, 128
Lewis, Ron 6, 34, 36, 43, 177, 194, 197, 198, 215
Lincoln, Abraham 4, 16, 22, 23, 55, 84, 88, 94, 97, 98, 99, 100, 105, 112, 118, 120, 121, 133, 159, 160, 167, 169, 170, 174, 185, 187, 191, 192, 198, 199, 208, 210, 213, 219
Lincoln Conspiracy Trial 19, 75, 139, 155, 158, 191, 217, 218
Lincoln, Mary Todd 118, 133
Love, Robert 15, 158, 159, 215, 216
Luallen, Crit 12
Lucas, Grant 20
Lucas, Maurice 11, 97, 99, 101, 117, 127, 128, 158, 161, 207, 208, 209, 210, 211, 212, 214, 215, 216, 218, 221
Lyddan, Dana Beth 84, 126, 180, 200, 201

M

Mackevich, Eileen 202, 203
Martin, Judge 197, 198
Martin, P.J. 154
Marton, Andras M. 10, 138, 182, 183, 184, 218
Mattingly, Alison O'Donoghue 12, 117
Mattingly, Kelly 21
McConnell, Mitch 8, 14, 84, 127, 193, 194, 196, 197, 200, 201, 202, 209, 220
McGarry, Sean 9, 164, 165, 167, 168, 214, 215, 216
McNeill, Tammy 13
Meade County Archaeological Historical Society 21
Meek, Janet 218
Meeks, Janet 212, 213
Mercer, Heather 202
Meredith, Steven 15
Miles, Suzanne 14, 200
Miller, Jackie 12, 202
Miller, Jeffery A. 10, 63, 164, 165, 166, 167, 168, 217, 218
Miller, John W. II 8, 60, 62, 138, 175
Mink, Philip B. 20, 139, 188, 206

Minor, David 47
Monarch, George III 6, 37, 43, 46, 47, 124, 193
Moore, Scott 12, 107, 108, 202
Morgan, David L. 5, 6, 36, 37, 38, 41, 43, 46, 49, 92, 104, 113, 123, 124, 125, 177, 178, 179, 185, 186, 192, 193, 194, 197, 198, 203, 213, 214, 217, 220
Morris, Connie 219
Most Endangered Historic Places 19, 193, 194, 196, 199
Mudd, Dr. 172
Myers, Isaac 148, 213, 214

N

Natcher, William 35, 40
National Register of Historic Places 18, 34, 36, 40, 52, 53, 94, 100, 177, 178, 190
Neary, Donna 195, 196
Newton, Tommy 21
Nikolao, Konkadu 217
Nikolao, Konrad 15, 160
Nyberg, John 16, 157, 188, 211, 218
Nyberg, Kim 15, 16, 156, 157, 189, 208, 209, 210, 218

O

Obama, Barack 127
Obama, Michelle 164
O'Donoghue, Allison 202
O'Donoghue, Paul Joseph 20, 102, 188, 202, 203, 209, 210, 212, 215, 217, 219
Oldfield, Steve 212
Owen, Patty 18
Owsley, Bob 13

P

Parks, Elizabeth 14, 136, 206
Parrish, Chuck 122
Pate, Todd 19, 219
Pede, Charles N. 9
Piece, Judy 19
Piper, Jimmy 19
Porter, Fitz-John 23
Potts, Craig 17, 148, 181, 212, 213, 214, 217, 220
Powers, Ray 6, 7, 14, 48, 52, 54, 55, 59, 91, 107, 108, 109, 124, 125, 126, 127, 128, 137, 155, 179, 186, 194, 195, 196, 197, 198, 199, 200, 201, 202
Prather, Joe 200
Prather, Robert 49, 50
Pritchard, Christy 203
Prugh, George S. 60, 64, 84
Prugh, Patt 61

R

Ramolete, Analuisa 184
Ramsey, Dorothy 88
Ramsey, Dorothy Dowell 11, 86, 88
Redford, Robert 60, 61, 123, 169, 172, 174, 218
Rehmert, Chris 16
Reid, Celia Lynn 17
Revolutionary War 88, 159
Rifenburgh, Cmdr. 153, 154
Roach, Elizabeth 20
Robinson, Sarah L. 8, 57
Rogers, James 83
Rogers, Vestal 131, 133
Rollins, Jon 14, 18, 47, 71, 72, 73, 79, 148, 149, 208, 211, 212, 214, 215, 216, 218, 221
Roosevelt, Franklin 152
Rose, Cathy 15
Ross, Andrel II 218
Roush, John A. 16, 207, 209, 214, 216
Roush, Susie 16, 207, 214, 216
Rubalcaba, Leah 19, 170, 172, 174, 216
Ruskowski, Becky 47, 193

S

Sanders, Stuart 11, 195
Saylor, Andrea 203
Schamore, Dean 15, 97
Schmidt, Charlotte 21
Sebastian, Donna 11, 89
See, Larry, Jr. 17
Severance, Paul 19, 170, 172, 173
Seward, William H. 169
Shelby, Graham 211
Shepard, Gloria 11
Sheron, Ben 17, 219
Shipp, Becky 6, 37, 38, 91, 113, 123, 125, 126, 179, 180, 186, 194, 195, 196, 197, 198
Shuffett, Dave 7, 203
Sikes, Douglas W. 5, 7, 49, 50, 52, 55, 61, 63, 81, 82, 107, 108, 109, 110, 121, 126, 200, 202, 210, 216
Singer, Charlie 62, 64
Smallenburg, Gwen McCall 204
Smith, Brian 14, 199, 200
Smith, Margaret 147
Smith, Paul 7
Sowada, Kate 211
Sparrow, Marcheta 15, 55, 122, 201, 202
Spaulding, Timothy 215
Speed, James 169
Speed, Mrs. 32
Stanton, Edwin 23
Steele, Keith 121
Stephens, Richard 38, 159
Stinnett, Bobby 220
Stinnett, Lee 6, 44, 47, 200, 201
Stith, Rick 15
Stith, Sherry 20, 102, 188, 206, 208, 210, 215, 218, 219
Stivers, Regina 210
Storms, Mickey 204
Struble, Arthur D. 153
Surratt, John 173
Surratt, Mary 61, 172, 173, 174

T

Tabb, Kenneth 7, 49, 50, 130
Tabor, Kathy 12, 202
Taul, Charlotte 212
Taylor, David 217, 218
Terry, Mr. 40
Thomas, Carl 83, 84, 85, 207, 208
Thompson, Bill 18, 52, 94, 177
Thompson, Gwen 203
Thompson, Verbal 18
Tindle, Neil 19
Tivitt, Shannon 12, 97
Tobin, Myra 12
Tompkins, Kim 208, 221
Trawick, Greg 8, 61
Tucker, Hampton 196
Tucker, Shane 200
Turner, Tommy 6, 43, 46, 49, 55, 91, 108, 109, 110, 124, 185, 186, 193, 194, 197, 198, 202, 213

V

Vest, Stephen M. 17

W

Waitman, Richard 21
Wakefield, Sharon 12, 113
Wallis, Joe 36
Walters, Jim 191
Wardrip, Sarah 14
Washington, George 159
Wayne, Kendel 183
Wayne, Sheila 19, 121, 122, 150
Wayne, Todd A. 10, 19, 60, 176, 182, 183, 184, 218
Wethington, Becky 18, 107
Whayne, Robert 206, 207
Whayne, Suzanne 206, 207
Wheatley, Glenda 162
Wheatley, Janet 161, 162
Wheatley, Joyce 18, 104, 162, 216
Wheatley, Thomas 18, 104, 161, 162, 216
Whelan, Georgia (Davis) 207
Whinnery, Pam 20
White, Mr. 11, 91
Whitfield, Alisia 18
Whitworth, Kent 15, 91, 112, 179, 212
Wickliffe, Charles Anderson 39
Wickliffe Family Cemetery 33
Wickliffe, Robert 38
Wilks, Joshua 14, 85, 112, 205
Williams, David 221
Williamson, Jen 201, 212, 215
Willis, Ida Lee 204
Willoughby, Laura 18
Wilson, Charles Allen 8, 196
Wilson, Etta 5, 29, 105
Wilson, Roger 10, 99, 100, 101, 207, 208, 209, 210
Wimmer, Don 18
Wimsatt, James L. 7, 51, 52, 53, 107, 118, 156, 157, 206, 213
Wimsatt, Trudy 52
Wirz, Henry 23
Wise, Don 13, 214, 216
Wojcik, Don 20, 203
World War II 39, 52, 150, 151
Wright, Joe 12
Wright, Renee Allgood 13, 107, 109
Wright, Robin 174